SURVIVING DEATH

SURVIVING DEATH

Geoff Viney

St. Martin's Press
New York

Library of Congress Cataloging-in-Publication Data

Viney, Geoff.
Surviving death / Geoff Viney.
p.   cm.
ISBN 0-312-10436-7
1. Future life.   2. Spiritualism.   3. Near-death experiences.
I. Title.
BF1311.F8V55   1994
133.9′01′3—dc20   93-45295   CIP

First published in Great Britain by Warner Books.

First U.S. Edition: May 1994
10 9 8 7 6 5 4 3 2 1

For Elizabeth

'Those I would teach, and by right reason bring,
To think of death as but an idle thing.'

Ovid

CONTENTS

LIST OF ABBREVIATIONS

SPR	Society for Psychical Research.
ASPR	American Society for Psychical Research.
CSISOP	Committee for the Scientific Investigation of Claims of the Paranormal.
RSPK	Recurrent spontaneous psychokinesis.
SHC	Spontaneous human combustion.
EVP	Electronic voice phenomenon.
OBE	Out-of-body experience.
NDE	Near-death experience.
ESP	Extra sensory perception.

Introduction

'Afraid? Of whom am I afraid?
Not death; for who is he?'

Emily Dickinson

The narrow back streets of the southern Portuguese town of Faro hide a strange and unique place of worship. Much the same in outward design as any other, the building's peculiarity lies in its method of construction, or to be more precise, with the materials used: human skeletons. For this is the Capella dos Ossos, the Chapel of Bones. Built by monks centuries ago, its masonry is the femurs, spinal columns and knuckle joints of local people. The Capella dos Ossos is a true house of death and to stand inside on one's own, surrounded by walls decorated with over one thousand skulls, is an unnerving experience. Indeed, it was always meant to be so, for the chapel's original purpose was to remind those lacking in devotion of the inevitability and impartiality of death's hand. Confronted so starkly with the sight of the grim reaper's handywork, sinners would – it was envisaged – fall upon God's mercy and turn towards the Christian path of repentance.

I have no idea whether the place achieved its desired effect, though in all probability it was unnecessary. Those who lived in former times were already aware of death's central role in the daily round. Poor hygiene, impure water and a near total ignorance of medical care allowed plagues and other fatal diseases like cholera and typhoid to spread virtually unchecked. In the Europe of the Middle-Ages, infant mortality was appalling and the overall levels of life expectancy compared unfavourably with today's poorest developing countries. Far from needing to be reminded of the existence of death men were brought face to face with it every day of their lives. Yet while our ancestors saw the effects of death more openly and more frequently than we do today, there is much evidence to suggest that they viewed the prospect of dying with less trepidation than modern man. Their optimism was born out of a faith, or rather a belief that death was not the end of life but merely a transition to another state of being.

In truth the confidence of Medieval Man was neither new nor unique in human history. In all times and races an abiding notion has been maintained that hidden deep within us there is some central part, some final identity which survives physical dissolution. The idea can be found in the writings of eastern antiquity, upon the tablets and papyrus texts of the great Mediterranean civilizations, and in the myths and legends of the early South American peoples. The same belief remains central to each of the major world faiths and remains true today for committed religious devotees everywhere.

In the West, however, such adherents no longer form a natural majority. Since the beginning of the Age of Enlightenment three centuries ago, Western man's general acceptance of the reality of an afterlife has gradually given way to a deep suspicion of anything connected with the supernatural. The rapid advance of scientific rationalism during our own century has led to a further shift in opinion, a move towards a position where it not only seems illogical but almost insane to admit that one believes in ghosts or spirits. Yet whilst our attitude towards death has changed our terror of it has not. Psychologists tell us that fear of death is one of man's primal fears and this nihilistic vision of our collective futures can only serve to have a profound effect on society as a whole. It must come as no great surprise, therefore, to learn from sociologists that the self destructive attitudes displayed by so many modern people in their everyday lives springs from a sense of doubt about their true place in the scheme of things. Today most people in the West are left floundering in the belief that our last breath on earth constitutes an extinction of life, an annihilation of self. It is after all what science has taught us and for many science has replaced God. But is it the truth? Is an indefinable, indescribable nothingness all we really have to look forward to?

The answer quite simply is no. More than one hundred years of psychic investigations tell us otherwise, and it is a careful analysis of the known facts drawn from this research that forms the basis of this book. Along with many other paranormal investigators I have grown steadily convinced that the idea of human life ending in oblivion at the moment of death makes about as much sense as the theory that the world is flat. And I say it not on the basis of prayerful revelation or blind faith but after years of carefully, rationally assessing the various phenomena and their possible cause.

The title of this polemical work speaks for itself. In the following chapters I aim to put death, or rather the concept of death as final extinction, on trial. I am, if you like, self appointed counsel for the prosecution. The witnesses I call upon are those countless individuals who have experienced a personal contact with the unseen – ghost percipients, mediums, parapsychologists and researchers into the exciting new field of the electronic voice phenomenon. Considered also are the extraordinary testimonies of those who have died only to be revived, along with the recollections of people claiming to recall previous lives. If I am to give death a fair hearing I must necessarily also examine objectively and at length the many alternative explanations for paranormal mysteries promoted by sceptics and mainstream scientists, some of which undermine the probability of human survival. I do not hesitate from playing the devil's advocate on occasions and those called in death's defence include charlatans like Doris Stokes and Harry Price who have discredited psychic research with their fraudulent practices. It is for the reader – both judge and jury in this trial – to decide which argument is on balance closest to the truth. The only qualification required is a reasonably open mind.

Since death affects us all I hope this book will appeal to a universal audience. Perhaps I should, however, begin with a warning. The evidence for survival which I shall be presenting will stretch the imagination of most readers and shake the long-held certainties of others. The picture of the true reality of continued existence beyond death which emerges not only upsets committed atheists, but also challenges many of the most cherished beliefs of hundreds and millions of devout Christians and Muslims around the world. What we can say for certain is that our chances of making it to the next world do not depend upon membership of any religious group, attendance at church, or the observance of a code of conduct laid down by priests, rabbis or mullahs. No one has ever ascended to Heaven because they received the last rites and no one has ever fallen to Hell because they died unbaptized.

The sheer amount of survival evidence currently being gathered is truly astounding. Perhaps what is even more astounding is the fact that very little of it has filtered through to the wider public. Few people for instance are aware that the voices of the dead can be captured and replayed on a conventional tape recorder or heard through the medium of a normal telephone. Hardly anyone among the general population knows that technological research is now well under way to produce a televisual image of the spirit world and that the successful culmination of this research seems to be just around the corner. The majority of people remain blissfully unaware that during the last decade the existence of poltergeists as autonomous entities has been proven scientifically or that a case of genuine reincarnation is more likely to spring from a nursery school in Britain or the United States than it is from a remote ashram on the banks of the Ganges.

As the various strands of evidence begin to link together one is drawn towards the inevitable conclusion that none of us can ever really die. At the same time there emerges a clear picture of the new existences we can all expect to find beyond the grave. It is a very different vision of death from the one most of us have been led to believe in, and after reading this book many people may wonder why they ever feared dying at all. I guarantee you will never think the same way about the subject again.

A Door Left Ajar

'Die happily and look forward to taking up a new
and better form. Like the sun, only when you set in
the west can you rise in the east.'

Rumi
(Islamic poet of *The Koran*)

On the evening of 12 February 1977 a Finnish university
lecturer holding a reception in her Helsinki apartment
was surprised to see a female guest arrive who she did
not recognize. The stranger, dressed in a peculiarly
old-fashioned style and without an overcoat despite
the bitterly cold weather, seemed aloof and left half
way through the evening without saying goodbye. The
hostess assumed her to be the wife of an acquaintance
but upon investigation this proved incorrect. In fact,
when she spoke of the mysterious woman afterwards it
turned out that none of the other guests had even noticed
her. Though perplexed by the incident, the academic put
it to the back of her mind. But six months later she saw
the stranger's face once more – this time in a photograph
which accompanied a magazine article about the painter
Marie Genetz, who had died in 1943. She was certain
that Genetz was the woman who had gatecrashed her
party. When she told friends of her discovery most of
them laughed. Their attitude changed, however, when
deeds were found which proved conclusively that Marie
Genetz had once occupied the lecturer's flat. Though her

lease on life was up the painter still appeared to be in residence.

I am aware that many readers will find the Finnish lecturer's story hard to accept. At the time many of her friends felt the same way, even though they could see no conceivable reason why she should fabricate such a bizarre tale. Remarkable though it may seem however, the return of the artist Marie Genetz thirty-four years after her death must be counted as a relatively commonplace event in the supernatural history of our planet, just one example among literally millions of reported ghost sightings that have emerged during the past few thousand years. Faced with such a mountain of evidence the paranormal researcher who sets out to prove the existence of an afterlife might be thought hard pressed to decide which sightings to include and which to leave out. Actually, this is not the case. Tales of ghosts seen when witnesses are on the verge of sleep or immediately upon waking are of little or no value, since it increases the possibility that the percipient's vision is a dream or hallucination. Likewise, visitations lasting a few seconds and unaccompanied by external indications of a real presence might simply be a trick of the light.

As a researcher I would be the first to admit that many ghost sightings remain suspect, and over the past few years I have been alerted to innumerable cases which proved upon investigation to have a high probability of natural causes. I find this neither surprising nor particularly disappointing, since there is nothing worse than wasting time on a wild-goose chase (or even a wild-ghost chase!). Every time a new case arises I ask myself the following questions: a) Does the witness have a faulty perception of what really happened? b) Does he or she seem to have poor memory recall? c) Does the belief system of the witness prejudice the possibility of an objective impression? d) Do the manifestations reported match known elements of real phenomena or do they correspond to the story line of a recent popular film or book about the supernatural? Often natural explanations have proved childishly simple to construct for apparent anomalies. A vibration from passing traffic closing a door; a draught rattling the pages of an open book; an old house creaking as it settles due to the fall in evening temperature. But there are many other stories that cannot be accounted for so easily. For every event which can be put down to a person misidentifying a combination of circumstances, there is another that appears to indicate the genuine presence of discarnate forces. Even if we exclude every tale told by children, those of a nervous or hysterical disposition or those who wish to claim psychic powers for reasons of self satisfaction, we are still left with a hardened kernel of inexplicable cases that defy mechanistic interpretation.

It is these stories – the ones investigated and checked for reliability by genuine investigators past and present – which provide the hard evidence for the existence of apparitions, and it is these that form the subject of this first chapter. If you are hoping for a few scary tales of graveyard ghouls and headless coachmen you'll probably be disappointed. On the other hand if you are seriously interested in what happens to you when you die then I suggest you read on.

At approximately 11.30 pm on the night of 4 May 1980, a young waitress named Hilde Saxer left her restaurant work place in a small mountain township in the Austrian South Tyrol. Walking home by her usual route she happened to notice the slow approach of a grey Audi car which bore the distinctive registration plates belonging to the one owned by her sister's fiancé

Johann Hofer. As the Audi passed Hilde Saxer waved a greeting and her gesture was enthusiastically returned by Hofer. Yet somewhat to her surprise he did not stop to offer her a lift. Fifteen minutes later, on the other side of town, the same grey Audi was seen pulling into the family garage by Johann Hofer's father. Knowing his son had been out this came as no surprise but when, after a time-lag of some half an hour, Johann had still not come in, Mr Hofer went to investigate. To his astonishment he found the garage to be empty with no sign of either the youth or his car. Mr Hofer returned inside bewildered by the whole business. Had he simply daydreamed his son's return?

The truth was stranger still. For earlier that evening, at roughly 7.45 pm Johann Hofer had been caught in a roof caving which had engulfed traffic passing through a mountain tunnel twenty miles away – driver and car had been crushed flat under hundreds of tons of rubble along with many other motorists. Both the fact and the time of Johann Hofer's death can hardly be called into question yet if we are to believe the accounts of two independent witnesses, he was seen driving his car several hours after the tunnel disaster took place.

Another case of collective percipience was the phantom return of Captain Eldred Bowyer-Bower, a British airman shot down over France during World War I. The flyer was killed on 18 March 1917 and would seem to have appeared to two female relatives the following day. On the morning of 19 March, Bowyer-Bower's half-sister Susanna Spearman, who was living in India, purportedly saw her brother's uniformed figure materialize on her hotel balcony, standing a few feet away from her as she was feeding her infant daughter. Meanwhile, 6,000 miles away at the same moment (allowing for the Continental time difference) the flyer's form became manifest before

his eldest sister, Mrs Rosemary Chater, in the living room
of her house in the English Home Counties. Neither
visionary figure spoke but both women later wrote of
their belief that their brother Eldred had returned to
prove his personal survival of death.

When two people see the same ghost the possibility
of illusion begins to fade. When dozens of people see
the same ghost it disappears altogether. On the night
of 29 December 1972 an Eastern Airlines Tri-Star jet
liner bound for Miami plunged into the swamps of
the Florida Everglades killing one hundred and one
passengers and crew. Among the dead on board Flight
401 from New York were the pilot Captain Robert
Loft and the flight engineer Don Repo. Afterwards
there were stories of spectral figures in flying officers'
uniforms materializing inside the cockpits of Tri-Stars
operating the same route as the doomed aircraft but
initially they were dismissed by Eastern Airlines. When
reports persisted, however, the company's senior officials
had little choice but to take the phenomenon seriously.
Flight crews who saw the apparitions described them
as wholly lifelike, three dimensional solid forms which
never spoke but which sat stony-faced in the pilot's seat
on the airliner's flight deck. Witnesses who had known
the men insisted that these figures were the ghosts of pilot
Loft and engineer Repo from Flight 401. The identifica-
tions were even confirmed by passengers who matched
their own sightings with photographs of the two men.
Nothing could convince any of these witnesses that they
were hallucinating. As far as they were concerned the
ghosts had been there no matter who called them liars.

Fearing adverse publicity from the incidents, execu-
tives of Eastern Airlines instructed flight crews to keep
the strange tales to themselves. But rumours of the
manifestations in the sky gradually spread, despite the

order. Among those who became interested was journalist and writer John G. Fuller whose investigation into the phenomenon was eventually published in a detailed study entitled *The Ghosts Of Flight 401*. Already a seasoned investigator of psychic matters, Fuller quickly realized that the apparitions were not appearing exclusively on aircraft operating the same flight path as the crashed plane; they were manifesting most frequently on those Tri-Stars which had been serviced with spare parts salvaged from the wreckage of Flight 401. The writer concluded that some element of psychic energy had also been transferred – the life force of two human beings. Their souls were trapped in a dimension unsuited to their present condition.

Assisted by three Eastern Airlines pilots who were themselves spiritualists by faith and gifted mediums into the bargain – plus a Federal Aviation Agency technical officer who had known both Loft and Repo in life – Fuller set up a seance designed to make contact with the dead duo. In his book he explains how the seance helped the two men, who were both atheists, to comprehend their death state and travel onwards to the higher planes of existence – those other worlds to which spiritualists believe all humans are meant to ascend following physical death. According to Fuller's account the ghosts of Loft and Repo ceased to be seen aboard the Tri-Stars as soon as they realized that there was a better place waiting for them. For their part, Eastern Airlines ordered the removal and destruction of the elevators, radios, fans, seats, panels and other equipment that had been salvaged from the crashed plane. Company records show that after the last recycled part had been removed from their fleet of Tri-Stars there were no reports of further manifestations.

Can this extraordinary story of psychic rescue in

the sky really be held credible? Astonishing though it may seem, the only logical answer would appear to be 'yes'. As evidence supporting the existence of ghosts, the visions which appeared thirty thousand feet above America in the two years following the fatal crash of Flight 401 remain supremely impressive. Over twenty-five sightings were made, usually not by a single witness but by several persons, whose integrity would seem to be unimpeachable.

On one occasion, Don Repo's spectral form was seen by an Eastern Airlines senior executive; on another by a state senator. Even so, many people dismissed the stories as an elaborate fabrication and derided John Fuller's book without ever offering a shred of evidence to support their prejudiced standpoint. Sadly, this was an entirely typical reaction, for in the eyes of many the supernatural remains a taboo subject. It is a viewpoint which reflects the schism in our attitude towards ghosts. Today, in the last decade of the twentieth century, millions living on our planet claim to have seen spirits and tens of millions more attest to a belief in their existence. Nevertheless, among Westerners there remains a solid majority who vociferously uphold the opposite view, a core of hardened sceptics who prefer to dismiss all sightings as the product of hallucination, mistaken identification or wishful thinking. Those who claim to encounter ghosts are often labelled by the media as superstitious, feeble-minded, even mentally unbalanced. People whose word might otherwise be accepted without question are, on this subject, suspected of being liars, hoaxers or attention seekers.

As we shall see, however, it is the rationalists' scepticism and not the imagined superstitions of witnesses, that is beginning to lack credibility. Ghosts are nothing new. The testimony of ancient manuscripts and tales of folklore handed down by word of mouth over the centuries bear witness to the fact that the dead have been returning to earth to haunt the living since the beginnings of time. In the Old Testament Book of Job a terrifying spectre rose which caused the prophet's bones to shake and his hair to stand on end. The Romans likewise recognized the reality of the returning soul, and the first century chronicler Pliny describes a ghastly phantom in chains which led him to the spot where the remains of the murdered individual lay. In Northern Europe, early Norse and Celtic legends are full of spirits, whilst Saxon writings from the sixth century onwards suggest that the existence of ghosts was readily accepted by all levels of society. In his eighth century *History of the English Church and People*, the Venerable Bede attested to his own belief in ghosts and other pre-Norman writings uphold the same view.

Elsewhere in the world it was a similar story. From ocean peoples to jungle tribes, recognition of ghosts was central to the ethnic systems of faith and superstition and at all levels of Eastern society, educated and otherwise, there was a generally held belief in the existence of the spirit world and the ability of souls to return to the mortal plane in spectral form. It was, wrote one poet, as if a door had been left ajar by the Gods.

In Europe, the belief in ghosts, which continued throughout the Middle Ages and the Renaissance, ended abruptly around the turn of the eighteenth century with the advent of the so-called Age of Enlightenment. The march of scientific rationalism during the past three hundred years has made it necessary for Western Man to prove the existence of the phantom in order to believe in it. Some, it must be said, have been more than equal to the task.

*   *   *

The foundation in London of the Society for Psychical Research (SPR) in 1882, brought about a turning-point in man's relation to the phenomena of ghosts. The Society's original members were by no means a collection of credulous fools. Drawn mainly from Oxbridge graduates and other members of the educated upper-middle classes, the Society's ranks were soon swelled by such eminent Victorians as the writers Alfred Lord Tennyson, Mark Twain, John Ruskin and Lewis Carroll, as well as scientists Sir Oliver Lodge and J.J. Thurston – the discoverer of the electron particle. Even Prime Minister William Gladstone showed a keen interest in the Society's activities. Taking a level-headed view of psychic phenomena, the Society's early members recognized correctly that accounts of apparitions needed to be subjected to careful and painstaking analysis before they could be counted as genuine proof of survival. 'What is really required,' declared the Society's first annual report, 'is a large supply of first-hand, well-attested facts.' In its first decade the Society set out to achieve that objective, collecting an astonishing body of witnessed events.

To one study, the *Census of Hallucinations*, conducted between April 1889 and May 1892, some 17,000 replies were drawn forth in answer to the question: 'Have you ever, when awake, had an impression of seeing, hearing or being touched by a living being or inanimate object which . . . was not due to any external physical cause?' Of those who replied, almost 1,700, or roughly ten per cent, answered in the affirmative. Being serious minded academics, the SPR team recognized that these mainly anecdotal reports were far from infallible. So they investigated each one with persistence and vigour, wherever possible interviewing the witnesses personally. Most observations failed to stand up against the Society's vigorously applied criteria of genuineness.

Yet there was a consistent minority which indicated that contact was occasionally made between human beings and apparitional intelligences.

After suspect cases had been excluded, there still remained a formidable body of evidence for the continuing presence of the dead among us. Indeed if the census was an accurate reflection of the Victorian population in Britain, more than one million adults might have seen a ghost. The results of the census, and much more besides, was presented in a remarkable seven-volume work entitled *Human Personality and the Survival of Bodily Death* authored by a SPR founding member Frederick Myers, otherwise an academic at Trinity College, Cambridge. A hundred years later Myers' study remains one of the most important texts in the history of paranormal research. As a carefully documented record of evidence for the existence of an afterlife it remains unsurpassed.

The British SPR was not alone in drawing positive conclusions. Around the same period, a comparable study conducted in France by the writer Camille Flammarion was revealing a similar pattern. Some of Flammarion's research has recently been called into question, but a large proportion of his case histories, like those of Myers, hold true. Impressively, most came from men and women of substance – magistrates, doctors, high-ranking military officers and senior civil servants. The subjects who witnessed the manifestations were themselves so convinced of their genuineness, that they were prepared to put their name to their accounts despite the risk of personal ridicule.

Early research into accounts drawn from ghost-seers exploded some of the more common myths surrounding the phenomena. Contrary to public opinion, with its conjured-up visions of bed-sheeted figures or Dickensian chain-rattlers, there is no such thing as a 'typical' ghost. Nor are there specific times of day, types of location, or particular circumstances in which a phantom is most likely to be seen. Haunted houses do not all look like the Bates Motel, nor are graveyards particularly fertile territory for ghost-hunters. Thunder and lightning are definitely not required. Ghosts may very well appear nearly transparent or as a swirling wisp of mist, but more likely they will be solid forms, like the spectres of the dead airmen from Flight 401. They may be seen, heard or felt either in a tactile way or as some indefinable presence, but rarely all three. Spectres might attach themselves to a place or a person but usually seem free to materialize wherever and whenever they choose.

One American parapsychologist has coined the phrase 'semi-substantial' to describe the ambiguous reality of apparitions. It seems particularly apt, for although ghosts can affect the physical environment of matter they fleetingly inhabit (lifting solid objects etc.), they are also seen to appear and disappear suddenly, fade in and out of view slowly, pass through closed doors, walls and solid objects, float or glide rather than walk. Though they can talk out loud, more often they will communicate through gestures, symbols or telepathy. Precisely how a ghost achieves all this remains open to speculation. It would appear sure, however, that ghosts who behave with intelligence and intent are demonstrating the ability not only to interact with other minds but also the capacity to pull together some element of etheric or other substance in order to materialize. Ghosts with a less solid appearance may be returning via a different method, possibly the mental projection from their own minds into the mind of the observer – a sort of telepathically-spawned hallucination. Perhaps no single hypothesis is comprehensive enough to account for each and every type of ghostly manifestation. But whichever supposition we lean towards, the undeniable fact remains that the visionary entity we term 'ghost' either is, or is driven by, some form of autonomous consciousness, a part of the human psyche that has survived the death of the brain, and whose continued existence is independent of the blood, bone and tissue counterpart which emerged long before from the womb.

Many witnesses say ghosts appear as if they were still alive which raises the distinct possibility that people sometimes see ghosts without realizing it. Curiously, apparitions do not necessarily reflect the presence of someone who is dead, since there are many reports of 'living ghosts', visions of people who have remained very much alive in their earthly body. Some people even have the dubious pleasure of witnessing the sudden materialization of their own ghost or *doppelgänger*, though these instances are extremely rare.

Reports of 'living ghosts' are considered by some to undermine the possibility of the existence of 'dead' ones. In fact, they do nothing of the sort. The possibility that some part of the human soul or spirit is able to function independently of the physical body is central to the case against death. As we shall see in subsequent chapters, there is much evidence to suggest that we all have at least two (and possibly several more) bodies apart from the one made from blood, bone and tissue that we instantly recognize. The appearance of so-called 'living ghosts' does nothing to lessen that possibility. If anything, they increase its likelihood.

There may be no such thing as a typical ghost, but recent studies into the various types of ghost encounter suggest that some sensory experiences occur more frequently than others. In 1975, the Director of the Institute For Psycho-Physical Research in Oxford, Celia Green, made a detailed study of the SPR's archive for her book *Apparitions*. She found that the vast majority of reported experiences, eighty-four per cent, involved the phantom being seen, whilst just over a third, thirty-seven per cent, entailed auditory phenomena, and only fifteen per cent included the sensation of being touched. Although barely a handful of witnesses recorded noticing an odd smell of any sort, many reported feeling an unnatural coldness together with an indefinable change in atmosphere. As we shall see later, when we come to examine specifically the phenomena of hauntings, inexplicable drops in room temperatures have on occasions been measured by the thermometers of paranormal investigators – a fact which cannot be readily explained by reference to the human imagination.

Some have gone even further towards a comprehensive sub-classification of the supernatural. Another British researcher, G.N.M. Tyrell, postulated in his earlier study, also entitled *Apparitions*, that (excluding the ghosts of the living) there were really four main categories of true phantoms. First and most common were those Tyrell labelled 'place-centred spirits', who continued to inhabit the earth plane by choice. According to Tyrell, these were only rarely frightening to an observer. A second variety were 'post-mortem ghosts', which appeared soon after the person's death – perhaps to relatives in order to reassure them that all was well. A third category were 'crisis apparitions', which appeared at times when the subject underwent a moment of extreme stress – often a violent or sudden death. The British writer considered this to be a form of soul-sympathy, an extension of the facility of telepathic communication which he believed to be possible between the minds of living persons. Tyrell's fourth classification was that unfortunate variety of ghost forced to remain earth-bound, either against its wishes or because it is incapable of recognizing that it has died. Such spirits would, he felt, go on to haunt the places where they once lived and generally make a nuisance of themselves. Unable to visualize the reality of the true afterlife state, these entities behave as if they were still alive; their minds being obsessed with the earthly desires and pleasures they once knew. Tyrell believed it was from this fourth group of spirits that the majority of haunted house stories came. In cases where the spirits had been cruel and evil in their earthly existence he wrote that frightening and even violent phenomena might become manifest.

Of the types of ghost that G.N.M. Tyrell identified, some are more useful than others to the researcher engaged in proving the factual existence of an afterlife. Particularly worthy of consideration are those 'crisis apparitions' which have often seemed to return to earth with a purposeful intent – even relaying information to witnesses which they could not otherwise have known. In these cases the possibility of hallucination cannot readily be held up as an explanation.

A famous example of a 'crisis apparition' concerns the manifestation of a phantom at a dinner given in 1863 by the Baroness De Boisleré, attended by many notable personages in French society. During the last course of the meal the hostess saw a vision of her uniformed son Honoré appear at the head of the table. Badly bleeding, his eyes had been shot away leaving only a gaping wound in their sockets. The baroness fainted leaving the other guests bewildered. Two months later it emerged that the young man had died that day, shot through the eyes by a rebel bullet whilst serving in Mexico. Given the continental difference in time it would appear that young Honoré's grisly form had manifested itself at the exact hour of his sudden death thousands of miles away.

A strikingly similar example surrounds the last moments of Wilfred Owen, the World War I poet who appeared in London at the moment of his death in 1918. A veteran of the Somme, Owen survived the great battles of the trenches only to be killed a few days before the Armistice ended the conflict. Knowing the war to be close to its end, Owen's father had been hoping his son would be spared but when he saw him suddenly appear as a shining figure dressed in his officer's uniform he knew in his heart that the young soldier would not be coming home. Sure enough a week after Mr Owen saw his son's apparition he received an official telegram stating how Captain Wilfred Owen had died of injuries sustained in battle. If accurate, the time of his son's death in a French field hospital would appear to coincide precisely with the appearance of his spectral form in England.

Very often crisis ghosts are heard rather than seen. Camille Flammarion, in his book *The Unknown* (1900) recounts in detail a story told by the botanist Carl Linné, who was awoken one night in 1766 by the sound of somebody walking up the stairs towards his private study. Linné recognized the steps as the familiar approach of his close friend Karl Clerk, who had a peculiarly heavy way of walking, yet no one entered and when he opened the door the staircase was deserted. The next day Linné was informed that his friend had passed away in a tavern the previous evening, apparently at the same time he had heard the idiosyncratic steps in his home.

A far more recent example of a ghost who returned audibly comes from Indiapolis, Indiana. In October 1987 Christopher Evans was killed instantly when a pilotless jet plane crashed into the Ramada Inn Hotel where he was a receptionist. Yet ten minutes after the disaster Evans' parents received a phone call from their son telling them of the accident and assuring them that he was not hurt. Only when the couple went to the hotel to find Christopher's body laid out by rescuers did they realize that the voice they had heard was the voice of a dead man.

Some occultists (and more recently some scientists) believe that the moment of physical death can lead to an effusion of energy into the surrounding area. Should this be the case it may explain why some deaths are occasionally accompanied by outbreaks of spontaneous paranormal disturbance. Specific psychokinetic activities accompanying the passing of a human soul that I have personally come across in England include: locked doors mysteriously opening or closing; lights being turned on and off; glass windows shattering without cause; pets behaving oddly; heating systems malfunctioning and televisions being switched on of their own accord. Unless my peers in the parascientific community are deliberately and regularly fabricating evidence to buttress their own preconceived beliefs, my own experiences are in line with other investigators currently working in this field.

Clocks and watches stopping for no apparent reason at the moment of their owners' passing appear to be among the most common of all phenomena reported to parapsychologists. When James Hyslop, the American who ran the US Society for Psychical Research, died in 1920, not only was his spectral form to be seen floating along the corridors of his home, but his daughter's watch stopped and the grandfather clock of an old friend began to chime incessantly for no apparent reason. Several days after Hyslop's death, Gertrude Tubby, a fellow member of the Psychic Society, attended a seance with a trance medium whom Hyslop had never met. At the time neither she nor the medium knew of the watch-stopping incident but during the session a message was received in which the dead researcher described it and claimed credit for affecting the time mechanisms.

Throughout history there have been several other examples of clocks stopping for no apparent reason other than to mark the death of their owner. For instance, an elaborate clock made for Henry VIII was said to have stopped at his moment of death in 1547. It stopped once more beside the deathbed of his successor Edward VI in 1553, and has marked the passing of at least two other monarchs since. Now kept in Hampton Court Palace another inexplicable stoppage acknowledged the death in apartments there of one Miss Jane Cuppage during the early part of this century.

A contemporary example of the same phenomenon was the way in which the favourite alarm clock of the dying Pope Paul VI rang without warning at the precise moment of the Pontiff's demise on the evening of Sunday 6 August 1978. As usual the clock had been set for 6.30 am yet it stopped and began to ring – for no discernible natural reason – at 9.45 pm, seconds after the last rites had been completed in the papal bed chamber. One report suggested that Pope Paul VI's likeness was seen walking through St Peter's Bascilica the same night, though this was officially denied by a Vatican spokesman.

The eerie phenomenon of bells ringing at the moment of a human death but without the aid of human hands are almost as commonplace as the stopping of clocks.

In November 1930 vagrant Albert von Calow crept
into a hayloft in the village of Berkheim in Bavaria.
When he died in his sleep bells in the church next door
began preternaturally to peal and continued to do so
throughout the night. A comparable event awoke the
residents of Carpegna, a small town on the Adriatic
coast of Italy, in November 1970 after the death of
a Franciscan monk. The great bells in the tower of
San Niccolo Monastery rang all night and continued
to burst into song at random intervals throughout the
following months. Similarly, on the stroke of midnight on
6 February 1980 the small Scottish fishing village of Crail
was woken by its old curfew bell whose modern electrical
mechanism had been installed some years before by a
local electrician, Lawrence Nash. Council maintenance
men were unable to explain how the bell had begun
to toll, until the following morning when it became
clear that the sounds had coincided with the death
of Lawrence Nash in his cottage several miles away.

Crisis apparitions and related parapsychic phenomena cannot readily be explained in terms of natural
causes unless one chooses to challenge the honesty
of those who report them. It is significant that those
who witnessed the apparitions described above had
no way of knowing that the person they were seeing
had died. Certainly it is true to say that inanimate
objects such as clocks or bells cannot be affected
naturally by such events. How then can we explain
them without first accepting the reality of ghostly
energies?

Another category of spirit which goes a long way
towards building a case for the reality of human survival
are those instances where visions return to impart some
piece of specific evidence for their continued existence
to friends or acquaintances.

In the late eighteenth century a particularly impressive
spirit of this variety manifested itself before Henry
Brougham – a British Whig politician who was later to
become Lord Chancellor. As university undergraduates
Brougham and a friend (referred to as 'G') had con-
jectured upon the possibility of surviving death. While
still young men, both agreed that, upon their separate
deaths, they would attempt to return, and thereby prove
the existence of the hereafter to the other. In later life 'G'
travelled east to seek his fortune in trade and both men
lost contact. However, on the night of 19 December 1799
'G' returned in the form of a spectre which Brougham
found sitting in – of all places – his bathroom. The
ghost was not at all frightening but simply sat smiling
benignly. Nevertheless, the politician was so surprised
that he slipped and fell over backwards temporarily
losing consciousness. When he recovered the vision
was gone. Two months afterwards Brougham received
a letter from India stating that his old companion had
died on 19 December. Clearly 'G', had lost no time in
fulfilling his promise.

Though it may surprise some readers, astonishment
rather than fear is probably the most common reaction
to seeing a ghost. On 19 April 1957 two Finnish women
claimed to have shared an elevator with the country's
former President, Dr Juho Kusti Paasikivi, who had been
dead for some four months. At first neither of the women
recognized Paasikivi, but when he introduced himself
they stared open-mouthed in amazement. Chuckling in
a good-humoured manner, he assured them that they
need not be afraid, whilst adding little in explanation for
his dramatic appearance. 'Ladies,' he joked, 'you must
certainly be wondering why I am here when I should
be in the grave. But it is really so!' The ex-president

stepped off at the next floor, leaving the two witnesses dumbstruck.

The claimed return of the Finnish statesman leaves us with a few imponderable questions. Even if we accept that he appeared in order to prove he had survived, why on earth did he materialize in such an odd location and to two people he had never known? No answer appears to be remotely satisfactory yet this type of behaviour is characteristic of many phantoms. Less baffling in its choice of witness was the spirit of British Christian philosopher C.S.Lewis, who, soon after dying in 1963, appeared before the prominent theolgian Cannon J.B.Phillips, in order to offer advice. Phillips had met Lewis only once in life, though they regularly corresponded on matters spiritual, often arguing over the possibility and nature of a continued existence beyond death's door. According to Phillips, the radiant figure of Lewis appeared in a chair, whilst the theologian was watching television in his front living room. Only days after Lewis's mortal remains had been laid to rest in the earth, the ghost of the philosopher seemed to Phillips to be positively exuding health and happiness, grinning broadly at his host's unease. The precise nature of the advice Lewis offered is not made clear in Phillips' account, though the churchman maintained that it was particularly pertinent to problems he was facing at the time. In writing of the experience, Phillips describes how the ghostly form reappeared the next week at the same time, once more to impart a helpful suggestion. When asked how he was able to remain alive when his body lay under the earth, Lewis apparently replied with a chuckle 'My dear fellow this sort of thing is happening all the time.'

And so it was. The return of C.S. Lewis is simply one amongst thousands of examples recorded by paranormal researchers on both sides of the Atlantic. The very fact that such witnesses as Cannon Phillips and Henry Brougham were unlikely to concoct fantasies must surely lend credence to the probability that much of this reported phenomena actually happened. It is difficult to imagine what these men of reputation could conceivably have to gain from lying about their experiences and given the considerable detail contained in their encounters, one finds it hard to believe that they were simply fooled by tricks of light. After all, can an illusion talk?

Another example of a ghost returning, this time to fulfil a promise, is recalled by British author Robert Graves in *Goodbye To All That*, an account of the writer's experiences in World War I. The phantom in this instance was that of a young infantry man, Private Challoner, whom Graves had known whilst they were both undergoing training in Lancaster. Challoner's battalion was subsequently posted to France a few weeks before Graves' regiment, and on the day he was due to embark the young soldier had cheerfully told the author that they would meet again in France. In fact Challoner was killed in a battle near the town of Festubert, some days before Graves' troop-ship crossed the channel. A month or so later, however, Graves insists that he clearly saw the young man walk past the window of his billet room, smoking a cigarette. According to the account in *Goodbye To All That*, Challoner recognized his old acquaintance, saluted and walked on. When a shocked Graves reached out of the window, he found only a smouldering cigarette butt lying where Challoner's ghost had passed a few seconds before. Typically, the writer ends his description of the incident with a touch of irony – 'Ghosts were numerous in France at the time.'

*   *   *

Given the wholesale slaughter of the Great War, few would take issue with the British writer's analysis. But does it, I wonder, hide a more literal truth? Leaving aside the obvious implication that more deaths ought logically to lead to an increase in ghosts, are some types of death more likely than others to result in the manifestation of spirit? After all, though we all surely die, we do not all return in this way. Curiously, evidence has emerged to suggest that the manner of some deaths does make the emergence of a ghost more likely. In a 1961 publication entitled *The Supreme Adventure – an Analysis of Psychic Communication*, the eminent English scientist and psychical researcher, Dr Robert Crockall, claimed to have detected a marked division between the types of psychic phenomena which followed violent deaths and those from natural causes. According to Crookall, a low level of psychical phenomena – raps, clocks stopping, doors shutting by themselves – were found to be associated with those who died in their sleep, whilst a sudden death, like that suffered in battle or in a car accident, would often coincide with more violent and prolonged outbreaks of telekinetic energy. Thus full-scale hauntings were caused, wrote Crookall, by a 'sudden and uncontrolled release of psychic charge' into the surrounding etheric substance (a hypothetical soul-matter which occultists say pervades the entire physical and non-physical universe).

The beliefs of other cultures tend to bear out Dr Crookall's theory. In Bengal, India, the souls of those who have been executed or killed by a tiger are known as 'Bula' which means 'wanderers who have lost their way'. In other parts of the sub-continent, a woman who dies in her early years through suicide, accident or childbirth is believed more likely to be become an active ghost or 'Mohani', than one who sees through her full life cycle.

Elsewhere, the assumption that violent death leads to the return of angry or restless ghosts has characterized superstitions as far apart as Burma, Japan, Persia and the Slavic countries.

Interestingly, the findings of other researchers also tend to back up Crookall's assertions. When Italian investigator Professor Ernesto Bazzanno meticulously examined a total of more than three hundred reports of hauntings across Europe, he found that in two out of every three cases the disturbances could be traced back to a fatal tragedy of one form or another. Ivan T. Sanderson found a similar pattern repeated among a sample of over 150 hauntings he investigated from the United States and Canada.

Haunted houses have been familiar to man ever since he began to build a roof over his head. The walking dead have been reported to inhabit every kind of dwelling – not only the castles and country homes of literary legend but also tribesmen's huts in the Kalahari, crofters' cottages in the Scottish Highlands, slum dwellings on the outskirts of Rio de Janeiro and tenement blocks in New York's toughest ghettos. Hauntings are not even restricted to purely domestic surroundings. In my research throughout Britain, I have uncovered tales of haunted hotels and inns, theatres and opera houses, schools, factories, libraries, prisons, mines . . . the list is endless. Close to where I live in the English county of Essex there is even a popular discotheque which seems to have its own ghostly resident. Britain's reputation as the most haunted country in the world is perhaps unsurprising since there are so many ancient churches, castles and ancestral homes still standing, and because the history of these islands is rich in battles, murders and executions.

However, tales of famous hauntings from hundreds of

years ago are of more interest to the casual reader than
they are to the serious parascientific investigator. When
we are dealing with legends which have their beginnings
in a bygone era the likelihood of embellishment and the
lack of hard evidence are heavily characteristic. Their
usefulness to the case against death is subsequently
reduced to a minimum. Nevertheless, there is one ancient
variety of manifestation – the persistent haunting of
stretches of road – which I believe commands special
attention. Modern sightings, which have come to be
called the 'phantom hitchhiker syndrome', are not only
too numerous to ignore but frequently compelling in their
intensity.

The experience of English motorist Roy Fulton is
typical. Returning from a darts match in October 1979
Fulton picked up a young hitchhiker on a deserted road
near Dunstable, in Bedfordshire. It was roughly 9 pm,
dark and growing steadily foggy, when the driver first
encountered the youth half a mile after passing through
the small village of Stanbridge. The stranger on the
road looked real enough in the headlights; he was later
described by Fulton as being roughly nineteen years old
with dark, longish hair.

The driver even remembered what he wore – a dark
round-neck jumper over a white shirt. Once seated in the
car's passenger seat the hitchhiker was asked where he
was heading; he said nothing and simply pointed ahead.
They drove on in silence until they had almost reached the
next town of Totternhoe, at which point Fulton offered
his uncommunicative passenger a cigarette. It was not
accepted – the youth had disappeared. Minutes later
the shaken motorist was relating his story to stupefied
customers in a nearby public house.

Many readers will find this tale hard to take seriously
and I can understand why. It is certainly much easier to

believe that Roy Fulton was simply tired and imagined the whole thing. But the Bedfordshire man's experience is by no means an isolated example, and anyone who has researched the phenomenon cannot help but be struck by the way that phantom hitchhiker encounters follow a characteristically similar pattern. Usually the hitchhiker is seen at night in a car's headlights, is then picked up and says little or nothing, but otherwise behaves as a real person. Then suddenly he or she vanishes without warning, leaving the bemused drivers doubting their sanity.

On at least one occasion, however, the roles have been curiously reversed. By his own testimony, American actor Telly Savalas, famous for his portrayal of Kojak, was once picked up by a Cadillac-driving ghost after he had himself ran out of petrol on a lonely desert highway. Unlike Fulton's spirit-passenger, Savalas's lift engaged in friendly conversation, freely divulging his name and telephone number and other personal details, before dropping the actor off at a gas station. The following afternoon Savalas phoned the number to express his thanks for the good turn, only to learn from the distressed woman on the other end of the line that the man he had spoken to was her dead husband, killed three years earlier in an accident at the very spot the actor was picked up. Although the dead man had never driven a Cadillac in life, descriptions Savalas gave matched his appearance in every detail, as did the personal details. As soon as he saw a photograph of the dead man Savalas had no doubt that he had been assisted by a ghost.

Sometimes the same apparition is seen by several motorists. On the night of 10 April 1978 South African motor cyclist Dawie van Jaarsveld picked up a girl on a highway near the town of Uniondale. Ten miles on, stopping to refuel, he found his passenger gone and the crash helmet he had given her to wear strapped to the seat. When he went to the police they confirmed that an identical report had been received two years before from a motorist named Anton le Grange. Subsequent enquiries by paranormal researcher Cynthia Hind identified the ghost as one Maria Roux, killed in an accident on 12 April 1968 at the spot where both van Jaarsveld and le Grange had met the hitchhiker. A photograph of Roux was later recognized by both men. Reports from the past decade suggest that the young woman's ghost has continued to appear at the same location, always around the anniversary of her death and invariably to young men travelling alone.

Faced with this type of story the voices of the rational sceptics fall quiet. To begin with, accounts of phantom hitchhikers are a world-wide enigma whose numbers can be counted in hundreds if not thousands. Indeed, a whole book has been published by one English author devoted purely to the modern British examples he has uncovered. Secondly, these stories are clearly not the product of demented minds or attention seekers. Most witnesses to phantom hitchhikers are deeply confused by their experiences and many have been profoundly and, on occasions, unpleasantly affected by them. Few, when cross-examined, seemed to lack sincerity and while some road-hauntings turn out to be apocryphal tales, there are far more which bear the undeniable ring of truth. In their recent pot-pourri of the unnatural entitled *Mysteries of Modern Britain* writers Janet and Colin Bord include a chapter outlining several stretches of English road in south-west England – the A38 near Wellington, Somerset, being one – where sightings are particularly common. They also describe a number of cases where motorists have collided with apparently real people only to find an inexplicable absence of victim. Invariably, as with the South African experiences outlined above, such examples correspond to places where a fatal accident once occured.

Phantom hitchhikers are somewhat unusual because apparitions of the haunting variety rarely seek contact with the living. Usually all they do is to allow themselves to be seen and only seldom is some form of message communicated. This has led several paranormal researchers to speculate that ghosts which haunt the same physical location for centuries may in fact be an energy imprint, a fragment or residue of the psychic aura of the dead and long-since departed souls they represent. Such a hypothesis would do much to explain those curious spirits which apparently move in hologramatic fashion, performing the same duties or actions that they were once engaged upon during their mortal existence. The annals of the British Society for Psychical Research are packed full of stories of phantom monks deep in prayer, spectral servants sweeping floors and such like.

A possibly related phenomenon concerns the visions of long-since dead persons whose visual presence corresponds to structures, such as walls, floors, etc. that existed in their own time, rather than those of the present day structures in which they continue to appear. Perhaps the best example of a phantom tableau which meticulously observed the pattern of the past was reported by Harry Martindale, a heating engineer who, in 1952, witnessed the spontaneous manifestation of a column of Roman soldiers whilst repairing a heating installation in the cellar of York's Treasurer's house. Heralded by a loud trumpet blast, the Legionnaires, some fourteen or sixteen in number, came through a wall and marched diagonally in double-file across the room, completely ignoring the terrified onlooker. Unburdening himself the next day to a local historian, Martindale explained how, to his total bafflement, each spectre had seemingly walked thigh-deep in the stone slabs which paved the cellar floor. The historian became convinced that the engineer's tale was authentic and suggested that a Roman road might lay a few feet below the foundations of the Medieval Treasurer's house. Studies of Roman maps confirmed the hunch, suggesting that the spirits Martindale saw believed themselves to be (or were) still marching on the surface of the long-since buried road. Whichever explanation we choose to accept, the Legionnaires were no figment of Martindale's imagination. Seven years later, an archaeologist working in the cellar of the building witnessed the same phenomenon, complete with trumpet blast.

The idea that a psychic record or imprint might remain locked in the etheric substance of a particular place would also seem to provide a suitable explanation for one of the most enigmatic hauntings in the entire history of English ghost folklore – the mass apparitions of Edgehill which appeared repeatedly during the winter months of 1642/3. On 23 October 1642 Royalist troops led by Prince Rupert engaged the Rebel Parliamentary Forces at Edgehill, Warwickshire, in the first major battle of the Civil War. Though neither side gained a decisive victory, it was a bloody affair and bodies lay rotting in the open fields for months afterwards. Three days after the battle ended, a group of local shepherds saw another conflict take place upon the same slopes of Edgehill – a battle complete with men and horses, clashing swords and roar of cannons. Yet this time no real military action had taken place: the entire vision lasting several hours was an extraordinary illusion. Incredibly, the same vast tableau was re-enacted several times during that winter, including a display on Christmas Eve. Each time large crowds turned up from nearby towns and villages to witness the eerie phenomenon. When an account of the phantom battle was published by a London printer, Thomas Jackson, in January 1643, King Charles I became so interested that he sent a team of his most trusted officers to investigate. On their return they confirmed the tale, having seen the ghostly battle themselves and heard the screams of dying men with their own ears, not once but twice on consecutive days. Each Royalist was able to recognize the figures of comrades who had died the previous October.

The mass haunting of the Civil War battlefield witnessed by so many at the time (and if my own research is correct, on at least two occasions during the present century) must be one of the most compelling examples of the dead returning before the eyes of the living. Were such a visitation to recur with reliable regularity, say on the anniversary of the battle every year, then doubtless attempts would be made to capture the events on film. Unfortunately, ghosts are rarely so obliging as to pose for the camera but even if they did it is not altogether clear whether attempts to photograph them would succeed. Since the early days of the photographic process, attempts to capture phantoms on film have proved decidedly unsatisfactory and much so-called photographic evidence has been exposed as cheap fakery. However, the history of psychic photography is not quite the unmitigated catalogue of 'fraud, folly and fabrication' that one notable critic deemed it to be and some exposures really do seem worthy of the seal of authenticity. Easily the most interesting are those in which anomalous images spontaneously appear on family snap-shots, in situations when the photographer has noticed nothing untoward at the moment the picture was taken. During the twentieth century there have been many such examples.

In the summer of 1925, a holiday portrait of English aristocrat Lady Palmer, taken by a companion during a visit to the Bascilia at Domnesy in France, clearly showed a pair of priests outlined in the background. The figures were dressed in robes unlike any used by local priests for more than seventy years and the women insisted afterwards that they had been completely alone in the chapel. Another example of a 'phantomagraph' was the picture taken in 1954 by the Reverend Kenneth Lord in his own parish church of Nealy Hall, Rippon, where a straightforward interior shot of the church altar produced the shape of a cloaked and hooded figure. Again, Lord insisted that no person had been in his viewfinder at the moment he pressed the button and the shape was too clearly human to be a shadow or optical illusion. Another ghost was captured on film by Suffolk housewife Mrs Mabel Chinnery in March 1954. Mrs Chinnery's picture of her husband sitting at the wheel of his car, revealed also the clear imprint of her deceased mother Mrs Ellen Hammell occupying the back seat. Recent attempts to assess scientifically the validity of the Chinnery photograph by modern methods of computer analysis have established it as probably genuine and no satisfactory explanation has been put forward to explain the enigma. Positive proof that Mrs Chinnery's ghost had returned it may not be but there can be little doubt that something very odd indeed happened at the moment the photograph was taken.

Weird images continue to crop up with what seems to be increasing regularity. In the autumn of 1990 during a holiday to the Austrian Tyrol, Englishman George Todd took several pictures of a group of friends sharing a meal in their hotel. When he had the prints processed in his own home town of Scunthorpe he was amazed to see an extra guest at their table. The mysterious woman's form, slightly out of focus yet undoubtedly smiling, seemed to be floating just in front of the others present. The fact that two beer glasses on the table were clearly in front of her precluded the possibility that the photograph was simply an amalgam of Todd's picture and another holiday snap.

An equally odd picture was published for the first time in a British Sunday supplement in October 1991. Taken on the previous New Year's Eve in London's Covent Garden shopping area by a family named Webb, it clearly captured not only the couple's three-year-old daughter but also a floating phantom figure of a schoolgirl dressed in Edwardian black. The girl's form, seemingly legless, was partly obscured by other solid objects, thus indicating precisely her position and physical reality within the three dimensional framework of the picture. When it was carefully studied by Vernon Harrison, former president of the Royal Photographic Society and a world renowned expert on forgeries, he pronounced it to be genuine beyond reasonable doubt.

Perhaps the most famous example of ghost photography remains the most convincing, not only because of the quality of the image produced but also because of the dozens of witnesses. On 2 December 1929 an American-owned tanker, the S.S. *Watertown*, was steaming south towards the Panama Canal from San Pedro, California, when leaking gasoline asphyxiated two seamen working in the hold. Two days later James Courtney and Michael Meehan were buried at sea, following the usual service and the ship continued its voyage. The following morning something very strange was noticed by the ship's first mate. Looking through binoculars, the officer could clearly make out the faces of two men bobbing up and down in the waves off the Watertown's starboard bow. They appeared to be moving, keeping pace with the tanker. Alerted to the mystery, the ship's captain,

Keith Tracy, ordered his vessel to be steered towards them. It soon became clear that the shapes in the water were unquestionably the faces of the two dead sailors consigned to the waves the previous day. To the amazement of the terrified ship's crew, the apparitions continued to be seen alongside the ship for several days; only when the ship entered the canal zone just off Balboa did they finally vanish.

If the joint testimonies of all those aboard the S.S. *Watertown* were the only evidence to emerge from this curious incident, it would still remain an extraordinarily impressive ghost sighting. However, it is not. Captain Tracy had with him a box camera on the voyage and took a roll of film of the watery apparitions. All those who later saw the pictures, officials of the company which employed them and the friends and relations who grieved for their loss, agreed afterwards that the photographs showed the unmistakable features of the two seamen.

Fascinating though it is, the picture taken by Captain Tracy of the S.S. *Watertown* is sadly untypical of most purported ghost pictures. It is disappointing (although perhaps not that surprising since ghosts usually arrive unannounced) that 160 years after the development of the photographic process, photographers have only rarely been able to trap conclusive evidence of human survival in the eye of the camera lens. Faulty equipment, misidentifications, slow or double exposures, have all been proved responsible for so-called mysterious images. Moreover, just as fraudulent mediums have done much to discredit the cause of spiritualism, phantomagraphic hoaxers have wrought considerable harm to the overall case for the belief in ghosts. In the right hands the camera *can* lie, and many photographs that were once considered inexplicable by passionate

believers in the afterlife have long since been accounted
for by wholly material causes.

The damage caused by charlatans has not been confined
to spirit photography either. One infamous English
ghosthunter, Harry H. Price, has done more than most
to bring psychic research into disrepute, and sceptics are
ever-willing to cite his example. Price already had quite
a reputation for uncovering hauntings when, in 1929, he
began to investigate mysterious phenomena reported by
a clergyman and his wife, who were occupying a rectory
at Borley, a village on the Essex/Suffolk border. The
Reverend Lionel Foyster had spoken of many odd
goings-on, including strange sounds, broken windows,
cold spots and odd, unpleasant smells. These manifestations were followed by a series of physical attacks
upon the luckless Mrs Mariane Foyster, carried out by
an invisible assailant.

For a seasoned ghosthunter like Price, the case had
everything he could possibly wish for, and he lost no
time in persuading the vicar to allow him to undertake
a full investigation. Subsequently, the ghosthunter also
claimed to have strange experiences, seeing lights illumin-
ating empty rooms, hearing voices calling to him, and
feeling the presence of evil all around. Researching local
history, Price linked the manifestations to a medieval
legend concerning the elopement of a young woman with
a monk. Their story ended tragically when, according
to the tale, the lovers were recaptured and beheaded.
Price expressed his personal belief that the bones of the
sad couple were entombed inside the rectory walls and
shortly afterwards, triumphantly produced a skull which
he claimed to have found buried beneath the floorboards.
Following the abrupt departure of the hapless Foysters
who had had enough, Price purchased the property from

an estate agent and began an elaborate series of investigations aided by more than fifty volunteers. In 1940, after a decade of research, he published a book outlining his findings, pronouncing it to be 'without doubt the best-documented case of a haunting in the annals of psychical research'. It was a huge money-making success, won fame for its author, and earned Borley Rectory the reputation of being 'the most haunted house in England'.

As the years passed, however, Harry Price's findings began to be called into question. Shortly after the ghosthunter's death in 1956 the *Daily Mail* newspaper published a witnessed account by a journalist who claimed to have seen Price throwing pebbles across the room to indicate poltergeist activity. At the same time, another journalist photographer Cynthia Ledsham, who had also spent some time at Borley in 1944, raised doubts about the authenticity of a photograph purportedly showing objects levitating. This was only the beginning. The following year, a scathing book written by psychic researcher Trevor Hull entitled *The Search for Harry Price* depicted its subject as an overzealous hoaxer and unscrupulous liar. Price's image was further tarnished in 1959 when the British SPR delivered a damning 180-page report which challenged virtually every aspect of the Borley investigations. Echoing Trevor Hull's character assassination, the SPR's report concluded that Price had duped his own helpers into believing the stories and then ingeniously created 'happenings' to prove the existence of imaginary forces. Afterwards the reports of the ghosthunter's aides were heavily edited for newspaper and magazine articles. Editors keen to hear evidence of a genuine mystery were well satisfied and the general public lapped it up, never doubting the investigator's honesty.

Today the legend of the Borley ghosts, like the bricks and mortar of the building itself, has been comprehensively demolished and few remember that the original manifestations which terrorized the Foysters remain unexplained. The unmasking of Harry Price merely serves to confirm the suspicions of many sceptics, who point to the Borley affair as evidence that supposedly supernatural manifestations have their roots in human imagination, human gullibility and fraud.

Some have even claimed that all hauntings can be accounted for in much the same way. In particular a group of investigators known as the Committee for the Scientific Investigation of Claims of the Paranormal (CSISOP) have spent the last twenty or so years since their foundation trying to discredit the very notion of ghosts with the sort of frenzied conviction that borders on paranoia. Fronted by such figures as James 'the amazing' Randi, an American magician who has made a living out of debunking anything that smacks of the supernatural, CSISOP's team of rationalists only rarely take account of all known facts surrounding a given case. Far from approaching the subject with an open mind, they tend to attack not only the honesty of psychics but also those unsuspecting and otherwise innocent members of the ordinary public who just happen to suddenly find themselves in the same location as a ghost. In my experience, sceptics who operate on this level are almost impossible to reason with. Because they cannot come to terms with the possibility that genuinely strange events may occur, they often deny that they ever happened at all. As a rule they are highly selective in the cases they choose to focus upon and in the CSISOP journal *The Skeptical Inquirer* you will find only the least impressive of ghost sightings.

Everyone is entitled to his or her own viewpoint. The debunking fraternity quite clearly have theirs and I am not about to challenge their right to it. No doubt the phantoms that some witnesses claim to see are truly, 'all in the mind'. But if we allow ourselves an objective analysis of the accumulated evidence, it is difficult to see how such allegations can provide a satisfactory explanation for all ghostly encounters. Witnessed accounts of phantom forms have emerged down the centuries from every culture known to anthropology. These stories continue unabated to the present day, suggesting that ghost sightings are a phenomenon largely unaffected by changing attitudes and superstitions.

Literally millions of ghosts have now been seen and the encounters of thousands of percipients have been analyzed by scrupulous investigators who judge them to be true. In many ways it is the sheer size of this body of evidence that remains its most impressive feature. As the British SPR's first official report commented 'the point that impresses us most is not the quality of evidence but its overwhelming quantity.' Overwhelming to be sure and growing all the time.

Just as the SPR Census of 1882 drew a one-in-ten proportion of replies claiming personal contact, so more recent surveys conducted in a host of other countries have illicited much the same response. Some studies concentrating on specific groups within society have drawn even higher figures. In 1971, for example, a report appeared in the British Medical Association's journal the *Practitioner*, which focused on a survey conducted by Welsh GP Dr William Rees. Rees had asked bereaved women in his own catchment area whether they had ever seen their dead husbands during their widowhood. To his amazement he found that over half claimed to have done so. Rees felt that these findings amounted to rather more than a few random experiences and that the women's psychological condition could hardly explain evidence on this scale. In fact, the 1971 Welsh study is in line with other medical surveys. In 1980, for instance, a Californian clinical psychologist named Julian Burton began researching apparitional experiences after he saw a vision of his dead mother in his kitchen. Originally limiting his target groups to students already involved in the psychic research taking place in his own home city of Los Angeles, Burton later widened his survey to include people who had hitherto shown no interest in spiritualism or occult matters. From both sample groupings Burton discovered that over fifty per cent of respondents claimed at least one personal contact with the dead, confounding the commonly held superstition that ghosts were more likely to be seen by persons predisposed to believe in life after death.

Are such prodigous statistics simply a demonstration of the human mind's capability for self-delusion? A need for wish-fulfilment and nothing more? It seems implausible, and surely the psychological explanation cannot be applied to every case. Yet this is precisely the position held by most disbelievers in ghosts: to deny the existence of spirits one must throw out the evidence of *all* witnesses, no matter how many, no matter how reliable. In sharp contrast, those who have seen the truth for themselves tend to remain convinced of the reality of the phenomenon, often in the face of considerable pressure society puts upon them to reconsider their experience. Is it really so logical automatically to cast doubt upon the testimony of a ghost percipient when the testimony of the same person on a different matter would normally be accepted without question? I hardly think so.

*   *   *

If only a hundredth of all recorded sightings are true, then the case for ghosts could hardly be more overwhelming, by sheer reason of volume. Indeed, so widespread is the phenomenon of ghosts that most of us know at least one place that is reputedly haunted or has a close friend or relative who claims to have had an encounter. Whenever I lecture on the subject of the paranormal – something which I do regularly to all kinds of audiences, not simply psychics or spiritualists – several people invariably come up to me afterwards and relate a personal experience they have had of seeing an apparition. Occasionally one gets the impression that they are simply wanting to join in by telling a tale. Yet more often than not you can tell that they are relating an experience they believe they had in deadly earnest. Very often I am the first person they have spoken to about it.

Even in the course of everyday life I regularly seem to meet people who have had at least one brush with the unknown. Quite recently, for example, an A-level student I was tutoring, privately confided to having once seen a ghost herself. The experience had occurred when she was a young child; the ghost was that of her aunt who was due to be buried the next day. According to the girl's account, her relative's lifelike form entered her bedroom carrying a wreath of red roses, and the following day she saw the same wreath placed on top of the dead woman's coffin. Was this a case of my student making up the tale for my benefit, knowing of my own special interest in the subject, or did the incident really take place as she had described? Knowing her to be honest, I was naturally inclined towards the latter and see no reason to apologize for saying so. Perhaps the question 'Do you believe in ghosts?' should really be 'Do you believe other people?' Because we cannot summon a ghost and prepare an audience for its presence we are forced to form a judgement on second hand testimonies. Unsatisfactory though this may seem, the fact that some scientific observers continue to label all sightings of ghosts as misperceptions, errors of observation, or the mis-interpretation of natural phenomena is an insult to the intelligence of millions of people who have seen ghosts. What right have they to tell generation upon generation of percipients that they must really have been insane, too drunk or too stupid to know what they saw? In any case, if human testimony is held in such low regard, how is it that the judicial system has relied upon it for so long – often sending men to the gallows on the basis of a single eye-witness report? Why should an individual's word as witness to a crime be believed, and the same person's testimony as witness to a ghost be rejected?

Reasons for supporting the genuineness of apparitions are in fact numerous: descriptions often contain considerable detail; visions are frequently accompanied by other sensory stimuli; some occasionally perform physical actions – snuffing out candles, picking up objects, opening doors and so on. Even animals – which psychologists tell me tend not to suffer from hallucinations – regularly show sensitivity to a ghostly presence. Perhaps the strongest evidence of all for the existence of spirit manifestations are those accounts containing indications of external causation – examples where ghosts appear not only to one person but to several. Where a ghost's appearance and behaviour is corroborated by more than one mortal witness (such as the Flight 401 case) the 'all in the mind' hypothesis becomes untenable. But even if we accept the fact that apparitions do regularly appear with an element of realness, does it necessarily prove that they are true ghosts in the generally accepted sense, in other words that they are the living souls of personalities who once walked on the earthly plane?

To a writer researching the evidence for an afterlife, this is the key question. Whilst the realm of ghosts may be a fascinating area in its own right, its importance in helping to construct a case against death rests firmly upon the need to establish that the forms being seen are *alive*, and not some nebulous after-image of past events imprinted psychically on the ether. Are at least some ghosts precisely what they seem to be – the still living spirits of the so-called dead? Or can they all be written off as a residue of mental energy pulses?

As we have seen in this chapter, phantoms return for a variety of reasons: to deliver messages, to honour death compacts, to seek justice and, most commonly, to reassure loved ones of their continued existence. In order to establish the true nature of their reality the most useful examples to consider are those where a ghost returns with purposeful intent, either to impart some piece of information that the percipient knows nothing of (a phenomenon known as veridical hallucination) or to intercede physically in terrestrial events. Such examples are plentiful but a few stand out as being especially convincing. It will suffice to mention here just three.

The first, originally collected during the last century by the ASPR but re-published many times in paranormal literature, was reported by an American commercial traveller who witnessed the materialization of his sister who had passed away several years before at the age of eighteen. The witness, recorded only by his initials F.G., was not only shocked by his sister's sudden appearance, but also curious to notice an unfamiliar (and to him inexplicable) livid mark disfiguring the side of her cheek. Several weeks later, having returned to his own home, F.G. told his parents of the visitation and included the detail of the anomalous blemish. To the traveller's astonishment, his mother immediately dropped into a dead faint. Afterwards, having recovered, but still overcome with emotion, the woman explained through choked tears how, unnoticed by others, she had accidentally cut the face of her daughter's corpse while it lay in its coffin. Horrified that she had marred her beloved daughter's death mask, she had covered the wound with face powder and told no one of the incident. Understandably, all three family members became convinced that their lost relative had really returned with proof of survival.

An equally striking example was the return of Owen Harrison, a young British expatriate to South Africa who travelled to Europe to fight for the Allies during World War II and, as a result, lost his mortal life in the Italian Campaign of 1944. Though his immediate family had long since moved to Africa, it was to a Mrs Feakes, his English aunt, that Harrison's spirit appeared one evening, shrouded in a golden mist. He spoke just once, uttering the words 'Tell mum', before disappearing. Mrs Feakes was too upset to tell anyone, however, and even began to doubt her own sanity. But Owen's ghost was persistent, appearing again a few days later to make the same request and also mentioning this time the name of a girl, Helen. Before he vanished, he showed his aunt an exotic blue flower of a type she had never seen. It would, he said, be a sign which his mother would understand. After this second manifestation, Mrs Feakes did at last write to her sister in South Africa, describing the uncanny encounters in detail. The reply she received persuaded her that the vision of her nephew had been no product of her imagination. For it transpired, from Mrs Harrison's letter, that the blue flower was a rare, protected orchid which Owen had picked illegally from Table Mountain on his last leave. To avoid the possibility of being fined, he had shown it only to his mother and sister. If anything, 'Helen' was an even more conclusive piece of evidence, for although no one in his family had been aware of it at the time, investigation subsequently revealed that the youth had been secretly conducting a courtship with a girl of that name. Thus, for the grieving relatives of the dead soldier, the case against death was proven beyond reasonable doubt.

Of course for those of us who do not ourselves share such experiences, the leap of faith is less easy. Instances like those outlined above cannot, however, be put down to fragments of psychic energy. There was a point to the spirits returning, an end to be achieved – proof to their loved ones left on earth that their personality lived on. Their success in doing so challenges us all to reassess our own concept of the universe in which we live.

Ghosts which display an intelligent purpose in human affairs may be the rarest among all the sub-classifications of the spirit-world, yet they might also be the vital link that offers conclusive proof for survival of death. The example I have chosen to end this chapter is perhaps among the most unusual of all those that have emerged from the contemporary age – for it concerns a spirit which appeared not to demonstrate its own immortality but to save the life of a mortal threatened by imminent physical danger.

The curious incident occurred sometime in 1964 when a worker in an automobile assembly plant in Detroit narrowly escaped death after accidentally setting in motion a large piece of machinery above him. The endangered worker afterwards insisted, with his testimony confirmed by others on the factory floor, that a tall black figure had appeared at the vital moment to fling him bodily away from the threat. The survivor did not recognize the man who saved him but older men on the assembly line did. It was, they said, quite definitely the form of a worker who had been decapitated in a similar industrial accident more than twenty years before. The ghost had apparently returned to save a second victim from suffering a similar fate.

Was the appearance of the man's ghost simply a case of misidentification? A trick of the light? A fabrication expanded upon and embellished by successive generations of paranormal writers? Any of these interpretations could be true, yet to believe them we would have to have a pretty low opinion of human mentality. More likely is the fact that this last case and the two that preceded it are genuine examples of ghosts behaving in a way that no psychic after-image or telepathic projection could. Their deliberate interaction with the percipient greatly strengthens the probability that their appearance contained a level of objective reality. Through some process beyond our understanding these souls were able temporarily to draw together a combination of matter and energy which allowed them to clothe their ultra physical vehicle with something which was, for a few seconds, both substantial and visible.

How valuable then is this phenomenon of apparitions to our understanding of an afterlife? On the straightforward level of proof, it would seem very useful indeed. Ghosts provide visible evidence; some communicate intelligently; and their occasional fleeting presence suggests there could be a level of reality which does not involve matter as we know it. Their behaviour indicates the probability that consciousness, awareness, memory and personality can be preserved beyond bodily dissolution. On the other hand, they throw up many unanswered questions: why do so few dead people return? What happens if one does not become a ghost? Why do some people see spectres and not others? How can anything be alive which is not made of matter? What, if any, is the relation between the next world and the physical world around us, between the ethereal body and the body known to biologists? The answers to these and other riddles will gradually become clearer as we examine further the mounting evidence for the case against death.

Uninvited Guests

'Nothing is dead; men feign themselves dead, and
endure mock funerals and mournful obituaries, and
there stand looking at the window, in some strange
new disguise.'

Ralph Waldo Emerson
Nominalist and Realist

If ghostbusters existed they would probably be unemployed. Phantoms themselves may be numerous enough, but most people who encounter one recall their experience without the slightest trace of fear. As I wrote in the previous chapter, astonishment rather than terror is the most common sensation. This is by no means the end of the story, however, for if haunting apparitions are usually harmless the same cannot be said for all discarnate forces. The twin phenomena of poltergeists and possessions offer further proof that invisible intelligences operate on a level of reality which science does not recognize, and whilst Hollywood may embellish the truth, the facts behind the hype are real enough. Disturbing though it must seem to those of the rationalist persuasion, the evidence for the presence of these forces is now overwhelming. Moreover, since they leave the marks of their visitation – sometimes upon inanimate material objects, sometimes upon the minds and bodies of those they inhabit – their objective reality cannot be lightly dismissed as an optical illusion.

*   *   *

Poltergeists are among the more regularly reported
of all supernatural manifestations and although most
scientists are reluctant to dwell upon the subject, many
former sceptics have now come round to accepting their
existence. Like ghosts, they have been reported from
around the world and in a wide variety of situations.
A poltergeist may become manifest in a remote village
in Central Africa or in the heart of a modern Western
metropolis; the violent psychic intrusion may invade a
shanty dwelling in Manila or a state of the art office
block in Rome. The actual nature of the phenomenon
is scarcely less varied.

The German word 'poltergeist' literally means 'noisy
spirit' and the term is an apt one, for poltergeists often
announce their arrival by rappings on walls and doors.
However, their presence should not be confused with
the occasional bump in the night. In 1913 a spook
which invaded the residence of the Hugnet-Prousteau
family from Fougères-sur-Bièvre, France, caused bangs
in cavity walls of such violence that they not only shook
the house to its foundations but sent strong vibrations
through neighbouring buildings. According to witnesses,
the reverberations, which sounded like thunder, could be
heard several hundred yards away. When locals pounded
their own walls in an attempt to contact the presence,
it responded with the same number of percussions.
Interestingly, despite the force of these supernatural
resonations, no actual damage seems to have resulted
from the outbreak. Similarly there are numerous other
examples where loud noises, splintering wood, breaking
glass, furniture crashing etc. have, upon inspection, left
no visible traces whatsoever.

Nonetheless, most poltergeists *do* break things, often
to the despair of their unwilling hosts.

In the home of widow Mrs Beulah Wilson of Pearisburg,

Virginia, dishes, wooden chairs and other household
items were smashed with regularity by an invisible visitor
who arrived on the morning of 19 December 1976. Police
who investigated the destructive intruder assumed it was
a hoax until they saw for themselves the persistent movement of a kitchen cabinet weighing over 200 pounds.

When a poltergeist takes up residence, levitated items
are sometimes seen moving slowly through the air and
may even change direction several times in flight. Incredible though it may sound, floating objects have actually
been seen to pass through closed doors. In 1948, in
Vachendorf, Germany, a refugee family from Bohemia
was plagued by poltergeist activity which included the
regular bombardment (on them) of tools kept in a locked
wooden box and shoes left in a closed wardrobe. In
another German example from Nicklheim, which began
in February 1969, parascientists tested apportation stories
by placing perfume bottles in a sealed empty room and
calling upon the entity to move them. Soon afterwards,
the same bottles were seen outside in the garden, falling
gently from the sky.

The fact that the Nicklheim spirit responded intelligently to a spoken instruction supports the hypothesis
that a mind force is at work in poltergeist outbreaks.
Indeed, there is more often than not a human element
to the activity. In the case of a violent haunting from
Poona, India, earlier this century, fruit was left on the
doorstep as a bribe to make the ghost depart. The fruit
disappeared and sounds of eating were heard, followed
by the rematerialization of the rinds, bearing distinct
toothmarks. In 1975 an English poltergeist which moved
cars outside a house in Ascot, Berkshire, also listened to
telephone calls and regularly interrupted conversations
whenever its presence was mentioned. Speaking in a gruff
voice it seemed determined to intimidate its victims.

Communications from unwelcome visitors are by no means rare. In March 1920 a poltergeist which entered a sub-magistrate's home in Nidamangalam, Southern India, commonly left written messages on floors and walls. Purporting to be the handiwork of the magistrate's dead daughter, they bore strong resemblance to her familiar handwriting. Discarnate voices are also commonly heard during poltergeist activity though they are seldom coherent. A repetitive, unintelligible series of words is not unusual, and whisperings, screamings, or whimperings are quite typical.

The amount of trouble a poltergeist might cause varies greatly. In 1922 the Kogelnick family of Lieserbrucke, Austria, got so fed up with their invisible and untidy companion that they told it verbally to improve its habits. After watching Mrs Kogelnick sweep the kitchen floor the poltergeist promptly emptied several plantpots upside-down on the cleaned area. Another spirit with a sense of humour invaded the home of an American couple in Newark, New Jersey, in 1961. After a visiting psychic investigator, William Roll, explained to the frightened residents that their unseen guest was most unlikely to hurt them, the poltergeist immediately lifted up a sauce bottle and struck him squarely across the head with it.

Notwithstanding his bruised pride, Roll was probably right to reassure the Newark couple, since most poltergeists are mischievous rather than malevolent (and in any case usually leave after a few days). Whilst the majority of cases prove to be a temporary irritation, however, some others are extremely frightening. Few people who encounter these hostile entities forget the experience.

One of the most prolonged outbreaks of poltergeist activity took place in Britain during a thirteen-month period from August 1977 to September 1978. The location was a council house in the London Borough of Enfield, occupied at the time by a Mrs Joan Harper, a divorcee who shared her home with her four children. The Enfield poltergeist first made itself known audibly on 31 August when one of the Harper daughters reported raps and strange shuffling sounds emanating from the walls. Initially the girl's story was dismissed as imagination until Mrs Harper herself saw a heavy chest of drawers move along the floor. Terrified and confused, the woman called a burly neighbour into the house for protection. A search revealed no living intruders yet those who remained inside continued to witness the odd movements of furniture. Reluctantly the Harpers realized that something frightening had entered their home.

The following day brought even more bizarre manifestations: chairs were lifted into the air by unseen hands and children's toys were found whizzing around the front room at great speed. At the same time a man's voice was heard from nowhere. Deep, crude and swearing profusely, it claimed to be that of Bill Haylock, a dead Gypsy whose body could be found buried in Durrant's Park, a cemetery nearby. It boasted that he had come back to earth to 'make their lives hell'. A search of Durrant's Park Cemetery was made and Haylock's grave discovered.

As the phenomenon continued the police were called in to investigate and, when they retreated nonplussed, priests and spiritualist mediums were invited in to exorcize the house. All those who entered the place bore witness to the activity of the invisible force but efforts to get rid of the presence proved to no avail. After a few months the manifestations became more violent, centreing upon Mrs Harper's eldest daughter, Janet, aged eleven. On numerous occasions she was thrown around her bedroom and twice levitated to the ceiling floating in mid-air in front of astonished witnesses. And so the family's misery continued for over a year. Psychic investigators who were invited into the Harper household to help solve the mystery recorded nearly a thousand separate incidents which could not be explained. Over the same period, journalists, psychologists, local politicians and social workers were amongst those who bore testimony to the actuality of the reported disturbances. Photographs even appeared in newspapers depicting not only furniture but the terrified Harper daughters themselves in mid-flight. At no point was it seriously suggested that the Harpers had perpetrated some form of bizarre hoax; what was happening was happening for real. Eventually there was a respite when in September 1978, following the intercession of a Dutch medium named Dono Gmelig-Mayling, the poltergeist abruptly withdrew. The semi-detached house in North London has remained quiet ever since.

Frightening though their experience must have seemed to the Harpers some households have fared even more cruelly at the hands of uninvited guests. In the year 1817, the Bells, a pioneer family from Robertson Co., Tennessee, began to notice raps emanating from the log walls of their frontier home. In a pattern remarkably similar to the progress of the Enfield phenomenon, the noises were replaced by moving furniture, and the sound of strange guttural voices echoing from above the heads of the family members. If all this were not enough, the ghostly presence began to turn vicious. A rotting stench pervaded every room and invisible hands punched, slapped and pinched the Bells' young children. When a church committee was called in to investigate, its members were kicked, bitten and spat upon by the poltergeist, forcing the delegation to retreat in fear and confusion.

For the unfortunate Bells, the misery was only just
beginning. As the months passed, all were physically
assaulted, the most violent attacks being reserved for
the two teenage daughters who frequently had their
hair pulled out by the roots, their agonized screams
accompanied by raucous cries of delight from the unseen
tormentor. As the story of the manifestations spread,
hundreds of curious visitors arrived to witness it for
themselves, including a future US president, Andrew
Jackson. None who saw the scenes with their own
eyes doubted that the phenomenon was genuine. The
family's misery dragged on until, eventually, after four
years of terror, a despairing John Bell committed suicide, believing himself to be cursed by the Devil.
To the horror of his grieving relatives, the invisible
presence then assumed an exact likeness of the farmer's
voice, and proceeded to gloat loudly over its victim's
death. However, after Bell was buried the attacks ceased,
and the voice was heard no more.

So is the end of our search for conclusive proof of human
survival beyond death now at an end, or can there
be an alternative explanation for the poltergeist? Are
these outbreaks really influenced by the unseen realm
of souls beyond our physical senses – or are they, as
some psychologists have suggested, simply an extraordinary demonstration of the human mind's hidden
powers?

Perhaps we should approach this question by putting
the matter in its proper historical perspective. Like
ghosts, poltergeists have been recorded down the centuries and their manifestations attributed to a wide variety
of causes. Twelfth century writer Giraldus Cambrensis
encountered several whilst on a tour of Wales and
described them as 'foul spirits'. A hundred years later

'demons' were held responsible for the bites and scratches which appeared on the body of the blessed Christina of Stommeln. In 1521 Martin Luther witnessed a poltergeist outbreak whilst imprisoned in a castle in Wortburg and attributed the phenomenon to the devil. In 1681, the Reverend Joseph Glanville, chaplain to Charles II, investigated a poltergeist at the home of a magistrate and pronounced it to be an omen of doom.

Probably the earliest serious study of the phenomenon was conducted in 1599 by a Spaniard named Martín Del Río. Having examined closely the details of several cases, Del Río identified no less than eighteen types of demon capable of causing 'various commotions and annoyances'. Three centuries later a paper written in 1910 by a Fellow of the Royal College in London, Sir William Barrett, detailed those very same 'commotions and annoyances' in such mind-boggling detail that his work on the subject has become a classic reference book of the paranormal phenomenon.

The two commonest classes of phenomena reported were percussive sounds – knockings, rappings, thuds, crashes, bangs – and the tilting, displacement, lifting or other movement of material objects. Usually these two classes of happening would coincide. Where objects were levitated their movement might be slow or quick and with or without resultant damage. Sometimes fragile objects including glass might be hurled with great force and yet remain intact after collision with other hard objects. Yet at the same time incidences of crockery thrown and subsequently broken were found by Barrett to be particularly common, suggesting to the researcher that the force behind these disturbances might actually be enjoying the resultant chaos. As to the nature of that force, Barrett had little doubt. In the conclusion to his paper Barrett pointed out that several features noticeable

during poltergeist outbreaks such as human style noises
– panting, sighing, whispering and screeching voices –
plus the often intelligent behaviour shown during some
outbreaks, indicated the likely operation of a discarnate
intelligence. Of the absolute reality of the poltergeist the
researcher had no doubt, since outbreaks had been widely
reported from before the Middle Ages up to the present
day, from a diversity of cultures and with a uniformity
which ruled out the possibility that these stories were the
product of overheated imaginations.

According to Barrett poltergeists tended to be diurnal
creatures, unlike traditional haunting ghosts whose activities were more noticeable during the hours of darkness.
Most outbreaks he studied turned out to be sporadic,
temporary affairs lasting only a few weeks, though a small
proportion seemed to go on for much longer. In almost
every case the strange events would end as abruptly and
mysteriously as they began. Another key feature first
noticed by the Edwardian researcher, and the one which
put poltergeists in a markedly different category from
haunting ghosts, is the way in which a poltergeist entity
seems to attach its presence to a particular individual,
rather than a location. More often than not the focus of
a poltergeist outbreak is a teenager, and predominantly
one of the female sex.

One example included in Barrett's study which typifies
this aspect of the phenomenon was the 'Derrygonelly
Ghost' which haunted a farmhouse near Enniskillen,
Ulster, throughout the long winter months of 1871.
Investigating the outbreak, Barrett discovered that the
manifestations centred upon Maggie, aged nineteen, the
eldest daughter of the family. Stones and water fell from
ceilings around her, and loud rappings emanated from
rooms in which she entered. When the family put a
bible in her bedroom, the pages ripped themselves out.

Local priests were at a loss, until, through a system of raps, a code was developed by which one of their number was able to communicate with the unseen intelligence, and eventually persuade it to leave.

Thoroughly compiled though it was, Sir William Barrett's 1910 study seriously underestimated the variety of ways poltergeists can cause mayhem in the households they enter. In their book *Poltergeists* published in 1979, British authors Alan Gauld and Tony Cornell recorded more than fifty types of phenomenal happenings, from the preternatural falling from ceilings of various kinds of organic matter, to the tampering with of electrical appliances. Locked doors had been opened, messages smeared in blood upon walls, clothes ripped from the backs of those wearing them, excrement and other unpleasant substances spread about floors. Perhaps the most mystifying and potentially frightening feature of the poltergeist identified by the English authors was its power to cause fires, examples of which were by no means uncommon. In 1820, for instance, an outbreak of poltergeist phenomena centreing upon a servant girl in the London home of the prosperous Wright family, saw the disintegration in flames of Mrs Wright's clothes both in her wardrobes and upon the unfortunate woman's body. After the worst incident, Mrs Wright was badly burned but when the servant was dismissed the fires ceased. In Binbrook, Lincolnshire around the end of December 1904, the Reverend A.C. Constance reported objects being hurled around his rectory; two weeks later a girl was found nearby inexplicably on fire. From Antigua in the West Indies came the story in 1929 of a 'negress' whose clothes and bedding ignited upon contact with her body, whilst in 1932 a similarly peculiar affliction was visited upon a family in Blandenboro, North Carolina.

Unsurprisingly, those who attract fire spooks are often

wrongly suspected of being arsonists. In 1979 Carol
Compton, an English girl working as a nanny in Italy,
was accused by her employers of having the power to
start fires in their home. Tried for witchcraft in an Italian
court she denied the charge but admitted that she did
indeed hold regular mental communications with the
invisible fire starter who she considered to be a friend.
The Italian enigma has been repeated elsewhere many
times, often with tragic results. In 1991 Samantha Piper,
a twenty-year-old nursing assistant working in an old age
pensioners' home in Brentwood, Essex, was convicted
of the homicide of an old woman in her care, Mrs Elsie
De'ath. Mrs De'ath had been found engulfed in flames
one morning by other members of staff. Noting that
many fires had been started apparently inexplicably in
the past in buildings where Samantha Piper was present,
and taking into account her history of mental illness,
the court concluded that she must have deliberately set
her patient alight through malice. Yet Piper denied it,
and in reaching their verdict the court ignored the fact
that more than eight mysterious fires had been found
in the Brentwood complex during the previous few
months, none of which (as even the prosecuting counsel
admitted) could conceivably have been started by the
defendant. Samantha Piper remains behind bars although
a question mark over her guilt has not gone away.

No one should confuse the activities of these preternatural pyromaniacs with conventional fires. In 1941, in
a series of outbreaks at a farm near Odon, Indiana, individual items which went up in a puff of smoke included a
calendar hanging on a wall, a pair of wet overalls drying
on a line, and, most curiously of all, a book which, when
taken from a drawer, was found to be smouldering inside,
even though its cover remained unaffected. The same
year, small blue flames continually enveloped objects at

a Canadian country club near Windsor, Ontario. Files, telephone directories, tablecloths, towels, curtains and various other combustible materials burst spontaneously into ashes throughout a three week period yet no reason was ever discovered for the mysterious events. In all, forty-three separate fires were reported to insurance company officials.

Fortunately, no one was hurt in the Canadian outbreaks. Some people have not been so lucky. On the night of 7 August 1948 an invisible firestarter entered a farm ten miles south of Maycomb, Illinois. Small brown scorch marks on the wallpaper were its calling card; soon it began to blacken the timber frame of the house. Throughout that night and the next morning the farmer's family fought to keep the fires under control but to no avail – the numerous blazes eventually destroyed the house and neighbouring outbuildings. Maycomb fire chief Fred Wilson, who saw some of the unnatural activity for himself, logged the farmer's claim that over 200 separate fires had been found and extinguished before the conflagration got completely beyond control. Several men were seriously injured trying to fight the fires. Even more disastrous was the firestarter which plagued the Lucknow home of an Indian police inspector during June and July 1975. In this case, the spirit ended its six-week reign of terror by igniting the clothes of the inspector's wife, resulting in burns that were to prove fatal.

Examples of the callous activity of phantom firestarters continue to crop up. In the very week that I began to set out the final draft for this chapter in August 1991, a five-year-old English boy named Brian Hately was assumed to have burned down his family home in Pitsea, Essex, even though circumstances strongly militated against his personal involvement. Although the boy had never been seen playing with matches, he had on several previous

occasions been known to be in the vicinity of sudden outbreaks of fire. Following the incident which finally made
his family homeless, the Hatelys' residence was boarded
up and left for safe by the local fire brigade. Nevertheless
a few hours later a blaze was found once again raging
in the deserted building, an occurrence which local fire
officers put down to spontaneous combustion. Outbreaks
of unnatural fires which coincide with the presence of
poltergeists leave little scope for those people who prefer
to dismiss the supernatural as mumbo jumbo.

The commonly reported occurrences of stone-throwings
are equally hard to reconcile with the rationalists' viewpoint. Phantom stone-throwers litter the pages of paranormal literature. A European chronicle from as far bàck
as AD 858 describes how heavy stones were thrown at
residents of the small Rhineland town of Bingen. A thousand years on, the Parisian police authorities were called
to witness the daily demolition by phantom projectiles
of a house in the Rue des Grés. After three weeks'
bombardment the house was described as having been
'through a siege', though no one was seen throwing the
missiles, which appeared literally from out of the blue.

In our own century the activities of phantom stone
throwers have become even more pronounced. In October 1901 pebbles were falling in prodigious numbers on
Harrisonville, a small town in Ohio, causing widespread
alarm; four years later, in Port of Spain, Trinidad, stone
showers in and out of doors accompanied a whole range
of poltergeist phenomena centreing upon a reputedly
haunted house. In 1907, the Irish town of Magilligan,
County Derry, saw small rocks regularly hitting the roofs
and windows of a cottage owned by one Mr McLaughlin,
whilst in 1913 a similar force was breaking windows in a
street in Charleroi, Belgium.

Once again, eye-witness accounts tend to support

the theory that the energy involved in these incidents is intelligently directed. During an outbreak in West Bengal in 1919, a female ghost was seen stooping to pick up bricks before hurling them through windows and only after a holy man reasoned with her did the attacks ceased. In 1929, Fortean researcher Ivan T. Sanderson had a first-hand experience of a stone thrower's intelligent behaviour on the Indonesian island of Sumatra. Staying with a friend who found piles of small smooth pebbles every morning on his verandah, Sanderson suspected that a poltergeist might be to blame. To test his theory he marked several small stones with lipstick and hurled them into the darkening jungle, only to find, moments later, the same objects landing at his feet. Sanderson considered this to be absolute proof that a supernatural agency lay behind the phenomenon, since no human eyes could have detected the stones within such a short period of time and returned them from the tangled foliage which bordered his host's garden.

Sometimes the sheer distance that stones are propelled defies belief. In January 1923, following the four-month bombardment of a farmhouse in the Ardèche region of France, one local politician wrote: 'No mortal hand could have done this. It is impossible for a man to throw rocks across an open field 440 yards long, still more impossible for anyone to have been hidden undetected.' In 1977, officials in Spokane, Washington, were equally baffled by persistent reports of rocks falling upon a house owned by a Mr Billy Tipton. The following year Tipton moved to Hazlitt, New Jersey, where his home once more became the focus for a sky-born onslaught. Like most poltergeist outbreaks, the activities of phantom stone throwers is usually short-lived. As ever, though, there have been some notable exceptions.

One night in July 1987 stones began to fall on the roof

of the home of Simon and Beatrice Sithebe, residents of a black township near Durban, South Africa. The ariel bombardment lasted for weeks and gradually the strange phenomenon spread inside the Sithebe home. Not only were objects moved but some were projected with great force at the occupants. Most extraordinary of all, whenever the couple began to pray a bible would lift itself off the table and strike them about the head. The disturbances continued for many months and were filmed by a local journalist, Richard Compton. Also witness was an apostolic minister and exorcist, the Reverend John Hadabe, who was knocked unconscious by the invisible force as he attempted to banish it. Today, six years after the poltergeist arrived, the Sithebes only rarely experience disruption within their house but stones continue to fall from the sky upon their roof on a nightly basis, reminding them of the presence of their unnatural guest.

From Britain, perhaps the most compelling evidence for the objective reality of the poltergeist phenomenon was the nightly blitz of a row of houses in a street in the Ward End District of Birmingham. Early in 1982, having received numerous complaints of windows being smashed by stones thrown from the backs of houses in Thornton Road, the West Midlands Constabulary set up a team to watch over the afflicted premises. The police originally assumed that local youths were responsible for the nocturnal attacks but instead of finding human culprits they discovered an enigma which has defied explanation until this day. Although the vigilant officers heard the regular crashing of flying projectiles against the houses under surveillance, they could find absolutely no evidence of anyone hurling the objects. Sophisticated equipment, such as night-sights and image-intensifiers, proved of little practical value and, by the end of 1982, after 3,500

man-hours of fruitless observation, the police were no
nearer to solving the crimes. Today, the visitations have
ceased to plague the residents of Thornton Road but the
mystery remains unsolved.

Though a much rarer event, poltergeist spirits have even
been known to interfere with machines and electrical
circuits. Where this type of force becomes manifest
there is little room for doubting its preternatural origins. One particularly bizarre case, which emerged from
the Bavarian town of Rosenheim in 1967, centred not
upon moving objects but, of all things, on a series of
disturbances in a telephone switchboard. The German
oddity was first noticed by Herr Adam, senior partner
at a firm of lawyers, who complained bitterly to the
Post Office about his company's extraordinarily expensive telephone bill. Checking his own meter and staff
records, Herr Adam realized that dozens of unlogged
calls had been registered – all to the same number.
Upon investigation, this turned out to be the speaking
clock. When the Post Office flatly denied that a fault
existed on the line, the lawyer insisted that all phones in
the building be replaced. The authorities complied, but
the next month Herr Adam received an even larger bill,
this time indicating that over 600 calls had been made to
the official time-check! Things got steadily worse, with
fuses blowing, and electrical office equipment failing on
a daily basis. Electronic clocks ran backwards, fluorescent
tubes burned out, photocopying machines seemed to
have a mind of their own. Electrical engineers were
as baffled by these malfunctions as their counterparts
from the telephone company and so the directors of the
lawyers' practice were forced to accept that something
truly supernatural was happening within their premises.
    Soon afterwards a team of investigators from the

nearby Max Planck Institute of Plasma Physics were invited to make tests. They found abnormalities in electricity supplies so profound that they could assume only that 'an energy beyond our comprehension' was responsible. Herr Adam and his colleagues were at their wits' end, until one day someone noticed that the preternatural occurrences only took place when a certain employee, a nineteen-year-old typist named Annamarie Schneider, was present. On days when she was ill, nothing occurred. Likewise, the phenomenon always stopped when she went home. Though she was totally unaware of it, Annamarie had become the focus of the poltergeist. She was immediately dismissed and the odd manifestations came to an end.

Although careful investigation into the peculiar happenings by respected physicists from the Max Planck Institute rules out a natural explanation for the mayhem inside the lawyers' office, there were many other scientists who continued to insist that this poltergeist, in common with all others, was really nothing more than a hoax played by the person upon whom the activity appeared to focus. Twenty-five years on, such sceptics remain in the majority. Ignoring the paranormal evidence altogether, these people prefer to believe that moving objects are simply transported by sleight of hand, and that sensational stories appearing in the pages of the tabloid press are the imaginings of credulous journalists only too eager to be duped for the sake of a good headline. Can they really be right? Well in some cases perhaps but a careful reading of the literally hundreds of case histories documented in Fortean literature must give the lie to such facile explanations. As with manifestations of ghosts, the sheer number of poltergeist cases cannot be dismissed in terms of fraud. Moreover, like apparitions, they are a universal phenomenon. Michael Goss, a British writer, has recently produced a 350-page volume detailing over 1,000 separate eye-witness reports from nearly every country in the world. Colin Wilson in his book *Poltergeist* compiles a scarcely less comprehensive list. Add to these the earlier studies undertaken by the likes of Sir William Barrett, and the British writers Tony Gauld and Alan Cornell, and it is hard to believe that anyone can still claim that the poltergeist is a myth.

However, the outright refusal to accept the objective reality of these events is not the only objection that we must confront. For even among those paranormal experts who accept that poltergeist manifestations *do* take place on a regular basis, there is sharp disagreement over the nature of the force which lies behind its activity. One hypothesis which has recently found favour seeks to explain poltergeists in a purely parapsychological way. Its leading proponent is the aforementioned Professor William Roll, director of The Psychical Research Foundation in Durham, North Carolina. Investigating over one hundred cases during the 1960s and 1970s, Roll became convinced that a pattern was emerging between outbreaks of phenomena and the psychological state of the focus individual, found almost always to be a young person.

Many of these youngsters were, he concluded, 'seething with internal anger' and it was this suppressed emotional energy that was the true source of the uncontrolled psychic activity which became so obviously externalized. Unconsciously, through the medium of spontaneous telekinesis (the power of mind over matter) these young minds created their own poltergeist. In support of this theory, Roll pointed out that the behaviour of a typical noisy spirit often resembled the antics of an angry child. Furthermore, in girls it was noticed that poltergeist activity seemed most likely to erupt during puberty, and some outbreaks could even be traced closely following a stress pattern related to the menstrual cycle. So in these cases Roll suggested that researchers should best look no further than the person who seemed to be in the eye of the storm. It was really just another case of a paranormal mystery being all in the mind, for the root cause of the phenomenon lay deep in the subconscious frustrations of the agent, and not some invisible discarnate presence. For those parapsychologists who have adopted the American's ideas (probably the majority), poltergeists have ceased to represent supernatural phenomena, and having eliminated the possibility of a 'spook' aspect, they follow a person-centred approach to individual case studies.

Despite the attraction of Roll's theory, however, it fails to fit the jigsaw pattern of available evidence. To begin with not all those focus adolescents prove to be guilt-ridden, angry or sexually frustrated teenagers. Many are not adolescents at all. Moreover, not all poltergeists are playful or naughty; some can be simply malicious. No explanation drawn from within the parameters of current scientific laws can explain the apportations of stones and missiles from thin air, the levitation of solid objects, or the spontaneous combustion of inanimate material. No psychological explanation can account for the apparently autonomous behaviour of these invisible entities. Most important of all, Professor Roll's hypothesis fails completely to account for voices heard in houses haunted by poltergeists (often with definite personalities) and the occasional examples where spectres of the once-living have been identified as being in the vicinity of poltergeist outbreaks. Such an example was described in a detailed report prepared by L. Stafford Betty, associate member of the Department of Philosophy and Religious Studies at California State College, Bakersfield. Betty's paper focuses upon the frightening experiences of Mrs Frances

Freeborn who in November 1981 moved into a three-bedroom house in Bakersfield that had been vacant for nearly five years following the sudden death of its previous owner, Mrs Meg Lyons. Leased as a furnished property, the house had remained exactly as Meg Lyons had left it when the new occupant moved in. It was when Frances Freeborn decided to rearrange the place that odd things started to happen.

To begin with percussive sounds could sometimes be heard emanating from the wall, at first faintly and then growing in amplitude, whilst doors and cabinet drawers that she had purposely closed the night before were found to be open the next morning. Before long, lights in the house began coming on when she was absent. When she returned home on these occasions pictures and mirrors that she had moved from one part of the house to another were found to be removed, propped neatly against the wall below the spot where they had been hung years before by Meg Lyons.

As these events continued, Frances Freeborn gradually became aware of an ineffable sense of hostility in the atmosphere within the building. In early January 1982, after she had made up her mind to redecorate the house, the strange movements of objects intensified. It was almost as if some force within the place was determined to keep things the same. Matters came to a head one night when the entity, which Frances Freeborn had by then positively identified in her own mind with Meg Lyons, attempted to strangle the occupant. After this incident the woman left the house for ever, convinced that she had no choice.

Following his own investigation on this case, which lasted more than a year, L. Stafford Betty felt satisfied that the outbreaks were genuine. Frances Freeborn had not been the only one to witness the odd manifestations.

Others included the carpenter working on the property, an electrician who called in to check the lighting switches, various neighbours and Luke Cowley, Mrs Meg Lyons' son-in-law. He and Frances Freeborn had actually seen the apparition of Meg Lyons at one time or another. It was Betty's conclusion that although some of the phenomena experienced might have been the result of a coincidence of physical causes, most of the disturbances could only be explained by reference to the discarnate presence of Mrs Meg Lyons. 'The only explanation that covers all the phenomena,' he wrote in an edition of the journal for the Society for Psychical Research in 1984, 'is the paranormal one'.

Perhaps the clearest evidence that at least some poltergeist activity is linked directly to the spirit world was an outbreak of phenomena which occurred not in a house at all but in a tomb. The case of the moving coffins of Barbados, which has since become a *cause-célèbre* in paranormal literature, revolved around the Christ Church cemetery vault of the Chase family, wealthy plantation owners of the last century. On several separate occasions beginning in the summer of 1807, whenever the vault was opened for the laying to rest of a member of the Chase household, the coffins of those previously interred were discovered to be in violent disarray. Never in the same place where they had been laid by their funeral bearers, the coffins appeared to have been smashed about by forces of super-human strength. Yet the only access to the tomb was down a stairwell covered by a large block of blue marble. The Barbadoan authorities were baffled at the time and no amount of scientific research during the past 170 years has been able to bring forward a natural explanation for the enigma.

Though the most famous, the Chase family vault

is only one of several separate examples of moving coffins.

In his book *Footsteps on the Boundary of Another World* Victorian writer Dale Owen recounts an 1871 example from the Baltic island of Oesel, where faint ghostly cries were heard coming from a crypt underneath a small church. For a long time no one was brave enough to venture below, until poltergeist phenomena interrupted a funeral service and several members of the congregation gathered sufficient courage to enter the closed tomb. There, to their astonishment, they found a great number of the interred coffins laying in a rough pile. A commission of inquiry was set up, the crypt returned to its proper order and resealed. After three days, however, when the voices began again to be heard rising from beneath the stone floor of the chapel, another inspection was made. Although the entrance seal remained intact, the tomb had been violated even more devastatingly than before, with some coffins smashed open and others standing in an upright position with the head of the corpse downward. Several of those who witnessed the scene collapsed with shock.

The phenomenon of moving coffins may not be among the more commonly reported poltergeist happenings, but the relevance of these examples to the case against death is clear enough. Since the persons at the centre of these bizarre events were already dead, no parapsychological theory of the William Roll type could apply. Only an energy directed from a discarnate mind could have caused the chaos in the tombs.

The fact that these macabre tales would fit well into a gothic horror novel should not prejudice the late twentieth century reader into dismissing them as fabrications. The poltergeist is a well-documented phenomenon throughout all periods of history, up to and including our

own. Modern theories which seek to answer the riddle
of the poltergeist in terms of electromagnetic energy,
localized earthquakes or the vibrations of underground
trains simply fail to convince. Neither can mass-hysteria,
hoaxes or the more convoluted theory of Recurrent
Spontaneous Psychokinesis be held responsible for all
poltergeist outbreaks. Unpalatable though the thought
might be to the mind of the committed rationalist,
the most plausible explanation for poltergeist outbreaks
remains the original one that they are 'noisy spirits'
indeed – probably ghosts of the earth-bound variety,
unable or unwilling to ascend to the higher planes of the
afterlife sphere, trapped within a material world in which
they have no rightful place. Anger and frustration may
well be responsible for the poltergeist's violent moods,
yet it is not a living adolescent's mental energy producing
the psychokinetic disruption, as some have suggested, but
the mind power of a discarnate entity.

If some spirits are mischievous, then others are down-
right evil. In 1926 a pubescent Rumanian girl named
Eleanore Zugun claimed to have become the victim of
attacks by a ghost which only she could see. To begin
with no one believed her, but the incredulity of doctors
was soon shattered when deep scratches and bite marks
appeared spontaneously upon the face and hands of their
patient. Gradually, the medical specialists who examined
Eleanore became convinced beyond all possible doubt
that the contusions appearing on her flesh were not
self-inflicted. And when samples of the spittle that
frequently appeared together with them were analyzed
and found to be neither a secretion of her skin nor her
own saliva, it merely served to reinforce their belief.
    This is by no means the worst assault that I have uncov-
ered. In a still more violent attack reported from South

Africa during the 1960s, a farm worker named Jimmy De Buin was seen to suffer deep cuts and lacerations from an invisible assailant. Watched by astonished witnesses, the wounds opened up without apparent cause on De Buin's agonized body. It was, said one who saw it, 'as if an invisible sadist were carving him up with insane delight'. In the end the unfortunate De Buin died from his injuries. In 1965 an equally evil-minded entity plagued the life of Maria José Ferreira, a young child from São Paulo, Brazil. The unseen infestation would regularly burn and beat the young girl; on other occasions needles would be implanted fantastically into her flesh – sometimes appearing inside leather shoes which remained unpierced. After one savage attack a total of fifty-five needles were extracted from her skin. Not surprisingly, the girl went mad and committed suicide at the age of thirteen.

One of the most frightening cases to emerge during the last decade also happened to be one of the best documented. In November 1980 doctors at the Freiburg Institute of Psychology were alerted to the plight of a Spanish-born housewife, living in Mulhouse, eastern France. Having become the focus of poltergeist activity, the unfortunate woman, named Carla, found herself subjected to a series of brutal attacks from an invisible entity, culminating in a criss-cross network of deep cuts which opened up involuntarily on her shoulders and thighs. Carla also suffered the sensation of being punched savagely in the stomach. It did not take Carla and her husband Thierry long to convince the German specialists that the reported phenomenon was real. An investigation team from Freiburg not only witnessed marks appear spontaneously on her skin, but saw for themselves other poltergeist activity at the same time. Moreover, during their stay in the house, the German parapsychologists discovered that their equipment was regularly tampered

with and their films mysteriously ruined. To his amazement, Professor Hans Bender, the team's leader, found
thermometers recording a temperature of eighty degrees
fahrenheit in certain rooms within the house, even during
mid-winter and when the heating was switched off. On
another occasion a piece of sophisticated equipment set
up to monitor the temperature over a seventy-two hour
period revealed not only enormous fluctuations but
also broken horizontal lines on the printout that were
technically impossible to replicate.

The investigators unanimously concluded that an objective force of malevolent intent was present, but could not
think of a remedy until one of their number suggested
they try to make contact with the entity through glass-
rolling, a variation of the Ouija Board technique. After a
few aborted attempts, it seems contact was indeed made
with the poltergeist, a ghost who called itself Henry. Soon
afterwards Henry actually appeared (usually a dark and
menacing figure slipping in and out of sight), its form
not only seen by Carla and Thierry but also by a number
of the German investigators. Once, it was even captured
upon a radar controlled camera left running in an empty
room. Unfortunately, the identification of Henry in no
way assisted in persuading him to leave and so in April
1981, following an increase in violent activity, Carla and
her husband moved away. The house remains empty to
this day. Or does it . . .?

The cruel behaviour described above offers a clue to
the true nature of the spirits behind them. These are no
benevolent phantoms. Just as spiritualists consider that
ghosts of the haunting variety are earth-bound against
their will, so clairvoyants also believe that poltergeist
entities are trapped by the limitations of their own grossly
materialistic or possibly evil characters. Upon death such
persons would refuse to accept the loss of physical life

and the negative thought patterns and emotions of these unrefined souls stop them from ascending to the higher planes of enlightenment towards which all spirits are supposed to journey. So, held fast by the lower vibrations of the earth plane they blunder around in an attempt to contact those still living, causing chaos wherever they settle. They may actually derive pleasure from their antisocial activities, remaining unseen as they watch the growing terror of their human victims. According to spiritualists, it is usually only after the intervention of higher souls who form a sort of psychic rescue party that such depraved souls see the light. Finally made to confront the awful reality of their situation, they must purge their conscience of guilt before they can make the leap towards the higher mental levels which are the true destination of the dead.

Sinister tales of haunted houses, poltergeists and possessions have provided a rich seam of material for Hollywood movie moguls, and the popularity of the horror genre shows no sign of diminishing. What is less generally known is the fact that many of the cinema screen's biggest hits have been based directly or indirectly on reported, genuine phenomena. A notable example was the controversial 1973 blockbuster *The Exorcist*, in which the sex of the William Peter Blatty's fictional child-host was changed from the original story, but little else. Although most scientists and forward-looking churchmen remain united in their dismissal of the phenomenon of spirit possession, there is now a growing body of evidence to support the theory that possessions by spirits, like poltergeists and hauntings, are very much part of the real world.

Since the birth of their religion 140 years ago, spiritualists have constantly warned against the use of Ouija Boards and planchettes knowing full well that attempted

communication by the untrained may attract souls existing on the lower levels of the psychic planes. Those who
preach other creeds agree with this. Catholic priests,
whilst dismissing most other claims of spiritualists, regularly carry out exorcisms in Europe and the Americas,
casting out the spirits of those who have died only to
return and haunt the living. Even two recent Anglican
Archbishops of Canterbury, the Most Reverend Michael
Ramsey and Dr David Coggan, have voiced their belief
in demonic possession. Perhaps most surprising of all,
though, is the growing number of doctors and psychiatrists who are prescribing exorcism as a remedy for
conditions once thought to be the exclusive territory
of medical analysts. Just such a person is American
psychiatrist Wilson van Dusen who, whilst working in the
Mendicino State Hospital in California, gradually came to
the conclusion that the voices habitually heard by schizophrenics were not auditory hallucinations but the result of
contacts with discarnate entities. The Californian's theory
has since been supported by several other American
analysts, including Adam Crabtree and Ralph Allison,
(both of whom have written books on the subject) and
the highly respected Boston physician Dr Walter Franklin
Prince, who claims a high success rate through treating
cases of apparent mental illness as actual possessions.

During the past decade or so, the British medical
establishment has also begun to consider rather more
seriously the possibility of possession. Two figures who
have publicly stated their personal belief in the phenomenon include the well-known child psychologist
Dr Arthur Guirdham and a former consultant psychiatrist
at Mapperly Hospital, Nottinghamshire, Dr David Gill.
Another is Dr Richard Mackarness, a psychiatrist from
Hampshire who caused something of a storm inside medical circles when he claimed to have cured six hopeless

schizophrenics by seeking the advice of exorcists. The recognition of possession continues unabated. In the same week as I began writing this chapter, an article published in *The Independent* newspaper suggested that the ideas of the radical doctors mentioned above are no longer being treated as heresy within the closed world of British mental institutions.

If some part of the human personality can continue to exist beyond the dissolution of the physical form to possess the still-living body of another person, then our whole concept of death must necessarily be revised. So just how convincing is the hard evidence for possession? Apart from those medical practitioners and leading church figures mentioned above, who else should we look to for proof? Perhaps the most obvious answer is to consider the opinions of those who deal directly with the phenomenon – the exorcists themselves. Some practising exorcists are reluctant to talk of their work. Others are only too happy to do so. Father Ian Hazlewood, Church of England official exorcist in the diocese of Gloucester, was quoted at length in Leslie Watkins' 1982 study entitled *The Real Exorcists*, describing several individual examples he knew of where successful exorcism coincided with outbreaks of poltergeist-type phenomena. On one occasion, during the exorcism of a young soldier, holy water sprinkled on the possessed man's head began to sizzle. During another ritual, a man Hazlewood exorcized was levitated into mid-air. A second exorcist quoted in Watkins' book, Anglican Priest Reverend David MacInnes of Birmingham Cathedral, recalled being physically assaulted and choked by invisible hands whilst exorcizing a parishioner.

The Real Exorcists contains plenty of other examples at least as dramatic. As trained practitioners will point out, the casting out of evil spirits is a difficult and sometimes dangerous task, and when things go wrong the results can lead to tragedy.

In 1976 two Roman Catholic priests in Germany were jailed for six months for allegedly mishandling the exorcism of a possessed Bavarian teenager named Anneliese Michel. Three years earlier, the girl had begun violent tantrums, tearing her rosary and swearing during Mass. When two years of psychiatric treatment did nothing to produce a cure, the girl's parents sent her for exorcism at a nearby monastery. Imprisoned alone in her room Anneliese screamed blasphemies, vomited at the sight of a bible or crucifix, and viciously clawed at her own face and those of her exorcists. After nine months she died of exhaustion and the priests attending her were held responsible. They received six-month jail sentences for negligence but were they really to blame? Many among their own calling doubted it.

An even more appalling story of failed exorcism was the case of Michael Taylor, a British man who became possessed by spirits in September 1974. No one could understand Taylor's violent fluctuations in mood and personality until his plight was recognized by several local ministers who arranged for him to be exorcized. In an all-night session, dozens of evil spirits were supposedly cast out. Tragically, at least one remained. The following morning Taylor returned home and murdered his young wife in an orgy of bloodlust – literally tearing her face away from her skull with his bare hands. Afterwards he remembered nothing of the killing, insisting that he had been compelled by an outside influence and doctors agreed. Jailed for the homicide, the killer was nevertheless pronounced sane and harmless by psychiatrists at Broadmoor maximum security jail, and was released after serving only three years of a life sentence.

The violence displayed by the unfortunate Michael

Taylor may be thankfully rare in cases of possession, yet the strange behaviour of those under the control of invisibles provides strong evidence for the reality of the phenomenon. Levitation, insensibility to pain, the exhibition of super-human strength and the contortion of limbs into impossible positions, are just some of the manifestations which psychiatrists cannot explain. Others are even more incredible. During the infamous 'Devils of Loudun' outbreak from the seventeenth century, the body of a French prioress became swollen to twice its normal size; similarly, the possession in 1928 of American teenager Anna Ecklands caused her previously emaciated form to enlarge so grossly that medical staff summoned to her aid shrank back in terror. Eye-witness accounts of Eckland's ordeal described how she would continually be thrown upwards to hang fantastically from the ceiling, whereupon prodigous quantities of a foul substance would pour forth from her mouth. Some said her lips grew to the size of a man's fist during the fits.

Yet another extraordinary possession was that of Canadian woman Esther Teed of Amherst, Nova Scotia, who in 1878 not only began to talk in the languages of other nations but showed alarming signs of blowing up like a balloon. Her fits were accompanied by all manner of preternatural events. In the presence of the local doctor, bedclothes moved about, writing appeared spontaneously on a wall and pieces of plaster flew from a ceiling. When the town's minister, the Reverend A. Temple, arrived, a bucket of water boiled itself in front of him. The manifestations, which only occurred in Esther's presence, grew more dramatic by the day until eventually the unfortunate woman was imprisoned for the arson of a barn, though witnesses attested to the fact that on many occasions lighted matches appeared to drop out of thin air all around her.

This example from Nova Scotia is just one of many where an apparent possession has been accompanied by poltergeist phenomena. During the past decade such related activity has included sudden localized drops in temperature to freezing point, foul stenches pervading rooms where the possessed person is sleeping, and the anomalous appearance of blood or slime on walls. It is hard to imagine how schizophrenic hysteria can be responsible for such paranormal outbreaks. Certainly they fail to fit in with the standard psychiatric viewpoint which holds that those possessed are merely mentally deranged.

Whilst the split-personality theory may very well explain some cases of apparent possession, it falls far short of a believable interpretation for all. It is particularly inappropriate for those cases where the possessing entity is clearly indentified as being a dead person. Though rare, these instances provide some of the strongest evidence for survival.

On 11 July 1877 a thirteen-year-old girl named Mary Vennum of Watseka, Illinois, suffered a fit and fell into a trance-like state for several hours. Every day for the next few months she fell into the same swoon, afterwards attesting to remarkable visions of heavenly angels and other non-human figures. Her fits were accompanied by bouts of severe depression and eventually she became possessed by the ghost of an eccentric local woman named Katrina Hogan who had died the previous year. On the advice of neighbours, her family brought a doctor in to examine Mary. To their relief he concluded that she was not insane and used hypnotism to bring back the girl's normal personality. However, the next day she became possessed once more, this time by the spirit of a local girl who had died twelve years before – Mary Roff. Like

Mary Vennum, Mary Roff had during her own short lifetime suffered strange fits; she had also demonstrated extraordinary psychic feats – such as reading whilst blindfolded. Upon seeing the Vennum family, Mary Vennum/Roff recognized Mr and Mrs Vennum as her own former parents and told them numerous details of their daughter's life which only the real Mary Roff could conceivably have known. With literally hundreds of incidents described and confirmed by the amazed couple, the case became famous and was investigated by a sceptical Australian writer, Richard Hodgson, who had previously made a name for himself by exposing a number of fraudulent mediums. In this case however, Hodgson quickly concluded that the Vennum/Roff enigma was no hoax; it was, he said, 'the clearest example of genuine possession that could reasonably be imagined.' A hundred years later that verdict has not changed. No alternative explanation has been found that goes any way to account for the plethora of correct assertions which characterized Mary Vennum's descriptions of her earlier life as Mary Roff.

Although most possessions end with the original personality returning, there are some notable exceptions. In 1954 Jasbir Lal Jat, a three-year-old Indian boy from a poor village near the town of Vehedi seemingly died of smallpox. After an illness which lasted several days he stopped breathing and his body turned cold. However, the following morning, on the day scheduled for his funeral, Jasbir's body stirred, to the amazement of doctors and relatives alike. But this was only the beginning of an incredible story. To the astonishment of his parents the boy's personality had entirely changed. Speaking with a different accent and mannerisms far in advance of his age the child now claimed his name to be Sobha Ram Tyagi, the eldest son of a Brahmin family who were bereaved at precisely the same moment that Jasbir Lal Jat had passed away. It was Sobha Ram's soul which now inhabited the body of the smallpox victim, and not the child of the lower caste family.

Despite the scorn of all those who encountered his story, the boy remained firmly convinced of the truth of what he said, refusing to consume food handled by his own family who he considered to be unclean. Most people thought the boy had gone mad until one day by chance he recognized a passing stranger as Sobha Ram's aunt. True enough the woman confirmed it was so and her own version of the boy's death from a head injury concurred with his own. More importantly it became clear that the two children had expired at precisely the same time on the same day. Eventually taken to the village where he claimed to have lived before, Jasbir Lal Jat was able to greet Sobha Ram Tyagi's relatives by name and all agreed that his descriptions of his old home were too detailed to be the product of guess work.

For the afterlife researcher, this story poses an imponderable question. Since in the Indian example the shadow of death fell upon both possessed and possessor, should the case rightly be classified as an example of reincarnation or possession? Either seems possible and for this very reason the case could just as easily be discussed in my later chapters dealing with transmigration. But whichever angle we approach it from it would appear to buttress the case I am trying to build against the extinction of the human personality at the point of physical death. Be it possession or palingenesis (rebirth), the simple fact remains that some form of life continued in the once-dead body of a young smallpox victim. This then would seem to be a genuine example of the mind's, or rather the soul's triumph over matter. To put it another way, it is evidence of the victory of life over death.

Perhaps the examples which most clearly suggest the reality of possession are those instances where the invading spirit communicates in a tongue unknown to the host (a phenomenon which medical experts label 'xenoglossia' but cannot satisfactorily account for).

In 1974 a female lecturer at Nagpur University in India underwent an extraordinary change in personality. Uttara Huddar, a shy, somewhat introspective woman of thirty, suddenly became a vivacious extrovert who called herself Shadara. Formerly uninterested in religion, Shadara proved to be an obsessive devotee to her faith; more strangely, she spoke in Bengali, a dialect entirely different from Uttara's native Marathi. Mystified colleagues at Nagpur University confirmed that Uttara Huddar had no previous knowledge of the Bengali tongue. To them she was simply another person. Even her handwriting was totally different.

A second case from the 1970s seems, if anything, even more conclusive. In 1977 doctors at a state penitentiary in Ohio, USA, discovered that a convicted rapist named Billy Milligan had become possessed by two new personalities, both of whom communicated in their own highly distinctive language. As Abdul, Milligan could read and write in flawless Arabic; as Rugen, a Yugoslav, he spoke perfect Serbo-Croat with a thick Slavic accent. Doctors treating the prisoner found that not only did these new personalities perform as psychologically autonomous entities, but each emitted peculiar brain wave patterns when analyzed by neurological experts. Altogether Milligan's personality switches seemed to involve changes which could not be duplicated naturally.

Could such cases as these have been the result of a schism in the normal consciousness of the subject involved? The answer is surely no. If we exclude a paranormal cause it is hard to imagine how any individual might suddenly and without training or practice begin to use a vocabulary, syntax, and system of grammatical rules entirely different to their own language. Nevertheless, those who manifest xenoglossia achieve just this and, what is more, often speak with the appropriate accent and pronunciation. So does this prove literal possession or is there a still another possible alternative explanation? According to psychologists the human mind has a faculty known as cryptomensia or hidden memory which allows it to unconsciously pick up and store vast amounts of information which may become exhibited later in life, often in the most surprising fashion. For many this is a likely explanation for xenoglossia. But as any linguist will quickly point out, access to a foreign language is a mental feat of an entirely different order to simply remembering. For many people, learning to communicate in a new language requires long and arduous training of the muscles which operate the tongue and lips. Neither Uttara Huddar or Billy Milligan received such training prior to the exhibition of their new languages, yet they achieved the feat instantaneously.

Xenoglossiac examples of possession in children surely destroys any last possibility that a natural explanation lies at the bottom of the enigma. In his *Beyond Supernature* author Lyall Watson describes an exorcism of a ten-year-old child he personally observed whilst staying in the Philippines. A member of the Igarot Indians who live in the remote Cagayon Valley, the boy had never had any contact with a culture or language other than his own. Even so, whilst under the control of the possessing spirit he communicated freely in Zulu, a tongue he could not have conceivably heard. His family thought the words were simply gibberish until Watson, who had spent his early life in Africa, recognized it.

An equally inexplicable case was that of a young

English girl from Blackpool, pseudononymously known in SPR files as 'Rosemary', who in 1931 became overshadowed by the personality of Telika-Ventiu, a Babylonian woman who apparently lived sometime during the Eighteenth Dynasty of ancient Eygpt – approximately 1400 BC. Although the child's new character spoke in a curiously old sounding dialect, psychiatrists treating her found the idea of possession hard to swallow, until one of their number, Dr Frederic Wood, copied down some of Telika-Ventiu's phrases and sent them to Eygptologist Howard Hulme.

Hulme found the utterances demonstrated a remarkably high degree of grammatical accuracy, and contained many archaisms, peculiar popular terms, ordinary elisions and figures of speech appropriate to pre-Christian Egyptian. 'It was,' he claimed 'very evidential that the mind controlling "Rosemary" must have considerable knowledge of the language and customs which characterized Egypt under Pharoah Amenhop III.' To probe the enigma further Howard Hulme went to Blackpool to interview Telika-Ventiu at first hand. He was armed with a set of twelve questions concerning obscure details of everyday Babylonian life which required detailed answers – the sort of replies only he and perhaps a dozen other historians around the world might be able to deliver with confidence. In his presence the small girl from the north of England was able to do just that, in a tongue unheard outside academic circles for thousands of years. Over a ninety minute period the girl also wrote down sixty-six accurate phrases in the lost language of the hieroglyphs and by the end of the session Hulme was convinced that he had really heard a voice speaking from across the sands of time. It was, he insisted, difficult to imagine a more striking piece of evidence for the survival of the human spirit.

*   *   *

The twin phenomena of poltergeists and possession may or may not be interrelated. Certainly the disturbing possibility of their existence may be something which most people would prefer not to believe in. However, in order to dismiss them the rationalists have got their work cut out – and to date they have not even begun. As one paranormal researcher wrote at the beginning of the century, 'If the probability of the survival in some form or other of the human personality is not on balance the most likely cause of the unseen, then we have waited a long time for a better explanation.' We are still waiting.

Whispers of Immortality

'Whether man dies in his bed or the rifle knocks him
dead, a brief parting from those dear is the worst
man has to fear.'

W.B. Yeats
Under Ben Bulben

Thankfully, very few of us end up as ghosts, poltergeists
or possessing entities. Earth may be the right place for
love as Walt Whitman wrote, but it is no place for the
dead to love. So where do most of us end up? According
to mediums, for those who pass through the valley of the
shadow of death there are other places appropriate to
the discarnate condition. Just as Christians and Muslims
believe we will be collectively reborn on some future
resurrection day, so spiritualists believe that immediately
following death we are individually met by guides who
lead us towards higher psychic planes where we continue
to exist in a state no less real but far more wonderful
than the world of matter. Among these spiritualists are
some who claim to contact those rarefied regions of the
human consciousness. As proof positive of the survival
of the soul these contacts from the other side have
occasionally imparted significant evidence, for instance
information which only the dead personality who returns
could have possibly known. Other mediums, assisted by
their guides, have performed miraculous feats of healing
and mind over matter quite impossible to comprehend

within a mechanistic world view. Perhaps most important of all, these contacts have offered vital clues as to the real nature of the afterlife state and the purpose of our present lives.

To many their vision of the next life makes the most profound sense. Others see it as absurdly optimistic. So what is the truth? Can we really be surrounded by other dimensions, worlds populated by discarnate souls only too willing to make contact with us? Or are these stories just further evidence of humanity's endless capacity for self-deception, the manifestation of a collective need to believe in survival? It is for the readers of this book to make up their own minds. However, it may surprise some to learn that a belief in the reality of an afterlife is shared not only by spiritualists and religious devotees, but also by scientists, doctors, psychiatrists and most recently by members of criminal investigation agencies throughout the world. The army of believers is growing all the time.

A court of law might seem an unlikely place to debate the existence of eternal life. Yet in 1979 an American jury in Evanson, Illinois, reached a decision which was incomprehensible unless one accepts the survival of the human spirit to be a fact. The reason was simple: the chief witness for the prosecution in this case was a ghost.

The trial centred upon the brutal murder of one Teresita Basa, a Filipino nurse who had been stabbed to death in her apartment two years previously. Initially there had seemed little chance of ever solving the brutal crime. Forensic evidence was inconclusive and conventional police enquiries offered few clues to the identity of the assailant. All that was clear was the motive – robbery, for Teresita Basa's expensive jewellery had been stolen from her home. It was not until many months after the murder that police investigations took a dramatic and unexpected turn, after Remy Chura, speech therapist, spiritualist and close friend of the dead woman, began having the same persistent dream. In these nightly visions Teresita's spectral form would appear over Chura's bed asking her friend to avenge her. The Filipino nurse named her murderer as one Allan Showery, a small time thief who had called on the fateful day posing as a TV repair man and then attacked her once inside. According to Teresita's ghost, Showery had now given her stolen jewellery to his girlfriend, a woman she also named, and before disappearing Teresita would always implore her old friend to go to the police with this information.

For some time Remy Chura refused, sure that her story would be ridiculed. Eventually, however, she relented. It was the right decision for although the homicide investigation officers found Chura's tale somewhat fantastic, Allan Showery was known to them as an persistent offender and they called him in for questioning. To begin with Showery denied any knowledge of the killing but his nervous manner aroused enough suspicion amongst his interrogators for them to instigate a search of both his and his girlfriend's homes. The raids revealed a large quantity of stolen goods including a ring which proved to be an heirloom from Teresita Basa's collection. Under pressure Showery broke down and confessed to the slaying, though later at the trial he changed his plea to not guilty on the advice of a lawyer, certain that a ghost's testimony would be thrown out of court. In the event the hearing made legal history. Showery's defence attorney insisted that the testimony of a disembodied spirit was inadmissable. But the presiding judge, Frank Barbero, ruled otherwise. Faced with the condemning evidence of his unseen victim, Allan Showery changed his plea to guilty and was sentenced to fourteen years in gaol.

Although the outcome of the Illinois trial provoked controversy in legal circles, it was by no means the first time that a case has been solved by a spirit. In the annals of criminal detection there are literally hundreds of instances where mediums have used their psychic powers to aid police investigations. The previous month to the Teresita Basa trial, police in Los Angeles called in a clairvoyant to assist in the search for a missing child and it was a huge success. The medium correctly reported not only the whereabouts of the vanished boy's corpse but also named the child's killer who admitted his guilt upon arrest.

Examples of psychic detection from across the Atlantic are scarcely less spectacular. In 1922 an ex-British army officer named Eric Tombe was blasted with a shotgun in the back of his head by a former business partner, Ernest Dyer. Dyer threw Tombe's body into a cesspit at his Surrey racing stables and covered it with a large stone slab. The murderer escaped justice until Eric Tombe's ageing and spiritualist mother received a clairvoyant impression of the whereabouts of her son's body. Initially sceptical, police nevertheless drained the cesspit to find Tombe's badly decomposed corpse. His dark secret uncovered, Ernest Dyer shot himself before he could be arrested.

While they may not advertize the fact, many police forces throughout Western Europe regularly turn to the spirit realm for help. During the pre-war years Dutch medium August Droist helped solve more than one hundred robberies across the Low Countries. Until his death in 1980 Utrecht born Dutchman Gerard Croiset aided police in more than a dozen countries to track down missing persons. Peter Hurkos, whose work with police forces was no less impressive, once picked out the face of an arsonist from the files of over 500 youths. Once again across the Atlantic, American Dorothy Allinson was credited by US law enforcement agencies in 1977 as having materially assisted in the location of twenty-six missing persons and solving six homocide mysteries.

Even when psychic assistance is not sought there is often evidence to suggest it might have been useful. In October 1979 an English medium named Nella Jones claimed to have received a message which included details relating to the identity of the notorious Yorkshire Ripper, the serial killer whose reign of terror across the northern counties of England was every bit as horrific as that of his Victorian namesake. In an interview given to London journalist Shirley Davenport, Jones described the Ripper as being a long-distance lorry driver by trade, whose Christian name was Peter. A Bradford man, he lived, she said, in a large detached house set back behind wrought iron gates. His actual surname and full address remained unclear to her although she was certain that his house number was six. She had one further detail, the date of his next atrocity – 17 November. Although the journalist became convinced of the story's authenticity the Northern Constabulary took a different view. Having already decided that the killer was a Geordie (a supposition based on a tape which subsequently proved bogus) they had already wound down investigations in the Bradford area and saw no reason to change their strategy on the uncorroborated advice of an eccentric and possibly demented housewife. When 17 November 1979 passed without incident nobody wanted to hear anything more from Nella Jones. But the police had got it wrong. There were no further murders for more than a year until on 17 November 1980 the Ripper struck for the thirteenth and final time. Shortly afterwards he was arrested, largely through a stroke of luck, and finally unmasked, the murderer did indeed turn out to be a Bradford man, Peter Sutcliffe, a long-distance lorry driver whose home, number six Garden Lane, concurred exactly with the description given by Nella Jones to Shirley Davenport the previous year. Since then the Yorkshire Constabulary have regularly used mediumistic advice, with, I am assured, a fair degree of success.

Striking though the feats of modern mental mediums might seem they pale into insignificance when set against the careers of past giants. Born in 1688, the son of a Lutheran bishop, Emmanuel Swedenborg grew up to be a genius in the field of physical sciences. After becoming his country's Royal engineer while still only in his mid-twenties Swedenborg travelled the length of Europe learning new disciplines. In a glittering academic career he became by turns a mining specialist, geologist, astronomer and gifted tutor of mathematics. It was for none of these things, however, that Swedenborg is remembered today. Alongside his interest in conventional science, the Swede had always been deeply fascinated with life's greatest mystery – the nature and destiny of the human spirit. During his childhood he described having visions of angels and, many years later, even claimed to have had the honour of meeting Jesus in person. It was following this Christly apparition that Emmanuel Swedenborg became convinced of the reality of an afterlife and for the next thirty years until his death he demonstrated the ability to talk to the dead whenever he chose. Indeed, so powerful a medium was Swedenborg that to him a conversation with a ghost was as natural and as unexciting as a chat with his next-door neighbour. Hundreds witnessed these strange spontaneous communications; many attested to seeing the ghosts themselves, whilst others received messages from their own dead relatives which convinced them of the genuineness of the phenomenon. By the time he himself died many had come to regard him as one of the most remarkable men of all time.

The types of evidence Emmanuel Swedenborg gave as proof of the soul's existence were many and various. On one occasion, for instance, he was approached by the widow of the former Dutch ambassador, Countess de Montville. Swedenborg claimed to make contact with her husband and to show that he was not lying, told her how the ambassador had paid a sum of money to a business acquaintance shortly before he died. The receipt for this payment, said Swedenborg, lay undiscovered in a secret compartment in the family bureau. Sure enough, the piece of paper was found in a hidden drawer just as the medium had indicated; the Countess herself had not even known that the compartment existed. On another occasion, in 1761, Queen Ulrica, sister of Frederick the Great, asked Swedenborg if he would attempt to contact her deceased brother Augustus. The message of proof Swedenborg received made her faint with shock: it turned out to be a cryptic phrase of which only the Queen herself knew the meaning. 'No one apart from God knows this secret', she is reported to have exclaimed and then professed a belief in spirits for the rest of her life.

Swedenborg also had the gift of second sight and remote-viewing, on one occasion seeing the assassination of Tsar Peter III of Russia and on another, reporting the outbreak of a fire that was raging many hundreds of miles away. But it is Swedenborg's mediumship and in particular his descriptions of the afterlife which are most interesting. The Scandinavian firmly rejected the idea prevalent among some religions that the human soul remains in some form of limbo state until a future resurrection day. According to Swedenborg, a person who has just died continues to exist consciously in much the same way as before. 'The spirit of a man recently departed', wrote the mystic, 'could be easily recognized by his friends.' Yet the spirit body was not entirely the same, for a discarnate soul had the ability to move, feel pain or joy, and travel in an instant over great distances by the power of thought. In appearance, the spirit world was altogether similar to the material world only more *real*. Spirit man had senses, tactile sensation, smell, hearing and sight – all of which were 'far more exquisite' than his earthly counterpart. As for the personality of the departed soul this remained unaffected, at least for an initial phase. In his new domain, spirit man found himself with almost God-like powers, the world of the dead being created and modified by the mind. It could be dull and dreary or light and happy depending upon the soul's preconceptions, ideas or established behaviour patterns. Thus a mean-spirited person would find himself in a somewhat miserable existence, whilst a generous person would end up in a sunny, life-exuding landscape. However, these differences were not rewards and punishments dictated by some higher authority but simply the natural consequence of the person's mind. On this plane, imagination rules supreme and just by thinking a thing it appears. Once deceased the ability of each soul to transform their self-created environment would depend upon the speed of their spiritual development which in turn would depend upon their willingness to face up to past errors.

By the time Swedenborg's own soul left its material body the medium claimed to have spoken to thousands who had passed beyond the veil of death. So commonplace did these communications eventually become that on one occasion he wrote in his diary of the death of a friend, 'Henrik died on Monday. He spoke with me on Thursday.' Unsurprisingly, the Swede's matter-of-fact

acceptance of his gifts contrasted sharply with the blink-
ered prejudices of many of his contemporaries who flatly
refused to accept that he was really contacting spirits. But
his critics never particularly bothered him. The medium
steadfastly refused contention of the subject, preferring
simply to assert his own belief with the words, 'I have
seen, I have heard, I have felt.'

In some ways Emmanuel Swedenborg was fortunate to
have lived when he did; during the preceding four centuries a man with his psychic talents might well have found
himself burned as a heretic. The idea of contacting the
dead goes back long before the Middle Ages, however.
The first mediums were probably shamans, medicine men
and witch doctors, those gifted individuals through which
early tribal cultures contacted the gods and spirits of the
underworld. Centuries later, the ancient Mediterranean
civilizations of Egypt, Greece and Rome sought advice
from seers who they believed held the same power.

The *Chronicles of Porphrey* tell of the numerous
attempts by contemporary magicians to call up the
dead, describing seances which bear remarkable similarity to those gatherings attended by Victorian physical
mediums. There is no suggestion in these writings that
necromancy was regarded as dangerous or illegal. The
attitudes of the Hebrews and early Christians are more
difficult to define. In the Old Testament *Book of Samuel*,
believed to date from roughly 1,000 BC, it is written that
under no circumstances should men 'consult ghosts or
spirits or call up the dead,' though ten centuries later
Saul of Tarsus thought more favourably of such practices.
In his first letter to the Corinthians the Saint described
the 'gifts of recognizing spirits' to be a sign of God's
grace, an honour to be set alongside prophecy and
the healing touch. Despite the Saint's positive words

Christian leaders in the centuries following the Messiah's death effectively outlawed the practice of mediumship, so that by the early Middle Ages a person suspected of consulting with the agencies of the unseen invariably found themselves executed, often in a slow and hideous fashion.

Today in the late twentieth century, though not burned as witches, those who profess to talk to the dead are treated with precious little respect. Instead of hunting down clairvoyants as criminals, modern society chooses in the main to ridicule or simply ignore a gift which has continued to defy rational explanation since its advent in the earliest civilizations. To a largely incredulous media, the spiritualists' associations which have grown up across the western hemisphere during the past century and a half are unworthy of attention beyond a line in a gossip column or the occasional spread in some third-rate human-interest magazine. More often than not, it is the outrageous and unauthenticated claims of the more eccentric mediums that hit the headlines and as a result most people have come to see spiritualists as a group too credulous and naïve to know when they are being duped.

The millions who remain active spiritualists in spite of the social stigma attached to their religion, believe the truth to be very different. Like Emmanuel Swedenborg 300 years ago, modern mediums believe they too have heard, seen and felt the presence of an invisible world beyond the mortal sphere. Moreover, unlike scientific rationalists, spiritualists can take comfort in the fact that they have developed a belief system which encompasses many of life's most inexplicable mysteries, a vision of the death-state which accounts satisfactorily for the otherwise impossible phenomena of ghosts, poltergeists and possessions. No search for survival-proof can afford to ignore them.

*   *   *

The history of modern spiritualism began not with Emmanuel Swedenborg, who was something of a lone pioneer, but in 1848 with an outbreak of poltergeist type phenomena in the small community of Hydesville, New York. A poor farmer, J.D. Fox, could hardly have guessed that his small clapboard cottage could one day become the focus of a series of events which would have a profound influence on the lives of millions. For that he would have his daughters to thank, Margueritta, fifteen, and Kate, eleven.

The first indications that the Fox sisters possessed mediumistic powers occurred when both reported strange nocturnal percussions on the walls of their bedroom, noises which soon spread to other parts of the house. Convinced their home was haunted, the girls responded to the raps with a series of signals of their own, simply snapping their fingers in the air whenever they heard anything. Soon contact was made and a two-way dialogue began. Apart from the immediate family few took the claims of the sisters seriously. But when the communications were subsequently performed in front of dozens of witnesses inside the cottage and later in the open air before even larger audiences, the doubters fell quiet. Certainly the vast majority of people who were present at these displays believed they had seen the supernatural at work and few if any could otherwise account for the mystery. From the ghostly raps it soon became evident that the unseen presence was the spirit of the murdered peddler whose bones, he said, lay buried in the house now occupied by the Fox family. A walled-in skeleton was duly found (convincing even more people that the ghost was real) and the sisters became celebrities. They were not alone for long.

Fuelled by the interest generated by the Hydesville phenomenon, a veritable craze of spiritualistic activity spread like wildfire across America and thereafter throughout the world. In dimly lit rooms everywhere the dead apparently returned with awe-inspiring frequency, accompanied by evermore extraordinary manifestations. As one Victorian writer commented wryly, 'It seems as though the spirit world, having at last hit upon a means of communicating, cannot get enough of it.' But quantity was not matched by quality. Whilst spiritualism rapidly assumed the status of a fully fledged religion for many people, others expressed profound disappointment at the content of the messages so frequently received from beyond the grave. After attending a number of seances himself and having heard very little of note, the philosopher Thomas Huxley denounced spiritualism as 'the chatter of old women,' and added that if he were himself to die and had the facility of returning, he would decline the privilege of being made to 'talk twaddle with a medium hired at a guinea a seance.' Huxley's disenchantment was entirely natural for a man of his intelligence.

The characteristic paucity of so many transmissions was blamed by the mediums themselves on the mundane minds of their contactees – less enlightened souls who had ended up on the lower planes of vibration. But many remained unconvinced by the excuse.

There can be little doubt that some mediums who claimed clairvoyant powers during those first heady days of spiritualism were in it for the money alone. In other cases, though apparently genuine, the sheer banality of messages given to sitters would make anyone wonder why the dead bothered returning at all. As always however, there was another side to the coin. Some spiritualists produced a clear, imaginative view of what an afterlife existence might be like, whilst the phenomena produced by the best physical mediums was truly out of this world.

Daniel Dunglas Home, the most famous medium of his day, is a case in point. An American of Scottish ancestry, Home made his name by demonstrating his incredible powers to the aristocracy of Europe. A genuine miracle worker, if alive today he would make the psychokinetic feats of Uri Geller look tame. D.D. Home could make objects appear and disappear at will, levitate his own body and heavy furniture (on one occasion a grand piano) and even had the ability to handle red-hot coals with his bare hands. Indeed, there seemed almost no limit to Home's powers. At the age of thirteen he began receiving messages from the deceased and by the time he was twenty he was already producing evidence of survival, the clarity of which surpassed any of his peers.

In 1852 during a seance held at the home of a silk manufacturer Ward Cherey, Home levitated for the first time. According to one witness, the newspaper editor F.L. Burr, the medium's body floated involuntarily to the high ceiling 'palpitating from head to foot with the contending emotions of joy and fear'. When Home repeated the feat in front of a room full of investigators from Harvard University, their leader Professor Wells concluded a report of the event with the words, 'It is true. We know we were not imposed upon or deceived.'

After that, levitation became a regular feature of Home's seances. On one occasion in London's Belgravia, he rose into the air and floated out of a third-floor window, where he remained for some minutes suspended in space eighty feet above the ground. Perhaps even more remarkable was Home's ability to levitate other sitters as well as himself. In Florence, at the court of Napoleon III, he apparently lifted the Countess Chrisini into the air along with the harpsichord she was playing! Home could handle fire at will and his incombustibility was

also transferrable. In a London seance he laid red-hot
cinders on the head and hands of a senior officer in
the British Army, Lord Adare, without the soldier
feeling any ill effects. On another occasion he placed
live coals in his mouth. It was to investigate such
apparently inexplicable powers that the British Society
for Psychical Research was set up in 1882. Among the
SPR's founding members was Sir William Crookes, a
scientist of repute who was later to win the Nobel
Prize. Crookes was himself a sceptic of spiritualistic
phenomena but his disbelief was shaken when upon
meeting Daniel Dunglas Home for the first time, the
medium manifested an ectoplasmic hand for the scientist
to shake. As Home went on to display miracle after
miracle he had no option but to accept the evidence of
his own eyes.

In his first formal laboratory test, Crookes asked Home
if he could press the keys of an accordion whilst standing
away from the instrument at a distance of several feet.
To the scientist's amazement Home did so without
hesitation. But this was only the beginning – after a
short time the accordion was flying gaily around the room
playing *Yankee Doodle Dandy*! By the time his first series
of tests were completed Crookes was convinced that his
earlier scepticism was misplaced. In a detailed report to
the Royal Society of Science, the academic expressed his
'single incontestable conviction' that the wonders he had
witnessed were 'real and unaccountable'. They were, he
felt, proof positive that life continues beyond the grave,
for only a supernatural agency could have achieved them.
Ironically many of those who marvelled at Home's powers of physical manifestation were occasionally less than
impressed by his mental mediumship. Elizabeth Barret
Browning, poet wife of Robert, became a close friend of
Home and never doubted for a single moment that the

unseen world was the source of his miraculous powers. Nevertheless, she once wrote testily to a friend that his seances usually contained 'much such twaddle as may be heard in fifth-rate conventicles'. It was a common complaint amongst intelligent witnesses who were both fascinated and repelled by the evidence for spiritualism. Even so, whilst much spirit communication remained tedious, disjointed and unconvincing, an overall picture of the type of world the spirits inhabited *was* gradually emerging and many of the assertions received through spirit guides during the last century remain fundamental to the beliefs of today's channellers. Just as Emmanuel Swedenborg insisted over two centuries ago, modern psychics are convinced that the newly dead emerge in their resurrection body looking and feeling much the same as they did on earth. Typically, they are met by friends and relatives who comfort them in their supreme moment of crisis and educate them as to the rules of their new life. Immediately following mortal death some time is spent on a plane of existence which is very much like our own world although infinitely more beautiful. It is a place which occultists describe as the 'paradise rest' and spiritualists more commonly label the 'summerland'. However, it is not the everlasting heaven of biblical legend but simply a stopping-off point in the soul's spiritual progress. From here the soul chooses to ascend to higher levels of consciousness or, if its development is incomplete, it will reincarnate once more in an earthly body. Thus, most spiritualists, even those who adhere to what is known as Christian spiritualism, believe firmly in the doctrine of rebirth and karma – the concept of soul development through a cause and effect system of reward and punishment. Although spiritualism is itself a relatively new religion, much of that which it holds to be true mirrors the ancient faiths of Hinduism and

Buddhism, whose own reincarnationist doctrines will be discussed in much greater detail elsewhere in this book.

For those who do not wish to see death as oblivion, the religion of spiritualism has much to commend it, and mediumistic communication has proved to be an effective way of offering comfort to countless bereaved people. Spiritualists who lose their own loved ones can rest assured that they will meet once again in happier and less troubled surroundings. Even those unfortunate enough to lose a child need not wonder why God allows a human life to be cut short so cruelly, since they believe the same child will be allowed to grow to adulthood in the spirit world. Spiritualist funerals, in marked contrast to the religious death ceremonies of most other faiths, are often cheerful affairs.

Not all souls who pass through death's portal can look forward to a happy time in the afterlife however. Spiritualists believe that one reaps as one sows: those who have been greedy, avaricious and mean-spirited, or even worse, those who have been deliberately unkind, cruel or evil during their earthly days will find themselves surrounded by other souls of a similar mental development and the lower planes to which such individuals gravitate are much more like hell than heaven. Liars, boasters and other antisocial elements often find themselves earth-bound ghosts. Others remain tied to the material world because their disbelief in an afterlife will not allow them to accept the fact of their own death or because their desires for the pleasures of the flesh outweigh any ambition for spiritual fulfilment. The souls of those who have descended to truly despicable acts, such as murder, rape or torture during their earthly life find themselves surrounded by an aura of darkness, created by their own psychic evil, from which there is no easy escape.

Within their self-created prisons they would be forced
to confront the fact of their own wrongdoing and a
long period of remorse would inevitably pass before
they could forgive themselves sufficiently to pass on to
the higher planes.

No soul is ever entirely alone, however, nor is hope
for any individual ever lost, no matter what crimes they
may have committed on earth. Spiritualists believe that
to each and every incarnate being there is assigned a
discarnate soul whose task it is to direct that person
towards the path of enlightenment. (It is these same
guides which mediums say assist them in communicating).
In the period immediately following death, even those
people who have not been particularly bad in life, yet
lack a dimension of spiritual enlightenment, may need
help from the guides. Created by thoughts and emotions
on a level some have described as a ideoplastic dimension,
the afterlife world inhabited by the newly discarnate souls
may not be truly suitable to their long-term development.
For example, an intensely materialistic man may initially
create luxurious surroundings with his desires for leisure
and sensual pleasures. For a while he will be satisfied but
soon, with the help of guides, he will come to recognize
the self-serving nature of this imaginary paradise and
begin to turn his mind towards worthwhile thoughts and
action.

The upward route of all souls involves many trials
and stages. On the higher planes souls have come
to realize that true satisfaction and purpose is only
possible through service to others. Here, on a level
some spiritualists have labelled 'first heaven', the soul
is shown the step-by-step story of its own nature whilst
on earth. Self-knowledge is gained through a long and
complex re-evaluation of past mistakes and personality
failings, as well as a recognition of worthy thoughts and

actions. Everything is laid bare without excuses, and the judgement which follows comes not from on high but from the soul itself. At this stage, as with all phases of the afterlife process, the purpose is to teach and not to punish. The reward for those who achieve is not fame, riches or glory, but the opportunity to be of service. The prize is the chance to fulfil one's destiny, to find the true identity of the real self, a far greater, more complete being than any individual incarnate person has considered themselves to be. Seen in this perspective spiritualism is a profoundly optimistic philosophy. We all share eternity, no matter what we may believe now. Dying itself, far from being the absolute event so many fear, seems to be little more than an altered state of consciousness.

So far so good. But the central question remains: can we believe these stories or is it all in the mind? For committed spiritualists, mediumistic communication may have provided answers for many of death's mysteries, but how convincing is this evidence for non-devotees of their faith? Just where is the hard proof?

Among those who doubt whether channelling is possible are those who argue that so-called guides are simply fragments of the medium's own subconscious mind. As a psychological theory it certainly has its attractions since it has been proved that the human mind can create new identities. However, this explanation of spiritualistic phenomena goes no way to account for those numerous instances where mediums gain access to information of which they themselves could have no knowledge. A particularly remarkable example, uncovered by Dutchman Nils Jacobsen and included in his book *Life Without Death*, serves to prove how difficult these enigmas are to account for within a rationalist framework. In 1928

Jacobsen's uncle was knocked down by a lorry; with his head smashed against a brick wall he died several days later in hospital without ever regaining consciousness. The family had always assumed that a fractured skull led to his death until, many years afterwards, a mediumistic message offered a contradictory version of events to Nils Jacobsen who was attending a seance. After accurately describing the circumstances of the road accident, the returning soul of the author's uncle explained that he had really died of a condition which 'came from the bones'. It seemed unlikely until Nils Jacobsen checked the post-mortem report. The hospital records showed that his uncle had died not as a result of brain damage but from an embolism originating from a blood clot in his thighbone – lower bone thrombosis. As Jacobsen wrote, it was a significant fact of which none of his family was aware, let alone the medium who received the message.

There have been plenty of other examples no less evidential. Typical is the communication given to the English woman Mrs Elizabeth Dawson-Smith in 1921, through the mediumship of Gladys Leonard. The returning spirit in this case was Mrs Dawson-Smith's son who had been killed a year before while still a young man. The message concerned an old purse her son had hidden which contained a receipt for a large sum of money previously paid to a Debt Clearing Office in Germany. Mrs Dawson-Smith knew of the transaction but had searched in vain for the piece of paper, unsure of where it was kept. When she found it in the place that Gladys Leonard had indicated she had little choice but to believe wholeheartedly that it was her son who had given the message for he had been the only person who knew of its whereabouts.

It was no means the only spectacular example of proof

that the English medium gave. During the late 1920s the psychic researcher Reverend Charles Drayton Thomas conducted a series of personal sittings with Leonard during which the medium gave him (through her guide Feda) a total of 124 factual elements; according to Thomas 70 were 'absolutely correct', 12 'close' and 22 contained a 'lesser element of truth'. Only 10 (less than 10 per cent) were wholly inaccurate. The churchman was immensely impressed but knew that if survival were to be conclusively proven it was necessary to banish all possibility of other factors – even telepathy. To achieve this Thomas introduced an element of precognition into his tests, asking Leonard's guide to read aloud stories which would be printed in *The Times* the following morning. In his book *Some New Evidence For Human Survival*, Leonard describes how Feda achieved this impossible feat on numerous occasions. In addition to his newspaper tests the churchman developed an even more complicated system of communicating proof, once more designed to rule out telepathy. During each seance Thomas would be told by the spirit to return to his home library, and there to look at a book on a certain shelf. On the page and line reference given previously he would inevitably find a phrase which meant something to him and him alone. For Thomas this not only provided proof that telepathy was not at the root of mediumship but also demonstrated that the mental capacities of the spirits far exceeded those of mortal minds.

Automatic writing – a process through which mediums in trance states seemingly take down notes on paper dictated to them direct from the unseen – has also produced some remarkable pieces of evidence. In this way, the famous English barrister Sir Edward Marshall-

Hall learned, in 1924, of the death of his brother who had been living in South Africa. Medium Katherine Wingfield, a guest at Marshall's home, wrote a message for the lawyer indicating that a letter he had received that day had been sent by a person who was now dead. In fact Marshall-Hall had received only one letter that morning, from his brother in South Africa. Two weeks later the barrister discovered that the prophecy was true; his brother had died on the very day that Katherine Wingfield's spirit friends had guided her pen.

A similarly inexplicable piece of evidence was received in the early 1970s by a group of English psychical researchers who conducted a series of seances using automatic scripts. Made up of scientists, rather than spiritualists, the team approached the possibility of an afterlife with an open mind. They ended up convinced of the possibility of spiritual communication. Initially very little useful evidence came through during the group's sessions until, in August 1973, a message was received from an entity calling itself 'Grace'. The spirit claimed to be that of a woman who had only recently died, and in subsequent sessions she gave further details, including her address in the London Borough of Hackney, plus the time, date and cause of her earthly demise. The details were thoroughly checked and found to be absolutely correct to the last degree, though no one in the group had ever known or had any contact with the dead woman. The evidence was conclusive – as one group member said at the time, 'a case that seems impossible to account for unless we accept that Grace herself had spoken to us'.

Perhaps the best evidence for the existence of genuine spiritualistic communication is the series of automatic scripts which form the basis of the celebrated SPR 'Cross

Correspondences'. These scripts were unique in the annals of mediumship in that the communications were received not by a single person but by a dozen individuals from around the globe, most of whom had never met. The background to the 'Cross Correspondence' case was the deaths of three distinguished Cambridge scholars, Edmund Gurney, Henry Sidwick and Frederick Myers, all of whom were founder members of the British SPR. The transmissions were received by means of automatic writing, the process described above, through which a medium in trance-state allows her pen to be guided across a blank page. They began being collected shortly after the death of Frederick Myers on 17 January 1901 – Myers being the last of the SPR trio to pass over to the next life, and the first to return. Determined to prove the reality of the afterlife state, Myers had left a message in a sealed envelope with a friend – the distinguished scientist Sir Oliver Lodge; its content was secret and the envelope to be kept sealed until some medium reported a contact. In the event, the first medium to receive a message was Margaret Verall, a lecturer's wife from Cambridge. In the communication, Myers' ghost explained both about the letter and its hidden message, identified as a few lines from Plato's *Symposium*. When Lodge unsealed the envelope it confirmed Verall's communication. Subsequently, Sidwick and Gurney also came through to the same medium, each giving accurate information about their own lives.

This was merely the beginning. All three SPR founding members then began to send messages to other mediums around the world – messages which made little sense in themselves but became deeply meaningful when the fragments were pieced together. Like an intricate three dimensional jigsaw, each transmission was signed by one of the dead investigators through the automatist in a precise representation of his earthly signature. Many of the messages included details of past meetings, conversations etc. of which the various mediums involved knew little or nothing. Often they contained sentences in a classical language which the medium had never learned. When the content of these communications was relayed to those still-living investigators who knew the men in life, they were invariably confirmed as being an accurate record of past events. Clearly the returning men were attempting to draw together a body of evidence which would make the case for the existence of an afterlife incontestable. In all, the scripts continued to be collected for a period of sixteen years, at the end of which the messages ceased, abruptly and without explanation.

The many hundreds of examples of automatic writing taken down in relation to this remarkable case are still to be found in the files of the British Society for Psychical Research in London and, arguably, they remain the most striking evidence for human survival to date. Since many of the automatists who received the messages lived as far apart as the USA, London and India, a straightforward case of collaboration must surely be ruled out. No one who has ever researched the enigma of the 'Cross Correspondences' has come up with an alternative explanation for the mystery which seems more likely than the probability that the three men *had* survived their own deaths, and chosen to return to prove the fact to those left behind. Yet this is just a single outstanding example of a much wider phenomenon; tens of thousands of people who have consulted clairvoyants have heard for themselves mediumistic communications, which seem explicable only if we accept the involvement of a supernatural agency.

*   *   *

Of course spirit communications are not always seen to
be correct, nor does every piece of evidence offered
prove particularly convincing. Most psychic communications are very much of the hit-or-miss variety, a fact
which sceptics readily highlight. I am fully aware from
personal experience just how frustrating this inconsist-
ency can be.

My first direct contact with clairvoyance took place in
the London headquarters of the Spiritualist Association
of Great Britain in 1979. During the sitting, a private
one-hour session for which I paid five pounds, I received
information which was startlingly accurate – in fact, I
reckoned there was not really a single detail given by
the medium which could have been meant for anyone
else. Her Tibetan guide genuinely seemed to know about
my past and present circumstances, as well as being able
to offer some indication of my future destiny. Correct
assertions included my then occupation (student) my
subject of study (English literature) the unusual Christian
name of a recently dead relative (right first time) and the
precise nature of my mother's serious illness. Incredibly,
the spirits even knew what I had been doing the previous
afternoon! Predictions for my future, which subsequently
proved correct, included the fact that I would become a
school teacher, that I would travel extensively (I have
in fact travelled to more than twenty countries including
Africa, India and the Far East) and that I would become
a published author one month before my thirty-fifth
birthday. In the fullness of time this last detail has proved
to be astonishing. When I signed a contract on my first
book *Unnatural Causes* in July 1989 I was still thirty-two.
It was due to be published within twelve months but
circumstances beyond my control delayed the final date
of publication for two years. In the end *Unnatural Causes*
appeared on the bookshelves in Britain on 25 July

1991, twenty-seven days before my thirty-fifth birthday. Perhaps most impressive of all at the time, though, was the way in which these spirit guides seemed to know an extraordinary amount about my own personality, my likes and dislikes, hopes, fears and ambitions. Sceptical when I entered the building, I left with very little option but to believe that the woman I had seen possessed genuinely incomprehensible powers.

When I visited the spiritualists' association again a month later the story was very different. On this occasion, the medium – different from the one I had seen before – proved unable to offer me any conclusive proof that she was in touch with unseen intelligences. Her stumbling performance was so inept as to be embarrassing. Deeply disappointed, I knew that had it been my first contact with the world of clairvoyance I should simply have found my former doubts reinforced. Nevertheless, as the saying goes, you only need to find one white crow to demonstrate that not all crows are black. In the same way the inability of the second medium to deliver a single word of note could not eradicate the extraordinary powers demonstrated by the first.

Why is it that so many mediumistic communications are disjointed, confused or only partly relevant to the sitter? Two possibilities seem to stand out from the rest. The first is that a medium's mind works on the level of a telephone exchange – not only must clairvoyants take care to tune in to the right wavelength, they must also occasionally get crossed lines. This picture of mediumship seems wholly plausible and may very well be at least part of the answer. Another possibility is that the medium herself may misunderstand or misinterpret the meaning of the message she is being given. An example from my own experience tends to make me lean towards this misinterpretation theory. In 1981, while sitting in a

circle in London I was told that a series of words were
appearing before the medium's eyes, directed to me. The
sentence read: 'Michael. Three weeks. This side of the
world and the other.' When I asked the psychic what
she thought it meant, she replied that she felt her guide
was referring to this (material) world and the alternative
reality in spirit. In fact I had already deduced that the
message was connected with my own cousin Michael who
was at that time on a three-week holiday in Australia.
Interestingly, my example would appear to rule out
a telepathic basis for the message, since, although I
knew of my cousin's whereabouts, the medium did not
correctly interpret the content of her communication.

The possibility that telepathy or some otherwise
undiscovered faculty of the human mind could be the
true basis for mediumistic channelling, rather than direct
transmission from discarnate entities, is a consideration that must be taken seriously. Indeed, given that
extrasensory perception has virtually been proven in
parascientific laboratories around the world it is difficult to doubt that information is occasionally and
unconsciously transmitted from sitter to medium in this
way. However, in such cases as those transmissions
delivered to either Mrs Dawson-Smith or the barrister
Edmund Marshall-Hall, the telepathy theory would
seem inappropriate. Certainly it can have played little
part in the SPR 'Cross Correspondences', or the newspaper tests conducted by the Reverend Charles Drayton
Thomas.

Where they have been carried out independent studies have tended to support the probability that some
form of genuine afterlife communication lies at the root
of much spiritualistic phenomena. In 1937 a report into
mediumship was commissioned by the then Archbishop
of Canterbury, the Reverend Cosmo Lang. A panel of

senior churchmen were appointed to conduct a study over two years. By a majority verdict, the working group concluded that there was a *prima-facie* case that mediumship was evidence of survival. Afraid of the controversy the report's finding might engender, the Archbishop kept the report under lock and key; only during the past few years has its conclusions become general knowledge. Yet the 1937–9 study was by no means unique; in the post-war years several independent studies have put the mediumship enigma on trial and reached the same verdict. Their testimony leads us inexorably towards the conclusion that the dead are still very much alive.

Russell's Law states that 'the resistance to new ideas increases by the mathematical square of their importance.' In just this way some people flatly refuse to accept the possibility of spirit communication no matter how powerful the evidence produced. A particularly determined sceptic was Harry Houdini, the world-famous escapologist who conducted a personal crusade to expose the 'myth of spiritualism' during the early decades of this century. An brilliant illusionist himself, Houdini believed he was perfectly placed to detect fraud in those who pretended to possess supernatural abilities. Upon those who resorted to trickery he heaped insults, regularly using the pages of the press to describe them as 'leeches', and it was partly due to the magician's highly publicized campaign that laws were eventually introduced prohibiting proven frauds from continuing to practise mediumship. Non-believer though he was, Houdini did paranormal research a favour. The ugly spectre of fraudulent mediums has done much to damage the cause of spiritualism since its beginning a century and a half ago. Astonishingly the late nineteenth century saw the appearance of an estimated 20,000 clairvoyants, many of whom claimed powers they did not possess. Often their tricks were embarrassingly simple.

One famous English medium named Florence Cook, whose seances were invariably conducted in near-total darkness, would sit inside a specially made cabinet from which she produced a spirit form clothed in white linen. Sitters were fooled for years until an SPR founding member, Sir George Sitwell, suspected a trick and seized the ghostly apparition. The 'spirit' turned out to be none other than Florence Cook herself, covered in a sheet. Sitwell was one of several investigators who unmasked fakery. On other occasions flashlight cameras smuggled by journalists into dimly lit seance rooms revealed purported apparitions to be none other than cheap stage props. Even the mediumship of the Fox sisters from Hydesville came under suspicion. Many years after the original event, a by-then alcoholic Margueretta Fox publicly denounced her own powers as fraudulent, suggesting that all along she and her sister had used the device of cracking the joints of their big toes to represent the supposed aural manifestations which had previously emanated from the walls of their home. However, in this case the likelihood of fraud is a little more difficult to credit. Given the level of documented evidence from hundreds of eyewitnesses it seems improbable that so many could have been fooled for so long. Her sister Kate continued to communicate with spirits, often in the open air and in front of very large audiences. It is perhaps significant that Margueretta had, by the time of her self-denunciation, lost her own powers and fallen out with her sister; it is also worth remembering that she had been paid a huge sum of money for her confession at a time when she was virtually destitute. Given the circumstances it is hard to come to any firm conclusions on the basis of her 'confession'

The decline in physical mediumship over the past half century has done little to alleviate the suspicion amongst some people that the most conclusive evidence for human survival of death has been brought about through deliberate collusion between medium and sitter. A parallel objection is that most sittings are judged by the sitters themselves who are likely to be emotionally involved and therefore unreliable witnesses. Sadly, the charge is not altogether without foundation particularly since it is always easier to fool people when they want to be fooled. We may no longer suffer the bizarre ectoplasmic fabrications of the Edwardian seance rooms, but fake mental mediums continue to flourish and prosper.

Probably the most famous British medium of recent years, the late Doris Stokes, is a case in point. Author of several books, star of numerous television chat shows and a general household name, Stokes held huge meetings in theatres and cinemas across the country. Without the aid of any devices apart from her invisible spirit guide, the smiling grandmotherly figure seemed to many to possess powers which were truly out of this world. Few went home disappointed and even sceptics grudgingly agreed that she put on a good show. For many people an evening with Doris Stokes provided the only proof of an afterlife they were ever likely to need. But was she the genuine article? Author Ian Wilson, who attended a Stokes demonstration at the London Palladium in 1986 whilst researching his book *The Afterdeath Experience*, is one person who definitely thought not. A firm disbeliever himself, Wilson expected to find Stokes' mediumship based upon the time-honoured technique of fishing for clues, making intelligent guesses and giving evidence so vague that it could apply to almost anyone. Instead, to his surprise, Stokes gave out a series of details so exact that they defied natural explanation, the messages including the Christian names of dead persons, the numbers of the houses in which they lived, descriptions of family heirlooms etc. So accurate was this information given and so moved were the members of the audience who received it that the atmosphere inside the packed theatre became, as Wilson put it, 'electric'. At the end of each communication Stokes urged the bereaved relatives not to worry about their departed ones who, she said, were really safe and happy, living in a world so much better than the one they left behind. None could doubt that the channeller's performance had been a remarkable one; the messages contained details much too specific to be put down to coincidence or successful fishing for clues.

Upon investigation though Wilson came to realize that the whole thing had been a classic setup. Having taken down the names and addresses of those members of the audience for whom the most accurate transmissions were received, the writer was shocked to discover that, without exception, each knew Doris Stokes personally and had been offered front row complimentary tickets only the week beforehand! In every instance Stokes had known in advance the identity of the dead relations she was supposed to have received from the 'other side'. Wilson concluded that he had been witness to a charade along with hundreds of other people, all paying five pounds a ticket for the privilege. In the event Doris Stokes died before Wilson's exposé was published and whether or not she ever possessed a level of real mediumistic power is anyone's guess. Yet her willingness to dupe audiences was perhaps not so surprising, since her self-confessed role model, the English psychic Helen Duncan was, in 1944, prosecuted at the Old Bailey for fraudulent mediumship and sentenced to nine months in jail.

The suspicion of trickery continues to do great damage not only to the young religion of spiritualism, but also to those researchers who spend years trying to assess the validity of the paranormal phenomenon. Exasperatingly, even some genuine clairvoyants have not been above using the odd hoax. Eusapia Palladino was, during the early years of the present century, one of the most remarkable physical mediums of her era, able to manifest bits of bodies including heads and hands firm and solid enough to shake, all in broad daylight. Still, many doubted that her apparent miracles were possible, so in 1908 the Society for Psychical Research organized a series of seances in Naples to be attended by policemen and SPR members experienced in exposing charlatans. It was written afterwards that Palladino was not 'detected in fraud in any one of the 470 phenomena that took place at eleven seances'. When investigated in 1909 by the American SPR in New York, however, researchers concluded that she had resorted to 'conscious and deliberate fraud on a number of occasions' as well as producing 'amazing genuine phenomena' which could not be explained. When she was faced with the damning evidence that she had deceived her investigators, Eusapia Palladino seemed not to think that it mattered whether the manifestations were real or not. A show-woman by nature, her only concern seemed to be that she gave a satisfactory performance. . . .

No discussion of clairvoyance can duck the issue of fraudulent mediums. Many people are desperate for proof that their loved ones still exist; some would prefer to be fooled rather than face the possibility that they will never see them again. There can be no doubt that many clairvoyants have unscrupulously exploited such credulousness, often for monetary gain. Others apparently manage to convince themselves that they really do possess special abilities.

Nevertheless, despite the tricks perpetrated by the occasional bogus medium: there is much in spirit communication which cannot be explained; and objections of fraud cannot outweigh the truly overwhelming evidence that genuinely gifted psychics have produced. D.D. Home, the greatest medium of the Victorian age, never accepted money for his seances. His preternatural feats, the levitation of himself, of others, of heavy furniture; the numerous demonstrations of personal incombustibility; the elongation of his body and his manifestation of disembodied forms were mostly conducted not in some darkened room of his own choosing, but in broad daylight, in or out of doors, and in front of thousands of witnesses. Over a period of thirty years, in a career which took him across three continents, no one was ever able to prove that the phenomena he produced was the product of trickery or illusion. In the words of the scientist Sir William Crooks who investigated Home for the SPR, '. . . to reject such evidence is to reject the value of all human testimony whatsoever.'

The phenomena produced by some other physical mediums has been scarcely less extraordinary. Shortly after the turn of the century, Carlos Mirabelli, a Brazilian teenage sales clerk from São Paulo, was locked up in a lunatic asylum because he said he kept hearing voices. Physicians only realized he was not mad when he began to manifest his acquaintances in three dimensional apparitions inside his cell. Those dead who were summoned by Mirabelli were completely visible to anyone and on several occasions the spirits even allowed themselves to be examined by doctors before they vanished. On his release Carlos Mirabelli was extensively investigated by the Cesare Lambrusco Academy of Physical Studies. In a total of 392 seances conducted in broad daylight he brought forth apparitions identified beyond question as the dead friends or relatives of the scientists investigating him. On one occasion the leader of the investigation team, one Dr Rivalino de Xavier, spoke with a visual likeness of his deceased mother for an hour and a half; on another occasion the phantom form of a drowned bishop returned so that a top medical specialist he had known in life could undertake a full examination of his semi-substantial body. Not surprisingly Mirabelli's fame grew. In 1930 he was investigated once more, this time by American writer and journalist Eric Dingwall. Dingwall afterwards wrote that the evidence he saw produced was 'frankly staggering to the intellect'. Pointing out that Mirabelli sometimes produced his manifestations in the open air and before huge audiences (on one occasion over 5,000) or in brightly illuminated laboratories under the close observation of scientists, Dingwall concluded, 'It would be easy to condemn the man as a monstrous fraud and the witnesses as equally monstrous fools, but I do not think that such a hypothesis will help even him who makes it.'

Perhaps the greatest evidence of all is not the messages mediums regularly receive but the extraordinary gifts conferred upon them. One notable example surrounds the life of Pearl Curgan, a medium from St Louis, USA, who inherited the literary talents of her spirit guide Patience Worth, a discarnate soul who had purportedly spent her life as an English Quaker in the seventeenth century. Under Worth's guidance Curgan took down sixty novels, plays and poems, although she was herself barely literate. One remarkable work was a 60,000-word epic poem which made astonishingly accurate use of Middle English pronunciations forgotten except by scholars. In other books Pearl Curgan reproduced in intricate detail the political intrigues of Caesar's Rome and Ancient

Palestine, demonstrating impressive knowledge of Arabic and Hebrew into the bargain. Members of the American SPR investigated the writings and concluded that these backgrounds could not have been researched by Pearl Curgan. In their view, only a person who had spent a lifetime studying the various historical periods could have produced such a body of material.

Some psychics have claimed to be the channel for new works by the greatest authors, artists and musicians of the past. In 1961 a British housewife called Rosemary Brown suddenly found herself able to play the piano brilliantly despite never having had lessons. Moreover, she was able to compose new material in the style of Liszt, Chopin, Brahms, Beethoven and Monteverdi. Although these achievements invariably fell short of the real thing, Brown's creations bore the indelible stamp of the masters and the phenomenon of the suburban housewife-composer remains unexplained.

As in the Pearl Curgan case, a gift sometimes given to mediums of a special order is the ability to speak in languages they are unfamiliar with (a phenomenon, as we have already seen, known as xenoglossia). Just as Jesus' disciples received the Holy Spirit and began to speak in tongues that were not their own, so mediums who can do this confound sceptics of today. A notable case of spontaneous xenoglossia was described in 1887 by John W. Edmunds, a New York judge whose daughter Laura regularly claimed to see spirits. The voice phenomenon began when a visitor from Greece arrived at their home. Without introduction, Laura spoke to him in Greek, a language she had not heard before. Laura's spirit guide subsequently took over and spoke fluently in many languages, including several dialects of Red Indian tribes. Examples from the present century are even more striking. American medium George Valentine could conduct seances in Russian, German, Spanish and Welsh, and the aforementioned Carlos Mirabelli, though not a well-educated man, used no less than thirty languages from the platform, including Syrian and Japanese. Rosemary Brown, the psychic composer mentioned above, has been known to communicate with the past giants of classical music in their native tongues of German, Italian and Polish, even though she has never heard the languages in normal life.

The mental feats of mediums such as these do not in themselves prove conclusively the existence of an afterlife any more than a bolt of lightning proves the existence of electricity. Even so, they defy explanation within a rationalist framework. The fact that mediums themselves insist the spirit world is the basis and source of such gifts should, at the very least, lead us to consider the possibility of an afterlife as a working hypothesis. Of course, just as many parascientists continue to assert that mediumistic communication is really the work of telepathy, so others prefer to believe that a similarly unknown mental faculty is at work in cases of xenoglossia.

The above explanation cannot, however, be so readily applied to the most fantastic of powers given to mediums – that of spiritual healing. Indeed, so incredible have been the careers of some healers that a search for non-supernatural causes seems futile.

As a child in the 1960s, the English psychic Mathew Manning was plagued by poltergeists; as a teenager he accepted his clairvoyance and went on to publish books about the afterlife and to perform psychokinesis. Not satisfied with his ability to transform inert physical matter, Manning persuaded his ghostly friends to help him learn the art of healing. Here again his abilities confounded the sceptics. In 1982, a British Anglia Television programme showed the psychic cure a woman suffering from a painful hip joint infection. Subsequently, before a team of medical scientists in California, Manning demonstrated that he could control and occasionally cure a wide variety of diseases. When he performed the same tests in England, working with Dr Hastead at Birbeck College, Hastead claimed the tests had demonstrated that the British psychic was 'able to exert significant psychokinetic influence upon a variety of biological systems'. That caused much heated discussion inside medical circles and some doctors openly questioned the validity of the Birbeck experiments. Particularly controversial were a series of tests which appeared to indicate that the psychic could control and even partially destroy cancer cells through the power of thought. To many doctors such a suggestion was laughable, but as time went on the evidence continued to grow. The following year Manning was tested again, this time at the Science Unlimited Research Foundation in San Antonio. Once again he achieved spectacular results – the partial destruction of cancer cells held within a glass flask. On twenty-seven occasions out of thirty, Manning's healing thought waves apparently worked, his cancer cell death-rate showing a one hundred per cent variation from the control flasks.

Fantastic though his various paranormal achievements have become, Mathew Manning is simply following in a long tradition of English psychic doctors. Britain's greatest healer for many years, Harry Edwards, had no formal medical training, claiming instead that his knowledge of the human body and his own psychic powers were based upon advice given to him by two past giants of medicine: the French genius Louis Pasteur, and Lord Lister, the founder of antiseptic surgery. Over a forty-year period tens of thousands made the pilgrimage to Edwards's healing sanctuary in the heart of the Surrey countryside, where the tough workman-like hands achieved miracles, remoulding deformed limbs, removing cancers and curing blindness. Foreign rulers, members of the British Royal family, cabinet ministers and showbusiness figures were amongst his patients, and many doctors attested to the medium's powers over illness.

Edwards had first become aware of his gifts in Persia in 1915, whilst serving in the British Army. A regular officer, the young Captain's duties included the demonstration of first aid to tribesmen helping the British. To the astonishment of both himself and his superiors, Edwards appeared able to heal even chronic conditions with an iodine rub. As news of his abilities travelled, a local sheik brought his dying mother for treatment at the British camp. Seeing that the woman was close to death Edwards knew he could do nothing for her but was unwilling to turn the Arab away; instead he prepared a placebo from carbolic tooth powder. Two days later the delighted tribal chief returned with his mother completely recovered.

Despite his notable healing success as a serving officer, Harry Edwards continued to doubt his gifts and, on his return to England, went into business as a printer. But the years of commerce ended in 1934 when, a middle-aged father of four, Edwards visited a Christian Spiritualist church in London where he was told that it was time to begin his true mission on earth. Initially sceptical of the prophecy, Edwards nevertheless attempted to heal a number of close friends who were suffering from minor ailments. These small-scale successes led him to become more ambitious and so he tried healing a person who he was told lay dying in a nearby hospital from tuberculosis and a haemorrhage. Whilst thinking of the man one evening during a moment of quiet meditation, Edwards found himself 'seeing' a picture of a hospital ward – a vision more vivid than any dream; this was his first experience of astral travel (a technique of leaving the physical form which will be examined later on). Within twenty-four hours of spiritual intercession the dying man's haemorrhage had ceased and three weeks afterwards he was discharged, with doctors unable to explain his recovery.

From that moment on Harry Edwards's life changed completely. Having turned to full-time healing he found his powers greatly increased: simply talking quietly with a sick person or laying his hands gently on the patient's head seemed enough to cure afflictions. As the numbers who wrote to him for help soon exceeded those he could treat in his own home, he began telling them to concentrate on his picture. Dozens who subsequently used this technique of 'absent healing' claimed to see his white-coated figure appear at their bedside and they usually made full recoveries thereafter. At the height of his post-war fame Edwards received some 9,000 letters a week from around the globe. Although he could have made a fortune he never accepted money for his aid, beyond the expenses needed for the upkeep of his sanctuary and the salaries of those who helped him run it. Though his demonstrations, in venues such as the Albert Hall, were often attended by 5–6,000 people, Edwards remained shy and entirely disinterested in material success. Central to his mission was a simple desire to spread the message that life was eternal, that physical death was transitional and that disease itself was neither an inevitable nor natural condition.

By the time Harry Edwards died in 1976 his fame had already been eclipsed by another English healer, Ted Fricker. In the introduction to his autobiography entitled *God is my Witness*, Fricker makes it plain that, like Edwards, he believed his own miraculous powers were achieved through the existence of spirits visible to him alone. Again like Edwards, Fricker's only medical training came through the advice of doctors who had passed away from the mortal realm. His own special aide was Abdul Latif who had been a Persian physician during his mortal existence at the time of the Crusades.

Ted Fricker's healing career began when he found that he could brush warts from the hands of his two young daughters, as if by magic. Soon afterwards, he received a series of clairvoyant messages which told him to give up his business interests to perform his true destiny. For a time Fricker feared that he might be losing his sanity but as apparition after apparition appeared to him, he gradually learned to converse with and trust his guides. Fricker's first miraculous cure took place when a paralyzed man was carried into his home on a stretcher. To everyone's amazement, not least his own, the mere presence of the healer was enough to affect a complete and immediate recovery – the cripple quite literally took up his bed and walked. Hearing of the apparent miracle a local journalist interviewed Fricker suggesting he prove his ability by curing the peptic ulcer the journalist was himself suffering from. The healer pressed his stomach with one finger and told him it was done, whereupon the reporter put it to the test by consuming six whiskies and fish and chips. The result – he suffered no pain whatsoever.

Ted Fricker's fame spread far and wide and after a few years he was able to open his own clinic near Harley Street. His often instantaneous cures were even more remarkable than those of Edwards and by the time he wrote his autobiography in 1974, Fricker could claim to have achieved over one million successful healings. Amongst his patients were VIPs (including the singer Tom Jones and actor Christopher Lee) and many have gone on record attesting to their belief in his powers. Most interestingly, a number of top medical specialists from across Europe held the same conviction for according to his memoirs, many doctors sent patients to his clinic in the knowledge that he alone had the power to cure them.

Astonishing though the careers of the English healers are, there have been other psychics whose cures are if anything even more difficult for the medical world to comprehend. Psychic surgery, which flourishes in many developing countries, is undoubtedly the most spectacular of all mysterious healing arts – it is also the most controversial. Aided by unseen spirits, the alleged miracle workers profess to cure cancers and other internal bodily disorders by tearing open the body with their hands and wrenching out the malignant tissue by main force. Afterwards there is usually not even the smallest sign of a blemish on the patient's skin. It is plainly evident that this type of surgical practice could not be explained in terms other than the paranormal and there is no shortage of sceptical medics who have tried to debunk it. Sometimes scepticism has been warranted. During the mid-1970s for example, investigations by American surgeon William Nolan and a team of documentary film makers led by a BBC television crew, exposed a group of healers in the Philippines as a bunch of highly skilled con artists. Elsewhere, however, attempts to unmask these extraordinary techniques as bogus have not been so successful. Some psychic healers, so far from being charlatans, would appear genuinely to achieve instantaneous cures through techniques which defy every established law of medicine.

José Pedro de Freitas (nicknamed Arigo), was born the son of a poor farmer in the Belo Horizonte district of Brazil in 1918 and as a child suffered from blinding headaches. These migraines were accompanied by hallucinations, both visual and auditory and to the astonishment of his parents and teachers, he often reported hearing voices speaking in a language that he could not understand. The voices continued to plague Arigo throughout adolescence until, at the age of twenty-five, he began to understand what was happening to him. The change took place after he was confronted by a vision of a man who introduced himself as Dr Adolpho Fritz, a German physician who had died during World War I. The apparition told Arigo that he had been chosen for a special destiny and must devote his life to helping the sick. However, it was not until some years later, in 1950, while staying in a hotel with a business associate called Bittencourt, that Arigo's career of psychic surgery actually began. According to Bittencourt, Arigo appeared one night in his room, opened his body with a cutthroat razor and extracted a malignant growth from his side. To everyone's surprise, including Arigo – who remembered nothing of the incident and had been entirely ignorant of Bittencourt's cancer – the story was backed up with physical evidence: Bittencourt's body displayed the neat incision that had been made in his side. A subsequent examination in a Rio de Janeiro hospital proved that an expert surgical job had been carried out and soon the news of the somnambulist surgeon made headlines across Brazil. Literally overnight, José Pedro de Freitas became a household name.

To begin with the publicity only served to frighten and confuse Arigo. Gradually, however, he came to trust in the wisdom of his guide, Dr Fritz. Setting up his own operating theatre in the kitchen of his home, he began performing regular operations without anaesthetic (as many as 300 a day), using rusty kitchen knives for scalpels and yet his patients never seemed to feel any pain whatsoever. The surgery would be carried out at breakneck speed, the incisions preternaturally sewing themselves together. Having seen one operation take place in which Arigo cut a large hole in a girl's neck and pulled out a tumour with a pair of workman's pincers, the American journalist and writer, Dr Guy Lyon Playfair, pronounced the healer to be genuine beyond doubt. An equally impressed witness was a local judge, José Immensi, who watched Arigo cure a girl who was blind. Afterwards Immensi wrote: 'I saw him pick up what looked like a pair of nail scissors. He wiped them on his sports shirt and used no disinfectant of any kind. Then I saw him cut straight into the cornea of the patient's eye. She did not feel anything although she was fully conscious . . . it only took seconds. She was blind but afterwards she could see. How, I've no idea, it has to be a miracle and nothing less.'

Not everyone was happy with the miracle worker, however. In 1956, under pressure from the Catholic Church (which was determined to stamp out the rise of spiritualism) and urged on by a medical establishment unable to comprehend the healer's powers, Arigo was charged by the local authorities with practising illegal medicine. Despite a plethora of supporters including journalists, intellectuals, politicians, and renegade medical figures who testified in his defence at the trial, Arigo was sentenced to fifteen months' imprisonment for fraud. The healer was unrepentant and on his release, began practising medicine again. With the connivance of a sympathetic police force he succeeded in avoiding the wrath of the authorities for several years.

In 1963 Arigo performed surgery on an American investigator, Andrija Pluhjarch, who subsequently made a three-year study of the Brazilian phenomenon. According to Pluhjarch's published account, on the first day his team of medical graduates arrived at Arigo's house they witnessed the healer go into a trance, adopting the German manner and language of his spirit guide Dr Fritz. After this transformation, Arigo operated upon his first patient, an old man with a cataract. Driving a four-inch stainless steel kitchen knife into his eye, Arigo appeared almost indifferent to the pain or physical injury he might cause. But there seemed to be no pain nor even blood. The knife was withdrawn after a few seconds, whereupon the old man, apparently cured, shook hands and gave thanks. Despite the evidence of their own eyes, Pluhjarch's team could find no sign of an incision to the man's eye.

Hundreds of equally bewildering operations followed, many carried out in less than a minute. Although the investigators found no apparent use of hypnosis, there was minimal bleeding in the area of the wound, even when incisions were made deep within the stomach and patients showed no sign of pain, nor even dis-comfort. Although the healer took few precautions against infection, Pluhjarch's men never once heard of a case of blood-poisoning. The US team were also massively impressed by the quality of diagnosis made by Dr Fritz. Taking a random sample of a thousand patients treated by the healer, they found that in almost every case the spontaneous diagnosis given proved to be exactly correct for the patient's condition. Writing some months later of his findings in Brazil, Andrija Pluhjarch made plain his absolute belief that the scenes he had witnessed were genuine. 'It's simply ridiculous,' he wrote, 'to deny that the phenomenon of Arigo exists. We cannot possibly deny the reality of his feats.' It would seem equally ridiculous to suggest that Arigo's skills did not spring from a truly supernatural source.

When in 1964, he was arrested again and sentenced to ten months in gaol, prison warders often allowed patients to be healed inside his cell. On his release he went straight back to his healing ministry which continued uninterrupted until his death in a road accident in 1971.

*   *   *

Among the thousands who eventually come to believe in the existence of a spirit world are many who were once violently opposed to spiritualism and everything associated with it. In some cases the change of mind comes about because of a personal revelation or through the development of latent psychic powers within themselves; in other cases it is the slow accumulation of overwhelming evidence gleaned through an evaluation of the testimonies of others.

Dr Richard Hodgson, who was a confirmed disbeliever in all psychic phenomena until he met the medium Leonora Piper in 1885, fell into the second category. After studying the medium for twelve years, Hodgson wrote a paper for the American SPR which concluded with the following words, 'I entered the house profoundly materialistic, not believing in the continuance of life after death, and today I simply say, I believe. The proof has been given to me in such a way and with such repetition as to remove from me the possibility of doubt.' William James, the great Harvard psychologist and another one time sceptic of supernatural communications, wrote of Piper, 'I cannot resist the conviction that knowledge appears to her which she has never gained by the ordinary working use of her eyes and ears and wits.' Like Hodgson, James ended his life convinced that the human personality survived death. The case which finally convinced both men involved the return of a friend, George Pellow, who died in a riding accident. In more than one hundred sittings with Leonora Piper, George Pellow made himself known to Hodgson, James and other friends who had known him in life, recognizing them by name and including details of obscure past events as token proof of his authenticity. None of those sitters left the Piper seances doubting that they had met their friend once again.

Piper's mediumship was held up by early SPR members as evidence of a real channel to another world, the living incontestable proof that clairvoyance existed. In reality there were many as gifted then and there still are today. Englishman Leslie Flint, a direct voice medium who communicates in the verbal likeness of his contacts, is perhaps the best current example. For decades Flint has defied all attempts to catch him out, allowing infra-red cameras to invade the privacy of his seances and throat microphones to be attached to his voice box. Throughout these rigorous tests nothing has been discovered to suggest that the other-world voices he produces could arise from any means other than the paranormal. In his autobiography *Voices in the Dark*, the medium wrote, 'I have been boxed up, tied up, sealed up, gagged, bound and held and still the voices have come to speak their message of life eternal.' For those who meet Flint, the fact of the afterlife is soon proven. Throughout my own research I have come across no one who has attended his circle and remained a disbeliever. Understandably, the medium is irritated with those who stay away, close their minds and remain ardent in their dismissal of the evidence he and others like him continue to produce.

This frustration is nothing new. Shortly before his death in 1929, James Hyslop, one of the earliest members of the American SPR, wrote a book entitled *Life After Death* which sought to justify the decades he and his colleagues had spent examining evidence for the unseen. In its final chapter he wrote, 'I regard the existence of discarnate spirits as scientifically proved . . . any man who does not accept the existence of discarnate spirits and the proof of it is either ignorant or a moral coward.' Given the sheer volume of witnessed testimonies that Hyslop and his colleagues had amassed over almost half a century, it is easy to sympathize with his condemnation of those sceptics who chose simply to ignore it. Even if only one-hundredth of the cases investigated by the SPR proved to be inexplicable, and the other ninety-nine per cent explained naturally, then we are still left with only one conclusion: that spirit communication does exist. In fact the proportion of unexplained communications is far, far higher than this. As a body of evidence it is certainly no less prodigious than that used to support many untested scientific theories which have long since come to be accepted by the mainstream scientific community as self-evident truth.

Even some of the greatest minds of the modern age have admitted that clairvoyance seems to have a basis in fact. During his last years, psychologist C.G. Jung wrote in a letter to a friend, that 'metapsychic phenomena could be explained better by the hypothesis of spirits than by the possibilities of the human unconcious'. Sigmund Freud, the father of modern psychology itself, stated that should he be given the opportunity to live his life again, he would dedicate all his energy to the investigation of the paranormal. Other scientific luminaries to have investigated spiritualism and been impressed by the probability of its truth include the eminent English Nobel laureate Sir William Crookes; the physicist Michael Faraday, Dr Charles Richet the renowned French physiologist, discovers of radium Pierre and Marie Curie, the great astronomer Franco Porro of Italy, and the German psychologist-physician Baron Albert Von Schrenk-Notzing. These great minds eventually bowed to the weight of evidence. Yet decades afterwards many lesser men than these continue to dismiss psychic research as an absurdity, a realm unfit for serious scientists to enter. Will the situation ever change? Can the world of the clairvoyant ever be taken seriously?

A Ghost in the Machine

'Of course you don't die, nobody dies, death doesn't
exist, you only reach a new level of vision, a new
realm of consciousness, a new unknown world.'

Henry Miller
(Interviewed in 1961)

In the late autumn of 1979 the elderly grandmother of a
friend of mine named John fell and broke her hip. At her
advanced age the woman's health rapidly deteriorated
and within days she fell into a coma. Doctors gave
her little chance so John, knowing that I had become
interested in spiritual healing, asked me if there was
anyone he could contact for help. I suggested Ted Fricker
whose London practice was not far from our home in
Essex. John wrote to Fricker that evening and received
a prompt reply stating that absent healing would be sent,
the process through which invisible spirits minister to the
sick. Fricker's most able spirit healer was named Abdul
Latif, a Persian physician at the time of the Crusades.

John's grandmother died the next week yet before she
passed away she apparently regained brief consciousness,
becoming lucid enough to talk of an Arab man she had
seen in her sleep and – if the reports of nurses are to be
believed – actually spoke several sentences in a tongue
which sounded like a Middle-Eastern dialect. Knowing
his grandmother had never left England, John became
convinced that Abdul Latif really had over-shadowed

the dying woman. Certainly there was no alternative explanation readily available, but since she was dead, proof of the healer's activities seemed beyond grasp.

This was not quite the end of the story, however. A few weeks later John answered the phone in his home to find his dead grandmother's voice on the other end of the line! She briefly thanked him for his efforts in contacting the healer and then rang off, leaving him dumbstruck with fear and incredulity. Retelling the experience to me, John described her voice as cheerful though somewhat detached. He told no one else of the phone call.

Can spirits use telephones? The idea seemed ridiculous and although I respected John I dismissed the story as a figment of his imagination. Until, that is, I came across a book entitled *Phone Calls From The Dead* by Californian writers D. Scott Rogo and Raymond Bayless which detailed many examples that paralleled my friend's experience. In one story from 1977, a girl named Mary Meredith got a call to her Oklahoma home from her cousin Shirley in Kentucky only minutes after receiving a letter describing the latter's sudden death. In another instance a mother received a call on Thanksgiving Day 1973 from her college student daughter, exactly two years after the girl had been killed in a car crash. Investigation uncovered that the telephone company had no record of the call. In a third even more outstanding example from 1971, two sisters named MacConnell from Tucson, Arizona, spoke for over thirty minutes to their old friend Mrs Enid Johnson, several hours after she had died in the Handmaker Jewish Nursing Home. Only afterwards did they realize they had been talking to somebody who was no longer physically alive.

Even though I had already come to believe in the possibility of mediumiship, the idea of ghosts on the line came as quite a shock. Clearly, the discovery of a process which allowed discarnate minds to send messages through a man-made device had the potential to revolutionize psychic research. Why hadn't it been exploited I wondered? Little did I know then that this momentous branch of paranormal research was already under way.

On the evening of 15 January 1983, a remarkable show broadcast by Radio Luxembourg, Europe's leading English language speaking station, caused a sensation across the continent. Hosted by Rainer Holbe, Luxembourg's senior presenter, the programme's subject matter was to be a live, on-air experiment to test the possibility of contacting the dead. Most listeners expected to hear an eccentric clairvoyant, but to their surprise the main guest was a quietly spoken German electronics engineer named Hans Otto Konig. For many years a private consultant to German industry, Konig had long been convinced that it might be possible to achieve, scientifically, a dialogue with those departed from the mortal plane. Believing, like occultists, that the spirit world vibrated at a different level to visible matter, Konig's chosen technique was to use ultrasound frequencies beyond the range of the human ear. To begin with, he had sent out a series of random messages into the ether, waiting months for a response. Eventually, when he began to receive signals back, he set himself the goal of building a machine which would act as a direct communication channel to the afterlife. By 1983, after eight years of largely empirical research, he claimed to have achieved his goal.

Naturally, many people were reluctant to believe the claims of the German engineer. When approached with the idea for a transmission, Radio Luxembourg's programme controllers accepted, but only provided Konig agreed to a series of very stringent conditions. First of all studio bosses insisted on inspecting Konig's communication equipment (or 'generator' as he preferred to call it) and he was told that during the broadcast only the station's own technicians would be allowed to operate the machinery. Radio Luxembourg warned their guest that they would not tolerate attempts at fraud or deception. Only their usual presenter would be able to ask questions once the programme had begun; Konig himself must remain silent throughout. Furthermore, the broadcast was to be a one-off – there would be no opportunity for rehearsal or retesting. If a conversation with the dead were really possible, then it must happen first time, live on-air, or not at all. To their surprise, Konig readily accepted all these preconditions without argument.

As the transmission began on the evening of 15 January, Rainer Holbe announced to millions of bemused listeners across a dozen countries how the programme for that night was to contain a live experiment attempting electronic communication with another world. There had been no trial run, he said, and no one knew whether it would be successful. He then introduced Hans Otto Konig who gave some background to the development of his research. Inside the broadcasting studio, tension mounted as a member of the technical staff switched on the machine and began with a single, straightforward question, 'Is anyone there?' Within a few seconds a disembodied voice answered from Konig's generator, clearly in the affirmative, 'We hear your voice,' it replied, in English, impassively. Then, 'Otto Konig makes wireless with the dead.' The tone of the disembodied contact was matter-of-fact, its brief message scarcely profound. But the fact that it had been heard at all was earth shattering. And heard it certainly was, by all present in the studio, as well as by millions across

Europe. It had not come from anyone in the room, nor could it have been received conventionally from outside. Presenter Holbe trembled with emotion as he broke in to reassure listeners that the broadcast they were hearing was not a hoax, 'I tell you . . . I swear by my children's lives, nothing has been manipulated . . . there are no tricks.' The exchange lasted several more minutes, punctuated by long, eerie pauses. There was much interference and a lot of static, yet the voices from beyond the grave were otherwise perfectly audible and afterwards all those present at the experiment attested to a belief that they had witnessed a genuinely paranormal manifestation. The highly charged atmosphere inside the studio was described by a witness as being 'electric', with some technicians actually moved to tears. Only Hans Otto Konig, who had heard the voices many times before in his own private laboratory, remained unmoved. Remarkable though the broadcast undoubtedly seemed, it was in fact but a single incident, in a much longer story. This was not the first time that such a scientific approach to spirit communication had been attempted. Nor was the existence of disembodied voices Konig's discovery. Though the German engineer had spent a large part of the previous decade working on the construction of his generator, the so-called 'electronic voice phenomenon' (EVP) had been recognized for more than twenty years, after being first identified by a Swedish film producer, Freidrich Jurgenson, who stumbled upon the voices by accident.

One evening in the late summer of 1959, Jurgenson, who was also a keen amateur bird watcher, decided to make a tape of birds singing in the garden of his villa at Mölnbo, near Stockholm. When the Swede played it back he was astonished to find a man's voice mixed in with the natural sounds. Faint but nevertheless audible, the man appeared to be giving a lecture, ironically on the subject of ornithology. Even more curious was the fact that the language spoken was not Swedish but Norwegian and since he was certain no one had been in the garden while the recording had taken place, Jurgenson became convinced that the voice must have been superimposed preternaturally. Intrigued, he began experimenting with a radio receiver, altering the frequency between conventional wavelengths. After a while he found he could make out coherent sentences amongst the background transmissions of radio stations, messages which seemed to come from the dead. This suspicion turned to certainty when he recognized one voice to be that of his deceased mother.

For several years Jurgenson told no one of his discovery and instead continued to record secretly the anomalous voices in the privacy of his own specially built laboratory. By the time he had collected the transmissions of over a hundred different discarnate personalities he felt ready to unleash his discovery upon an unsuspecting world. Most people scoffed at his story yet there were some who were impressed enough to try the technique out for themselves. In 1965 Professor Hans Bender, an eminent German psychologist and a director at the University of Freiburg, set up a team to try their own Jurgenson-style experiments. Months of positive results confirmed that under differing conditions and circumstances, a factory-clean tape would, after being run through a recording-head in an otherwise silent environment, contain the imprint of recognizable human voices which were not only audible to the human ear, but registered as visible oscillograph impulses. In his final report of the team's findings, Professor Bender wrote that the sound waves were clearly paranormal in origin. He was also reputedly said to believe that their discovery was of greater significance to the human race than the development of nuclear physics. Jurgenson, he claimed, might one day be spoken of in the same breath as Newton, Copernicus and Darwin.

Although the Swede continued his studies into electronic voice phenomenon for another two decades, his fame as a psychic investigator gradually became eclipsed by that of another researcher, the Latvian-born psychologist Dr Konstantin Raudive. Originally a disciple of Jurgenson's, the German-based Raudive tried a slightly different technique, introducing the manifestation technicians label as 'white noise'. Working mainly during the hours between sunset and sunrise, at his laboratory at Bad Krosingen, Raudive would precede his sessions with a brief invitation for the spirits to make themselves known. A small diode receiver (or 'cat's whisker') was then plugged into the microphone socket of the tape recorder and the recording level set at maximum. According to the researcher, diode recording gave the best results, the ghostly voices appearing slower, clearer and more natural. More importantly, the length of the ariel, less than two inches, effectively ruled out the possibility of picking up normal radio signals. Two respected scientists who worked with Raudive in the mid-1960s, Swiss physicist Dr Alex Schreider and Theodor Rudolph, a specialist in high frequency electronic transmission, had no doubt that his research was opening a bridge to a new dimension.

To Raudive these taped voices were conclusive evidence of human survival beyond death, but few others felt the same way. In 1967, when he released the results of his research upon a disbelieving world, it provoked considerably less enthusiasm than he had anticipated. It was pointed out that most messages were short, fragmentary and lacking in clarity or detail. Some transmissions even contained a number of different languages which hampered interpretation still further. Infuriatingly, the most interesting and important communications always seemed to be the faintest. Many phrases seemed to be thrown up at random and there was no single conversation which was clear from beginning to end. One particularly scathing critic suggested that the tape sounded like 'a very bad transatlantic telephone line'. The response of the general public was largely apathetic. The idea that spirit entities could address mortals through the commonplace tape recorder seemed too absurd to be taken seriously.

All was not completely lost, however. Despite their drawbacks, the research techniques pioneered by Freidrich Jurgenson and Konstantin Raudive continued to provide some truly startling, if occasional, examples of the voice phenomenon when repeated elsewhere. In March 1971 a British paranormal writer named Peter Bander persuaded publisher Colin Smythe to undertake a series of EVP tests at the studios of Pye Records in London. Using Raudive's diode, Bander had received messages from his dead mother which voice pattern analysis had virtually proved to be genuine. Sufficiently intrigued by Bander's story, Smythe arranged for a demonstration to be watched by two of Pye's senior recording engineers who guaranteed that no strange signals could enter the recording process.

The session, which lasted only eighteen minutes, took place on 24 March 1971. Throughout the exercise the diode constantly flickered even though Pye's engineers could hear nothing on their microphones. The playback, however, was a different matter. Over 200 voices *had* been recorded, twenty-seven of which were intelligible to all in the studio. One witness present, the chairman of Smythe's publishing company Sir Robert Mayer, even recognized the voice of an old friend, the

late concert pianist Artur Schnabel. Afterwards Roy
Prichet, Pye's chief recording engineer who supervized
the test, described the voices as 'astounding'. With a bank
of four recorders synchronized together and protected
by sophisticated instruments to block out freak pick-ups
from the high or low frequency transmitters of radio
hams, Prichet knew that the possibility of conventional
interference was nil. These voices were, he said, 'voices
from nowhere'.

Three days later a second experiment was conducted
by Smythe at the Enfield laboratories of Belling and Lee,
using a radio frequency screen laboratory that excludes
any form of electro-magnetic radiation. Supervizing the
procedure this time was Peter Hale, Britain's foremost
expert in electronic screen suppression, assisted by Professor Ralph Lovelock, a top physicist. Again voices
were clearly received, Hale admitting that they could
only have been made in a way that 'cannot be explained
in normal physical terms'. Ralph Lovelock concurred,
'They are beyond explanation'. Following this second
session, Colin Smythe persuaded his boss Sir Robert
Mayer to publish a book on the EVP mystery entitled
Breakthrough. Dealing mainly with recordings made by
Konstantin Raudive, its preface was written by Peter
Bander, the Englishman who first alerted Smythe to
the reality of the phenomenon. But *Breakthrough* failed
to break through the wall of intellectual opposition
towards EVP which surrounded mainstream science.
Whilst most scientists were prepared to accept that
the voices were genuinely weird, few were prepared to
risk their reputation by entertaining the possibility that
ghosts could talk through machines. To the end of his
life, Konstantin Raudive remained bitterly disappointed
that so few of his peers in the scientific community were
prepared to lend his work credibility. In fact, their

almost uniformly negative opinion continued long after his death.

Such a lack of interest by mainstream science is not surprising given the general antipathy towards psychic phenomena. And yet it is deeply ironic for in the earlier part of this century, two of the world's greatest scientific minds not only accepted the reality of EVP but were engaged in a markedly similar branch of research. Thomas Alva Edison, inventor of the phonograph and first incandescent electric lamp, had little time for those who believed that the human spirit perished with the material body. In 1920 the journal *Scientific American* carried a now famous interview in which the seventy-three-year-old genius stated his involvement in a project to construct an apparatus that could 'facilitate human communication with the dead'. This practical approach would, Edison felt, not only be more effective as a medium for communication than those 'present primitive methods' (Ouija Boards, seances etc.) but would serve to satisfy the ultra sceptical minds of his fellow scientists. In the article Edison was quoted as saying, 'I believe that if we are to make any real progress in psychic investigation, we must do it with scientific apparatus and in a scientific manner.' Unfortunately, his own mortality would appear to have come between Edison and his greatest triumph, for his research remained incomplete.

Another eminent name to become intrigued by the possibilities of spirit communication was Guglielmo Marconi, the inventor of the wireless radio. Marconi believed, like Edison, that life was indestructible, as was matter, and that a subtle form of electrical energy pervaded and underlaid the visible universe. Marconi therefore contended that not only was it possible to contact the dead, but that a recorded imprint of all the world's events existed upon the same etheric substance. All that was needed to view the past was a device delicate enough to capture these impressions. His own personal ambition was to record Jesus' last words on the cross. The Italian inventor was not worried by the laughter his ideas provoked in academic circles since the same critics had originally dismissed his claims that he might one day be able to send short wave, wireless messages around the world. In 1901, years after mathematicians had proved conclusively that wireless communication was limited by the curvature of the earth, Marconi succeeded in transmitting signals from Cornwall, England, to Newfoundland, Canada. When he went on to send a signal from Europe to Australia, bouncing the wireless impulses off the upper atmosphere, it proved to be the beginning of the modern global communication system. Having confounded the established wisdom of science once, the Italian genius had no doubt that it would be possible to contact other planes of existence. Unfortunately, in 1937 death once again cut short this momentous branch of research and the machine Marconi was attempting to build was never finished.

Despite their massive reputations, lesser men among the pre-war scientific community ridiculed the claims of Edison and Marconi. Among occultists, however, very little of what these two great figures said would have raised the smallest ripple of dissent. According to occult law, the so-called Akashic Records, which are believed by mystics to hold the key to all past events, would seem to correspond closely with Marconi's ideas of etheric vibrations. The word Akasha itself is the name given to the primal substance or soul-stuff, a material so subtle that the slightest whisper would cause an indelible impression to be made on its surface. Occultists claim that even thought patterns, no matter how fleeting, will remain locked eternally in this invisible psychic membrane. The purpose of this record is simple – to serve as a witness for the strivings of each human soul, through its many incarnations, until the spirit has reached a state of perfection. So, according to the occult fraternity, from the dawn of time there has been a complete record of the development and evolution of the race. Every deed, word or idea remains intact for all eternity.

Seen in this light the implications of EVP research become mind-boggling. Had Marconi developed his machine to capture these supernatural impressions, we might now be living in a very different world. Certainly our concept of the universe we inhabit could hardly remain intact in the face of such evidence. As it was, Marconi's premature death left the sceptics still with the upper hand, and the existence of the etheric records remains an unproven theory. Even so, occasionally one hears reports of anomalous audible phenomena for which there appears to be no natural explanation, phenomena which may indicate that the two great scientists were heading in the right direction.

For several nights running in November 1986, downstairs rooms in a small farmhouse in Somerset, England, became filled with what appeared to be the voices of former residents. Witnesses who listened to these peculiar conversations from the past claimed that they began and ended with a distinct 'click', just like a radio being turned on and off. Yet neither receiver nor transmitter was found and no natural explanation was put forward. A similar metallic click preceded manifestations which began to be heard inside Point Lookout, a converted lighthouse at St Mary's County, Maryland, in January 1973. The building's owner, Gerald J. Sword, was regularly awoken by a nightly cacophony of sounds which included doors banging, furniture moving and footsteps. In the morning, however, there was never any sign of disturbance. Concerned about his sanity, Sword set out to capture the sounds on tape, leaving a reel-to-reel recorder switched on. Sure enough, there were many extraneous noises on the replayed tape, including spoken phrases, some of which were apparently to do with the treatment of injuries. To Sword's astonishment, a local librarian researching the history of his home confirmed that the building had been used as a field hospital during the American Civil War.

Could the so-called supernatural sounds heard in some haunted houses really be a replay of past events, held in the fabric of the building itself? Some parascientists believe so and a significant experiment to prove the case was conducted in 1982 by two British researchers, John Marke, an electrical engineer, and Allan Jenkins, an industrial chemist. Hearing of reported manifestations in a Welsh public house, The Prince of Wales at Kenfig, Mid Glamorgan, Marke and Jenkins proposed to test their theory that certain conventional substances used in building materials can trap sounds like a conventional recording tape (some bricks contain combinations of silica and ferric salts, both of which are used in tapes). Their experiment involved the insertion of powerful electrodes into the inn's interior walls and running a huge current of more than 20,000 volts through the building in order to trigger electrons in the silica and so release the trapped sound energy. The test worked. During a four-hour period with the current on, many extraneous noises were picked up by recorders, including faint organ noises, a barking dog and voices speaking in an old Welsh dialect.

Following the experiments of Marke and Jenkins,

some researchers have come to the conclusion that sounds indicating a place memory also explain traditional hauntings. Many outbreaks, however, are less easy to classify. During the autumn of 1990, British investigator Peter Thorneycroft conducted a study into strange events taking place inside an aircraft hanger which housed a World War II Lincoln bomber at RAF Cosford Aerospace Museum. Aural manifestations included bumps, scratches, squeaks, human sighs and girls' voices; other peculiarities included the sighting by staff of spectral air crews, the movement of switches and the rotation of wheels, plus dramatic drops in temperature. Investigating the eerie events along with technicians from BBC Radio, Thorneycroft himself heard and recorded anomalous sounds within the aircraft and saw bright, moving pinpoints of light that could not be explained. Having had the sounds analyzed by BBC boffins, it became clear that outbreaks (most frequently noises associated with mechanical movements) always began with a discernable blip on the tape, of a type similar to that produced by a sudden burst of static. When the keeper of the museum, Len Wardgate, confirmed that the sounds could not conceivably have been produced by the 'dead' aircraft (which had no hydraulic pressure and was electrically disconnected) nor by the expansion or contraction of the aircraft hanger's metal structure, investigator Thorneycroft assumed that a place memory was in operation rather than some form of ghostly activity. However, when he returned one morning to find his tape recorder vandalized, even though the hanger had been empty and locked the night before, he began to have second thoughts.

Sounds from the past which are deliberately captured upon tape are fascinating; those which appear of their own accord can be very frightening. In 1978 a young woman named Joyce McCarthy from Whiteheath in Birmingham, England, found that her home-recorded tape of a Donna Summer album had inexplicably been wiped off and replaced by noises of men screaming, crashing timbers and rushing water. McCarthy had played the tape normally on dozens of occasions before the eerie sounds were superimposed. The tape was analyzed by a local university physics department who could offer no natural answer to the mystery. Local historians noticed, however, that the McCarthy's house lay above the site of a disused coal mine, known by the ominous name of Black Bat Pit. One historian, who was also a practising spiritualist, suggested there might be a link between the tape recordings and a disaster which had occurred exactly one hundred years earlier in 1878. Sure enough, when the voices were magnified, it was possible to make out the names of several miners who, according to records, had lost their lives in the flooded Victorian death mine.

In the years since Joyce McCarthy found a disaster replayed in her home, there have been several other examples of the same phenomenon reported. In 1986 thirteen-year-old Dawn Dearden from Kilnhurst, South Yorkshire, found a child's pleading voice superimposed on a cassette. Repeating phrases like 'Help me', 'Born again never to die', and 'Born into your family', the obviously distressed voice was never identified, yet Dawn Dearden's parents remain convinced that it had a supernatural origin.

Sound effects from the past tend to be faint or muffled but there are some notable exceptions. In the early morning hours of 4 August 1951, two English women who were staying at a guest house in Puys, France, were awoken from their sleep by a massive barrage of anti-aircraft artillery fire which seemed to be coming from the direction of nearby Dieppe. Tremendous sounds of battle – including numerous explosions and dive-bombing planes – continued for over an hour before fading away around daybreak. The following morning, with the experience still fresh in their minds, the women wrote an account of the manifestation, the timing of which appeared to correspond with an allied World War II raid on Dieppe on the night of 19 August 1942. No one else heard anything strange that night yet locals remembered that other people had reported phantom sounds of battle from time to time.

Another war-related curiosity surrounds the enigmatic noises picked up by the sonars on board US Navy vessels operating in the Pacific during the early 1980s. The huge rumbling sounds, emanating from the bottom of the world's deepest ocean, appeared to be an echo of battles that had taken place forty years earlier, during World War II. Garbled radio messages, Japanese and American, some in code, had been rising from the deep to haunt the latter-day sonar operators of the US Pacific fleet. Mixed in with these coded messages were the names of dead sailors and lost ships, as well as the explosions and gunfire of the naval engagements of yesteryear. According to a British newspaper report published in 1980, the phenomenon proved to be short-lived and no explanation was offered by military officials.

This, however, was not quite the end of the story. It was announced two years later that similar strange battle noises had been echoing around other oceans of the world – most frequently the North Atlantic – for many years. The US Navy's own network of supersensitive hydrophones – Sound Surveillance System (SOSUS) – is a security installation linked to land-based stations; its purpose is to detect and monitor the movements of potentially hostile submarines. Yet since 1952, when it was set up, SOSUS listeners had detected a plethora of quite different and inexplicable noises which could not be attributed to freak conditions under the sea. Commenting in an edition of the US News and World Report in 1982, a top-level Pentagon source insisted that the sounds of ghostly battles under the sea posed no conceivable threat to US security, though he admitted that many servicemen had found the phenomenon unnerving.

It would be quite wrong to suggest that all mysterious voices arrive through a replaying of past conversations. Some at least, become manifest in a way that indicates a still-living intelligence to be at work.

In July 1924 a strange voice was heard by mourners and other visitors to a cemetery in Butler, New Jersey. After ten consecutive days of reported disturbances, a committee, comprising police and locally elected officials, was set up to investigate. It confirmed that the voice, which hovered in the air above the grave of a recently buried citizen, could both ask and reply to questions. Similarly a voice which was first heard in a cemetery in Arapaho, Oklahoma in 1972 was quickly identified as being that of George Smith, and it was from his gravestone the sounds emanated. Smith's gravestone has spoken many times since to, amongst others, his widow, the local priest and Arthur Turcotte, a paranormal investigator. Other instances of talking graves have come from virtually every corner of the globe. In the Hunan Province of China there is a burial rock by the Dongting Lake which regularly holds conversations and in South Africa a tree near Daveytown, Witwatersand, is apparently haunted by a spirit which talks between September and February every year.

Phantom voices are not confined to a single location. The Blessed Clelia Barbieri was an Italian nun who founded a religious order, the Souore Minime d'ell Addolorata in Bologna, before tragically dying aged only twenty-three. On her deathbed Barbieri vowed to her companions that she would always remain with them wherever they should go. And so it has proved. Since her death in 1870 the nun's singing voice has continued to be heard in chapels used by her order in places as far apart as Africa and India. Curiously, hymns are sung by Barbieri's spirit in tongues appropriate to the location (Kiswahili, Malayalam) and messages of comfort are delivered with perfect ethnic pronunciation. Throughout the 120 years since the Blessed Clelia first returned, hundreds of people have heard the voice, including atheists and those unaware of the phenomenon's existence. Clearly this limits the likelihood of a natural explanation involving religious hysteria.

Occasionally a message will appear spontaneously on electrical recording equipment which seems to be a direct attempt at purposeful communication. Just such an occurrence took place in April 1969, in the small German village of Horb-am-Nackar. Hanna Buschbeck, then in her late sixties, had been widowed a year when she found her deceased husband's voice superimposed on a tape she had been preparing for private study. The voice came through clearly yet its message was cryptic, merely repeating Hanna's name several times which was followed, after a pause, with the word 'Freidhof' (the German for graveyard). Later that month another voice appeared spontaneously on the same tape. This time it was a different relative's voice that Hanna Buschbeck heard – her sister Freda whom she knew was still alive. 'At two o'clock life was ended,' said the voice simply.

Terrified, Hanna telephoned her sister's home, only to be told by her distraught brother-in-law that Freda had died in her sleep the previous night. The bereaved husband was bewildered when he heard the tape.

Given such clear evidence for the survival of her family members, the German widow became intrigued by developments taking place in electronic voice phenomenon research. Her case became something of a cause célèbre among those who steadfastly believed that the electronic medium would eventually prove the existence of the spirit world. During the early 1970s the small German village of Horb-am-Nackar hosted a conference into the subject, with delegates from parascientific research departments from around the world. Not surprisingly, Hanna herself was one of the main speakers to address the assembly and was afterwards quoted by German television as confidently saying, 'EVP shows that there is no such thing as the dead. We just go on living on some other level.'

As evidence continued to mount, more and more people from around the world were coming round to the same opinion. During the 1970s, with interest growing in EVP, some researchers were beginning to make startling claims on its behalf. In an edition of the *Psychic News* British expert Richard Sheargold wrote in 1973, 'There is no longer room for doubt that science has at last achieved its first real breakthrough.' Others remained less enthusiastic. In 1974, Cambridge physics graduate D.J. Ellis commented, after hearing tapes of the Raudive voices, that the phenomenon was interesting only because 'so many otherwise intelligent people had allowed themselves to be fooled into thinking that it was the supernatural they were listening to.' For his part Ellis believed there was no need to postulate paranormal sources for the sounds. They were, he maintained, probably just the indistinct fragments of radio transmissions

mixed in with casual utterances made by researchers
within the laboratory itself. Ellis's views were taken
up and echoed by many other confirmed sceptics of
EVP. Some scientists argued (with more than a little
justification) that Jurgenson's methods of control and
evaluation were sloppy; others insisted that Raudive's
interpretations of his voices were simply too amazing to
be taken seriously.

In fairness, both sets of criticisms held an element of
truth. On occasions, Jurgenson rather stupidly allowed
conversations of his assistants to intermingle with the
external communications he claimed to receive. For his
part, Raudive's analysis of some 'white noise' recordings
was eccentric to say the least. On one occasion, struggling
to make sense of apparent gibberish, he insisted that an
incoherent group of syllables were really a complex sentence spoken in five separate languages. Why the ghost
in question should choose to make his communication so
incomprehensible remained obscure!

As the seventies wore on without EVP producing the
unambiguous proof of an afterlife that so many had
hoped it would, interest in the research gradually waned,
even among the parascientific community. Some, however, continued to believe steadfastly in the possibility of
one day achieving through scientific methods unequivo-
cal evidence for life everlasting. Such an advocate was
George Meek, an American executive who left his highly
paid position on the Board of Directors of the US car
giant General Motors to form an organization called
Metascience, dedicated to proving the existence of an
invisible spirit world.

Using his considerable influence, Meek assembled
an impressive group of helpers including corporation
financiers, physicists and electronic engineers, as well as

spiritualists. Through conventional mediumistic channels Meek's group made contact with discarnate scientists eager to prove their existence, most notably Professor Francis Gray Swann, head of the physics department at the University of Chicago until his death in 1962 and two pioneers of early radio technology, Reginald Fessenden and Lee de Forest. Meek, who had already guessed that the construction of an electronic medium would be impossible without the active cooperation of the other side, welcomed the assistance of these minds.

The mechanism *Metascience* subsequently constructed was named the Spiricom. Comprising a 300-megahertz generator, with a powerful antenna and a radio receiver, it was more complex and more powerful than the equipment used by either Jurgenson or Raudive. It was also more effective. Using a spiritualist named Bill O'Neill to help synchronize the application of energies from either side, the results of the Metascience team transcended anything previously produced by their European counterparts. Together with his spirit guide, bizarrely named 'Doc Nick', O'Neill was able to assist matter and spirit finally to come together in a way that could be heard by all living people – not simply those with psychic gifts like himself. Through the miracle of radio wave transmission the world had not only grown smaller, but a vista of new worlds beckoned.

In the August of 1981 George Meek contacted author and journalist John G. Fuller, himself a believer in the afterlife and the author of *The Ghost of Flight 401*, to explain details of his extraordinary series of experiments. Meek's improbable story was backed up by a taped conversation in which the spirit guide Doc Nick gave detailed instructions for the Spiricom operators. The spirit spoke in a distorted monotone, metallic and gravelly, in stark contrast to that of the medium O'Neill whose voice was also heard. To John G. Fuller the tape was disappointing; sounding like a conversation between two radio hams, its content was unexceptional and undramatic. But unlike most EVP research up until that time, it did at least appear to be a definite dialogue. Fuller knew that if it proved to be a real conversation between the living and dead, then the quality of the transmission was largely irrelevant; the fact of its reality was all that mattered.

Though it took Meek many months to convince Fuller of the absolute genuineness of the phenomenon he first demonstrated in the August of 1981, the former executive did eventually persuade the author to make the construction of Spiricom the subject of a full-length book. The extraordinary story of the Metascience Project was eventually told in *The Ghost of 29 Megacycles*, published in 1985. The evidence which finally convinced John G. Fuller that direct communication was possible, was the testimony of another of O'Neill's spirit guides – a former physicist named George Jeffries Mueller, who died in 1967. Mueller, in order to prove his credentials as a *bona fide* spirit, told Fuller several factual details about his earthly life and academic career at Cornell University. He also gave his social security number and the whereabouts of his own death certificate. Both checked out as true. Still more astonishing was the way the disembodied voice of Mueller gave O'Neill three unlisted telephone numbers of high-placed officials in Government Security whom the scientist had known in his life on earth. Faced with such a level of corroborating evidence, the American writer had little choice but to accept that George Mueller had really returned.

At the same time Fuller knew that convincing the rest of the world would not be so easy. Having previously heard parts of Raudive's 'white noise' tapes, the writer had been unimpressed by EVP evidence emerging from

Europe, and he told Meek that Spiricom would need to be a far more reliable medium of communication if the Metascience Project were to stand a chance of being taken seriously. Meek assured him that under the step-by-step guidance of the spirits themselves, Spiricom offered a different set of possibilities to the research of Jurgenson and Raudive. He was soon to be proved correct. In December 1981 Mueller's voice began to be heard much more clearly through the Spiricom device. Several direct conversations lasting up to fifteen minutes took place all within the controlled conditions of the metascience laboratory. By the following April, Meek and Fuller had recorded over thirty hours of sessions with their disembodied contact. The author of *Flight 401* knew that the evidence they were amassing had awesome implications. Meanwhile, for George Meek the ex-industrialist, the breakthrough in communications with Mueller was a massive vindication of his faith in EVP.

Having convinced Fuller to make Spiricom the subject of a book, Meek now had to break the news of his invention to a sceptical and perhaps hostile world. To do so he formally presented his data to a gathering of journalists at Washington DC's National Press Club. At the press conference Meek outlined the developments and principles of the Spiricom device, before playing a tape of Mueller's voice. The representatives of the press were more bemused than overwhelmed, and as John G. Fuller had anticipated, most papers failed to endorse the findings of the Metascience researchers. One Chicago reporter likened the voices to 'a conversation between Dr Frankenstein and Igor on a windy night in Transylvania'. A couple of others voiced suspicions that they were being hoaxed. However, a significant number of journalists had been genuinely impressed by the evidence offered and urged their editors not to reject the possibility that the communications could be what the Metascience team claimed them to be. Of the numerous television and radio stations that carried snippets of the taped conversations the next day, half reported the researchers' claims in a fair and unbiased fashion. One radio station, based in Ontario, even went so far as to conduct its own phone-in, inviting listeners to express their belief or disbelief. More than 300 phoned through to say that they believed the voices were genuine, outweighing sceptics by more than five to one.

As a former journalist himself, John G. Fuller was relieved that the Metascience research team had not been subjected to outright ridicule; for George Meek however, the response to his announcement was something of an anticlimax. A born optimist, Meek had long believed that if an afterlife could be established in a tangible, technical way, then it would naturally lead to a revolution in man's acceptance of religious truth. Where the churches had failed to halt the decline in modern society's morals, Meek had hoped that Spiricom's evidence would reinforce that part of man's soul which had once been satisfied by simple faith. On any objective analysis, the evidence Metascience produced was never likely to achieve that. Yet the disembodied voice of Mueller did at least give Americans a taste of the peculiar evidence which had been slowly gathering from across the Atlantic over the past two decades – evidence which was continuing to mount all the time.

The 1980s saw a renaissance of EVP research. Shortly after his now famous Radio Luxembourg broadcast in January 1983, Hans Otto Konig demonstrated his 'generator' before a meeting of the German EVP association in Falda, a suburb of Frankfurt. It proved to be a far more exciting occasion than the Metascience conference held in Washington the previous May. Those present, including journalists, were allowed to put their own questions direct to the spirits, which were answered by the disembodied voices of Konig's contacts. A female reporter asked if it would be possible for the late Konstantin Raudive, who had by then been deceased for nine years, to make his presence known. A voice came through at once, proudly stating, 'I am Raudive. I have returned.' The moment could hardly have been more dramatic. Even Konig, who had never met Raudive, was stunned. A moment later another voice, this time one that Konig did recognize, came through the loudspeaker. It was that of Walter Steinneigel, a close friend and associate of the German researcher, who had died the previous summer. The utterances of both Raudive and Steinneigel were taped and later compared to those of their mortal counterparts. Computer analysis of the vocal pattern revealed conclusively that the voices of both living and dead were identical. The fact that Konig's voices were reproducible, unlike those of his European predecessors Jurgenson and Raudive, made them much more interesting to mainstream scientists who had previously rejected EVP. Their clarity and lack of distortion also helped to lend credibility to the phenomenon.

Elsewhere in Europe, other researchers working in the same field were also beginning to claim markedly more impressive results. Among their number was Alex Macrae, a middle-aged Scottish engineer who had previously made a name for himself by solving helium speech problems encountered by NASA, the US Space Agency. Working alone in his remote laboratory on the Isle of Skye, Macrae had been developing an electronic device to aid paraplegics, when he noticed a series of unidentified phantom utterances which seemed to appear spontaneously on his recording equipment. Coincidentally, the phenomenon began on 15 January 1983, the same day that Otto Konig had first announced his results and conducted his live, on-air EVP experiment for Radio Luxembourg. Working independently of other EVP researchers, the Scottish designer continued to record discarnate voices. He soon became convinced of their authenticity and subdivided them into categories. Some he felt were lower entities, souls living on an inferior plane of existence. These delivered messages in strange, somewhat sinister whispers; sometimes in a clearly hostile tone. Others, much more natural voices, Macrae felt to be evidence of souls existing on the higher plane of the spiritual world. These entities spoke consistently of truth, life, spirit and destiny. Most convincing of all were the numerous messages which responded directly to questions, or mentioned details unknown to Macrae which proved subsequently to have a factual basis.

Writing later of his findings on Skye, the Scot reached three central conclusions: firstly, that the manifestations were of a paraphysical origin; secondly, that the energy behind their creation involved direction by an intelligence; thirdly, that these intelligences were making increasing attempts to establish communication with the physical world. Although he himself was not a spiritualist, and knew very little of the the occultists' view of the universe, with its higher and lower planes of vibration, most of the conclusions reached by the Scottish engineer concurred precisely with the basic tenets of spiritualistic philosophy.

It is ten years since Meek, Macrae and Konig proved the existence of the Electronic Voice Phenomenon, and more than four decades after Freidrich Jurgenson first heard the strange disembodied voice of an invisible Norwegian lecturer talking over his recordings of bird songs. In all that time many thousands of voices have been identified, recorded and corroborated in experiments by independent witnesses. Much of the subject matter has been exhaustively rechecked and found to have a factual basis. Electronic voice-pattern analysis of disembodied utterances has even been matched to those persons whose bodies the souls once inhabited. Experiments into EVP have taken place in television studios, in live on-air radio broadcasts, and in front of audiences of sceptical journalists and scientists. It is hard to imagine how such demonstrations could be faked. Nevertheless, the validity of the electronic medium remains largely unrecognized by the contemporary scientific community. And the reasons for this unrelenting hostility? For an answer we must remember first of all the unsatisfactory nature of the original EVP researchers and the inflated claims made on their behalf. Certainly those early experiments with 'white noise' producing hour upon hour of distorted and unintelligible gibberish did much to damage the cause of EVP in the eyes of many. Raudive's notoriously imaginative guesswork plus the unforgivable disregard for scientific controls evident in Jurgenson's laboratory techniques, served only to diminish the significance of their findings.

All this has increased the frustration of today's researchers who have now answered most of the criticisms made by sceptics in the early stages of EVP experimentation. Unlike the interminable hours of random messages picked up by Raudive and Jurgenson, the communications taped during the 1980s have often been complete, clear and consistent. With laboratory discipline tightened, it is

no longer possible to attribute these voices to those
of ordinary conversations picked up by people working
within the studios. Nor is it likely that they could be
the transmissions of CB operators, police messages or
stray radio signals, since many of the spirit communications received were uncharacteristic of these wavebands.
Another doubt raised by sceptics – that the voices are
audio-hallucinatory – has now collapsed; demonstrations
have been heard not only by roomfuls of people but by
millions across an entire continent.

Could such effects be achieved by trickery? I doubt
it. Throughout the entire history of EVP research no
one has produced even the slightest proof of fraudulent
practice at any stage. Small wonder then that to many
people working in the field, the electronic medium proves
the existence of the afterlife just as surely as clairvoyants
demonstrate survival to a spiritualist. In the words of
Hanna Buschbeck, the German widow who heard the
voice of her sister the day she died, 'EVP has got
to be accepted by any open-minded person. It's there
on thousands and thousands of tapes . . .'. Yet in the
last decade of the present century, EVP is still *not*
accepted, like so much of the evidence which has gone
towards building the case against death. Rationalists
prefer the safer option – to ignore it. Perhaps the
situation will only change when a visual image of the
deceased communicator has been perfected so that a
world unwilling to listen to the evidence of its own ears
will be confounded by the proof before its very eyes.
At the time of writing, independent researchers on both
sides of the Atlantic are working towards this very end.
To date the most promising results have been achieved
by the West German team headed by Klaus Schreiber
and Martin Wenzel in their laboratory in Aachen. Using
a sophisticated opto-electronic feedback system which

bypasses the receiving parts of television sets (effectively turning them into eyes which look only inwards, as Wenzel puts it) they have collected remarkable images of people who are dead – including Klaus Schreiber's ex-wife. Simultaneous voice contact has so far eluded them but the research goes on.

Should the German team succeed in producing reliable televisual contact, the profession of mediumship will no longer be necessary. Science may yet have a vital part to play in widening our understanding not only of this world but the next one too.

Beyond the Body

'Why should one be startled by death? Life is a
constant putting off of the mortal coil – coat, cuticle,
flesh and bones, all old clothes.'

Henry David Thoreau

Centuries ago the French philosopher Descartes summed
up the certainty of man's existence with the immortal
phrase, 'I think therefore I am.' Its truth is obvious.
We all *are* otherwise we would have no awareness, no
consciousness, no being. But what exactly is a man? A
biological machine or something far more subtle? Let us
consider two opposing perspectives.

According to the mechanistic viewpoint we are what
we appear to be, that is to say our bodies – nothing more,
nothing less. Biologists tell us that we exist as a complex
organism of bones, flesh, cartilage, and blood, supported
by an intricate nervous system. Without these things
we could experience nothing; consciousness is simply a
function of the supercomputer we call the human brain.
The species Homo sapiens may have developed through
the evolutionary process to create a society wholly distin-
guishable from those which characterize the lower forms
of life, yet like any other animal, man is subject to the
same biological needs and constraints. If our vital organs
fail, we die just as surely as any other organism, and for
all creatures death is the inevitable end of life. We are a
collection of cells and nothing more; extinguish the cells

and there is nothing left. Man may have travelled to the moon and explored the furthest reaches of space through radio telescopes, built the pyramids and split the atom, written *Hamlet* and painted the Mona Lisa, yet he is really little more than an extremely clever monkey – a highly developed primate.

The dualistic viewpoint finds considerable support in the development of the world's religions. To Hindus, Christians, Muslims and Buddists alike, man has an eternal soul, an immortal counterpart to the earthly body which cannot be destroyed at death. It is a belief shared by occultists, theosophists and spiritualists and is in adherence with so-called primitive religions from the remotest corners of the globe. The 'soul' concept of the Zulu 'Zitunzela' bears close resemblance to the Eskimo 'Nappan'. Likewise that immortal part the Hebrews called the 'Nephesh' differs little from the 'Fulgur' of the early Teutonic races. The great civilizations of Greece, Rome and ancient China believed in soul immortality as did the lost peoples of South America. Almost nowhere, it seems, has there existed a highly developed belief system which limits man's span of life to the short period between birth and death.

As we have seen in earlier chapters, psychic phenomena such as the appearance of ghosts and the existence of messages communicated from a world beyond our physical senses, uphold the dualistic viewpoint. Perhaps even stronger evidence is now beginning to come from a new and unexpected source. Medical experts working in the field of the interrelatedness of mind, brain and body have been led towards the conclusion that we all possess more than one body, indicating the probable existence of other levels of reality vibrating beyond the range of our sensory organs. The implications of this new branch of research are clear: contrary to the generally accepted

biological view, the continuation of life is not entirely
dependent upon bodily life-support systems – indeed
the very opposite may be true. In the opinion of some
scientists, it is the human mind which supports the brain
and not vice versa.

For the purposes of proving the case against death,
these recent scientific breakthroughs hold enormous
significance, for if it can be proved that the human
consciousness extends beyond the confines of its physical
frame and normal sensory perceptions, then it seems
likely that our mind may also survive the dissolution
of our physical form. For some part of us at least, there
truly is life beyond death.

When he was a youth of nineteen, serving with a World
War I ambulance unit at the Italian front, the novelist
Ernest Hemingway was badly injured by a shell which
landed in the trench where he was sheltering. A brief
moment of blinding pain was replaced by a sensation
quite different and unexpected. Instead of writhing in
agony or losing consciousness altogether, Hemingway felt
himself ('my soul or something') leave his physical body.
It was, he said, 'as if a silk handkerchief had been gently
pulled from a pocket by one corner.' At first the young
writer thought he was dead, but the sensation lasted only
a few seconds, before he drifted inside his shrapnel-torn
body once more. Hemingway used the experience as the
basis for a fictional account in his novel *A Farewell To
Arms*, where the wounded hero Frederick Henry floats
momentarily above his mortal frame. Like his creator,
Henry believes he is dead until his soul slides back into
the world of physical sensation.

Celebrated though it has become, Hemingway's mystical experience is only one of dozens of similar experiences recorded by wounded veterans. Another typical

remembrance was that of a British officer serving in an armoured division which took part in the D-Day landings in 1944. After his tank had received a direct hit from a German shell, the man was blown several yards away from his wrecked vehicle, seriously injured, and with his battle dress aflame. At first the officer felt no pain and found himself floating above the ground, face down, watching his physical body writhing below. Only when he saw his own burning form roll into a water-filled ditch, dousing the flames, did he fall once more into normal consciousness and feel the agony of his seared flesh.

A still more extraordinary tale concerns a young army doctor who was involved in a biplane crash in April 1916 whilst serving as a medical orderly on the Western Front. Sitting helplessly in the passenger seat as the aircraft's pilot fought hopelessly to gain control, the man found himself facing imminent death. As the fuselage disintegrated on impact around him, he felt his physical body seemingly torn apart. However, the sensation of pain and panic was momentary. Seconds later he found himself floating high above the airfield, very much alive and apparently unhurt. Though confused, the doctor was also strangely detached and calm as he witnessed frantic attempts on the ground to revive his own body. Without knowing how, he abruptly returned to his natural state when an ambulance man began to pour a stimulant down his throat. For many researchers, this experience holds particular conviction. Following his full recovery in a field hospital, the doctor – who was later to become a distinguished member of the Royal College of Physicians and awarded the OBE – wrote a full account of his experiences for his commanding officer. Knowing his man to be neither a fool nor a liar, the CO made some inquiries into the incident's background. His investigations not only confirmed the

accuracy of the doctor's description of the attempts to
revive him but also tallied with other events taking place
at the time. Although he had been unconscious, his 'soul
vantage point' high above had, it seemed, afforded him
a proper view of the airfield.

Out-of-body experiences of the type described above,
(referred to as crisis OBEs), litter the pages of paranormal research. According to most accounts, experiencers
characteristically believe that they have been involuntarily projected some distance from their physical form
and, since they remain consciously aware of the goings-on
around them, they are able to observe their own body and
its immediate surroundings (even though their physical
body is unconscious). A curious lightness, a feeling of
general detachment and calm are typically associated
with the out-of-body or ecosomatic state, as some
parapsychologists have termed it. The new appearance
of the experiencer varies rather more: it may be a double
of the mortal form or a more ethereal, featureless essence
– a 'beingness', as some have described it. Either way,
they claim to feel entirely different in their new body.

Understandably, sceptics believe these tales to be
dreams, hallucinations, shock-reactions, or simply the
products of an overdeveloped imagination. Disbelievers in the phenomenon often point to the fact that
experiencers include many whose living has been earned
by such imaginative talent. In this respect, at least,
they have a point. Apart from the aforementioned
Ernest Hemingway, the list of writers who claim to
have experienced the sensation during their lives is
prodigous: Tolstoy, Dostoevsky, Tennyson, Edgar Alan
Poe, D.H. Lawrence, Emily Brontë and Virginia Woolf,
to name only a handful. But perhaps such a trawl of
literary giants is actually not so surprising given the
widespread nature of the OBE phenomenon. In the

1970s, for instance, a study undertaken by an American professor of psychology Dr Dean Shiels, analyzed over a thousand reports from no less than seventy non-western cultures; he expected to find distinct ethnic variations, yet he found the precise opposite. In the end, so universal was the nature of the recorded experiences that Shields concluded the phenomenon had to be genuine. Other studies support the American professor's contention. One, undertaken by an internal research institute at Duke University, showed that thirty per cent of students had experienced OBE, while in 1974 a survey of medical students in Charlottesville Campus, at the University of Virginia, uncovered twenty-five per cent of students answering in the affirmative. Remarkably, of those who replied positively in the Virginia study, over a third claimed to have been 'out' more than eight times.

Investigations in Britain during the 1980s reveal a similar picture. When psychologist Frances Banks conducted an out-of-the-body poll among 800 British church goers, 450 remembered leaving their body at some moment during the previous 5 years. In the light of her findings, Banks concluded that such experiences should perhaps be best viewed as an everyday occurrence, rather than an extraordinary event brought about by extraordinary conditions. Whilst accepting that moments of extreme pain, stress or nervous anxiety were likely to trigger spontaneous transference to the ecosomatic state, Banks felt that an OBE was best achieved in an atmosphere of quiet, peaceful meditation which ideally should have followed on from an exciting or cheerful experience. If this is true then one personal example would tend to bear out her opinion.

In the Easter of 1989, during a holiday to Goa, my wife Maggie and I had spent an enjoyable morning riding through the Indian countryside. After a few hours, hot, tired and hungry, yet spiritually uplifted by our exotic surroundings, we stopped off for some refreshment at a deluxe hotel on the coast. There we enjoyed a delicious lunch of spiced curry, sitting on a restaurant balcony high above an indoor pool. The hotel interior was splendidly designed in the style of a maharaja's palace, and with multi-coloured birds flying to and fro under the high domed ceiling above us a more peaceful setting would have been difficult to imagine. Whether it was these beautiful surroundings, the heat or the spices, or an amalgam of all the wonderful sights, sounds and smells she had experienced during that day, Maggie cannot say, but she told me later that while sitting on the balcony she consciously felt her 'self' leave her body and float away across the pool some twenty feet above the still blue water. The sensation lasted only a few seconds, but she insisted quite categorically that it was no product of her imagination.

Maggie's peaceful OBE in the Goan hotel is just one of a number of examples that have been personally reported to me. Among these, people have claimed to have left their bodies while writing, when on the verge of sleep, or while undertaking some menial repetitive task. Non-crisis OBEs seem most likely to occur when a person's mind has the time and freedom to wander and I have never heard of a person leaving their body during a period of intense concentration. Does this mean, then, that the ecosomatic state might be little more than a daydream? Personally, I very much doubt it. Leaving aside those low-level, temporary affairs like the one my wife described, a full transference to the ecosomatic state involves psychic voyagers going through a process quite unlike any other human experience. During this process of change the person passes through a series of distinct stages leading to a prolonged separation from their physical body. The recollections of those who go through these OBE stages are impressively consistent.

Initially the experiencer will often notice a peculiar rigidity in their limbs, bringing with it an immobility and a sense of frustration or unease. Once separated from the physical form, however, they rejoice in their discovery of a new found freedom – now clothed within a body strangely weightless and insubstantial, they are no longer constrained by gravity or the limits of physical matter. With their visual senses preternaturally sharp, non-physical voyagers see the world in brighter, more vivid hues; their insubstantiality allows them to pass ghost-like through solid objects. If this power brings with it a sense of shocked surprise, it is usually soon replaced by sheer delight as the voyager goes forth under the directive power of mental will. Normally, it is only when the experiencers fear they may not be able to re-enter their physical body that their journey ends. Some are relieved to return to mundane reality, some are saddened. But analysis of their recollections shows that psychic voyagers rarely regret their time away from the body, and each remains convinced that they have undergone an experience completely different from anything they have felt before. Tell these people that they were simply day dreaming and you will be given short shrift.

When English parapsychologist Celia Green surveyed a sample of over one hundred Oxford graduates in 1966, she found that of the thirty-four per cent who claimed experience of leaving the physical body, the vast majority did so whilst in a thoroughly relaxed frame of mind. They all rejected the notion that their experience lacked objective reality. Rather than feeling alarmed by the sensation of being 'out', the majority claimed to be elated by the experience. Disembodied within a small but definite location themselves, the Oxford undergraduates talked variously of being 'four dimensional', 'more real', and of seeing with a 'whole consciousness'. One said that she had never been so awake as she was when outside her mortal frame; another said that her physical body was but 'a shadow' in comparison to her true self. Many recalled a previously unknown sense of freedom and some spoke of feeling 'superior'. Most students felt calm and unmoved for the duration of their being out, though a few recalled after a time sensing an urgent need to return to the physical body – a sudden fear that they might not be able to get back to normal. In contrast, several were deeply saddened to face once more the mortal coil, wishing only to prolong the experience even if it risked their own deaths.

Continuing research into OBE during the last decade has produced much analysis which is consistent with Green's findings. Carlos Alverado, a graduate of the parapsychology programme at John F. Kennedy University, California, worked on an ecosomatic state survey for his Master's Thesis. According to Alverado's statistics, based once again on a sample of students who reported OBEs, forty-four per cent of all respondents said they had experienced out-of-body flights during sleep; twenty-eight per cent during the hypnogogic state on the verge of sleep; and thirty-two per cent when fully awake. Many of those involved in Alverado's study seemed to remember feeling consciousness in both places at once, suggesting to the parapsychologist that the mind might be able to send out a part of itself rather in the same way that a space craft might send out a sensitive probe.

*   *   *

Whilst serious scientific research into OBE may have begun quite recently, the phenomenon itself has been recognized for thousands of years. The concept of an astral or soul body runs through Eastern mystical philosophy and is mentioned in the ancient texts of Egypt, Greece and early Israel. There even appeared to be many examples in the Bible. The Old Testament prophet Elisha, for example, is said to have sent his spirit into the tent of his Syrian enemies where he was able to overhear their plan of attack. Likewise, Jesus appeared to have had the ability to leave his body at will.

Witchdoctors and shamans of ethnic cultures have long claimed the ability temporarily to leave their bodies through magic. Adepts and holy men in the highest reaches of the Tibetan Himalayas have demonstrated the capacity to cross great distances using an unrevealed process of Yogic superconscious concentration. During the nineteenth century, some theosophists claimed to have mastered the same skill – a process of mind-over-matter which they termed 'astral travel'. In our own century, spiritualists, and in particular those healers who engage in absent healing, recognize the reality of a similar technique.

In 1929 a pair of dedicated American occultists named Hereward Carrington and Sylvan Muldoon wrote a lengthy tome on the subject of astral travel, outlining in meticulous detail the techniques through which conscious projection of the astral double, or 'soul body,' could be brought about. According to their manual *The Projection of The Astral Body*, astral travel was within the capability of all people. The astral counterpart, made of an illuminous, translucent and etheric substance, invisible to the naked eye and much finer and more subtle than the world of matter, was in any case always withdrawn during periods of deep sleep, though in this state it was

neither conscious nor controlled. Likewise, according to
the writers, the astral body might involuntarily escape
under the influence of hypnotism, anaesthetics or other
drugs. The theosophists insisted that the voluntary or
controlled emission of the astral body could only be
willed through the application of the correct mental
technique which naturally they themselves claimed to
have mastered.

The Americans' book gave a number of precise instructions and tips for would-be travellers. A healthy diet of
fruit and vegetables, correct breathing exercises and a
mind free of material worries were held to be preconditions for achieving successful astral flight. External
factors, such as altitude and air temperature, were also
apparently linked though these were considered to be less
important. Would-be astral voyagers were advised to lay
down in a warm, dark room in a comfortable position
with the head pointing north. With the body and mind
gradually allowed to relax the subject should close their
eyes and breathe rhythmically, keeping their mouth
slightly open. In this state the individual should allow
their consciousness to drift towards sleep, but when the
state bordering wakefulness and slumber was reached,
the mind must focus upon an imaginary image at an
approximate distance of six feet from the subject's chest.
The purpose of this was to gain control of the vibrations
of both physical and mental planes so that they might
become harmonized. When this vibratory harmonization
was complete, the astral body would automatically leave
its physical counterpart and float upwards. Following
disengagement, it would then continue to rise horizon-
tally and gradually move away becoming upright. From
this point on, having achieved successful separation, the
experiencers would be able to move at the direction of
their own mind and unhindered by physical constraints.

To return to their physical self, they simply needed to focus upon re-engaging the two entities.

During their own soul flights the authors claimed total command over their non-physical doubles, enabling them to glide unseen into the houses of relatives and friends and observe what was taking place there. When they described the scenes the following day in the minutest detail, those same friends and relatives would always be amazed. This of course is the version according to Hereward Carrington and Sylvan Muldoon. Unfortunately since these tales were based almost entirely on their own testimony, they were pretty well impossible to verify. And so whilst *The Projection of the Astral Body* was avidly read by those who were already fascinated by the subject, few others took much notice.

For several decades the phenomenon remained largely ignored. However, since spontaneously induced reports of the phenomenon continued to come in from across the world in large numbers, it was inevitable that one day someone would attempt to construct a test under controlled conditions. In 1966 just such a series of experiments was begun by Dr Charles Tart, a respected professor of psychology at the University of California.

Initially Tart used as his main subject a businessman from Virginia named Robert Monroe who claimed to have experienced OBEs for some years. Although his OBEs had begun spontaneously, Monroe insisted that he had now learned to induce them consciously. Once out, the Virginian found himself able to float, glide or fly through solid matter – walls, floors, etc. On some occasions he said he even travelled across great distances in what seemed to him like a brief moment, mirroring the claims of Muldoon and Carrington. In order to test his subject's assertions, Tart designed a series of experiments in which Monroe had to 'fly' in order to get information he could not otherwise have known. The subject was placed in a cubicle set up like a bedroom where he could be alone and enter into the relaxed state he considered necessary in order to leave his body. During the whole time he was in the cubicle his brain waves, heartbeat and other bodily functions were monitored. Laying in this state of total calm Monroe was required to project his astral double to an adjoining room and there make a mental note of the actions of the technicians working. As a test it seemed simple enough to someone who claimed the ability to fly many miles. However, reclining in the bed with his head covered in uncomfortable electrodes, Monroe found it difficult to effect separation and although he thought he had achieved projection on a number of occasions his early descriptions of the room adjacent to his cell were disappointing.

Gradually though, his performances improved and, late in 1966, Tart completed a pilot physiological study of Monroe with surprising and interesting results. Electroencephalographic records during the psychic's 'out' phase clearly showed that he was not dreaming, nor properly awake, but producing slow alpha wave activity, suggesting that his body was in a state of semi-paralysis. Intriguingly, similar alpha wave activity had been recorded by Russian parascientists testing subjects during successful experiments into extrasensory perception. This of course did nothing to satisfy those sceptics who would not be convinced until Tart produced two lifelike Robert Monroes side-by-side. For a while Dr Charles Tart faced fierce criticism from those colleagues who had warned all along that the experiment was a waste of the university's time and money. All was not lost. A few months later the professor carried out a second series of tests which achieved far more impressive results. This time the subject was a schizophrenic patient, labelled in Tart's case notes (for reasons of privacy only) as a 'Miss Z.'

Miss Z claimed to have achieved numerous astral flights since childhood and to have developed total control over body-double projection. While wired up in Tart's laboratory relaxation cell, Miss Z was invited to travel to another room in the building in order to view a slip of paper featuring a five-digit number. No one but Tart knew the number, and the paper was placed on a high shelf, just below the ceiling and well out of sight of any member of staff. Incredibly, Miss Z reported correctly that the figure was 23132. As Tart was later to write, it is inconceivable that the correct answer could have been arrived at by guesswork. When the test was repeated many times using a random number generator, Miss Z continued to score hit after hit.

For many, Tart's results were all they were ever likely to need to prove the existence of astral flight. Soon afterwards, however, an even more convincing body of evidence emerged from a series of experiments conducted by Dr Karlis Osis, then director of research at the Manhattan headquarters of the American Society for Psychical Research. In this case the subject was one Ingo Swann, an artist who had first experienced the ecosomatic state at the tender age of three and thereafter on many subsequent occasions. By the time the American SPR began their experiments, Swann claimed the ability to project at will and travel wherever he chose. To try to prove this, Osis devised a series of tests in which the psychic was invited to sit in a sealed chamber and identify a series of everyday objects placed beyond the reach of normal vision. All through the experiments, he was wired up to equipment measuring fluctuations in brain wave activity, respiration and blood pressure. Unlike those of Robert Monroe, Swann's results were uniformily impressive. In his most successful series of tests he scored a total of 114 hits out of 147 attempts. Statistically, the American team of investigators calculated that the chances of achieving a similar result through guesswork would be around 40,000 to one. Intriguingly, electroencephalographic readings taken during Swann's OBE flights had recorded an unnaturally rapid brain wave pattern to be occurring while he was supposedly out.

Dr Karlis Osis continued research into OBE. In 1979, this time working with a college tutor named Alex Tanous, Osis set up a series of tests in which the subject was required to fly some distance to view an object placed elsewhere in the building, the target in this case being a series of pictures against different colour backgrounds. To reduce the likelihood of chance predictions, the picture/background colour sequence would be regularly and randomly changed. A protracted series of direct hits from the astral traveller Tanous, imprisoned some distance away in a soundproof room, was impossible to account for unless one accepted the reality of astral flight. In a total of thirty-eight trials carried out over a period of twenty sessions, Tanous achieved a sixty-five per cent ratio of success. Interestingly, sensors attached to his head detected a higher level of brain wave activity during the successful tests – confirming both the analysis previously undertaken by Dr Charles Tart and Osis's own work with Ingo Swann.

During the 1980s Alex Tanous has continued to work with Dr Osis in New York. His most recent experiments at the American SPR have been directed towards discovering whether immaterial forms (which in his own case Tanous humorously labels 'Alex 2') can affect instruments. Since these experiments began, Tanous has apparently been able to trigger off a number of devices such as strain-gauge sensors, thermistors which register minute changes in temperature, and photo-electric cells. Both Alex Tanous and Dr Karlis Osis soon realized the importance of their discoveries, not only to the realm of medical science and psychology but also to the very nature of life and death itself. For, if there was a second body existing on a parallel level with the physical flesh and blood form, then it seemed entirely possible that the consciousness within that body could survive the dissolution of the physical form.

The results obtained by researchers in California and investigators of the American SPR are far from unique. Similar tests in Western Europe and the then Soviet Union have achieved much the same degree of success. All in all, a dispassionate and unprejudiced person would surely, when faced with the weight of evidence, now have to accept the probability that astral travel is a reality. However, despite this bulk of data supporting the existence of the ecosomatic state, most scientists shy away from its implications, preferring instead to look for a psychological explanation that leaves established beliefs intact. One psychiatrist, Dr Jan Ehtenwald of New York, has expressed the opinion that OBEs are an expression of mankind's perennial quest for immortality, hallucinations in which individuals attempt to assert a wishful existence of the soul. They are evidence of the universal human desire to deny death, to avoid extinction but nothing more. From a psychological standpoint, Ehtenwald's opinion has much to recommend it but it can in no way explain the results achieved under experimental conditions in laboratories around the world. Nor can it be held to account for the prodigious number of spontaneous OBEs that are reported every year – often from atheists, agnostics and others who strongly disbelieve in life after death. OBEs are even regularly reported by those who refuse to believe in any form of psychic phenomena.

Few of those who have known the ecosomatic state for themselves, remain unaffected by their experience. According to Charles Tart, most astral travellers return to their bodies convinced they will survive physical death. Rather than having a vague belief in an afterlife, they know that their consciousness is capable of existing outside their own skin. Through their observations of dying patients, some doctors have also begun to accept this possibility. A typical example, and one which provides further evidence for the reality of OBE, has been related by the German cancer specialist Dr Josef Issells, of the famous Bavarian clinic at Ringberg. Dr Issells was doing his routine wardround, when a female patient he had known for some time, and who was close to death, stopped him. 'Doctor,' she said emotionally, 'Do you know that I can leave my body?' Issells was nonplussed until she offered evidence, telling him exactly what had happened a few moments earlier in a room at the end of the ward. The dying patient described a woman, whom she did not know, writing a letter and also outlined the contents of her correspondence. Impressed by the urgency of the patient's deathbed declaration, Issells hurried down to the room to check if there was any truth in her story. Everything was exactly as she had described it – even the precise details of the letter. When Issells returned to the patient's bedside, she was dead. Or was she? As the German doctor subsequently wrote, if she had really left her body before she expired, what was to stop her from doing so again afterwards?

*   *   *

Perhaps the most impressive evidence for the reality of soul projection are those examples where a visit made by an astral traveller is seen by someone else. In cases of absent healing, those who require help often claim to see the healer's form appear beside them to administer the laying-on of hands. The often reported phenomenon of 'living ghosts' may in the same way be the product of spontaneous unremembered astral projections.

Alleged examples of mutual recognition recalled by both parties – viewer and participant – are the most interesting of all. A typical case comes from the memoirs of an Indiana farmer, Walter McBride. One late evening in the autumn of 1935, having retired early, McBride awoke from a fitful slumber to find himself floating upwards in a room bathed in a preternaturally bright haze, a light which, as he wrote later, 'cast no shadows'. To his astonishment, McBride discovered he could move through ceilings and walls; seemingly involuntarily, he found himself flying across the countryside towards the home of his father, who was at that time seriously ill. Within seconds he was by the old man's bedside, looking down at the familiar face. His father apparently recognized him though he seemed unable to hear his son's voice. Seconds later, McBride was whisked abruptly back to his own home where he found himself once more within his normal garment of flesh and blood. The next day he visited his father to find him much recovered. McBride had dismissed his remembrance as a dream until, to his amazement, the old man verified his son's presence the previous night.

Another well documented case, this time from the last century, was the mid-Atlantic appearance aboard the steamship *City of Limerick* of the wife of S.R. Wilmott, a Connecticut manufacturer on board the ship at the time. Apparently having retired to her bed in her Connecticut home, worrying for her husband's safety, Mrs Wilmott's spectral form was seen aboard the ship not only by her husband, but also by four fellow passengers. The woman herself later claimed some vague recollection of the night's events though, like Walter McBride, she had initially put it down to a dream. Another 'dreamer' was the Italian Alfonso de Liguari who, while asleep on the morning of 21 September 1774, apparently travelled hundreds of miles from his chapel prison in Arezzo to the Vatican in Rome where he prayed beside the deathbed of Pope Clement XIV. Alfonso dismissed his memory of the scene as a product of his imagination until others in attendance at the pontiff's bedside recalled talking to Alfonso personally. The Italian is not the only Catholic saint reported to have demonstrated an ability to leave the body. Similar episodes have involved Saint Servens of Ravenna, Saint Ambrose and Saint Clement of Rome. In the year 1226, Saint Anthony of Padua was apparently preaching in a church in Limoges, France, when he suddenly remembered that he was also supposed to be reading the scripture in a monastery some distance away. The saint drew his hood over his head and knelt in silence for several minutes. During the same period, his *doppelgänger* was seen to materialize among monks at the monastery and read the appointed lesson before vanishing.

The numerous examples in folklore of the appearance of a living person's ghost may well be the product of out-of-body flights. Certainly there is no shortage of stories to be drawn from a variety of cultures and each country seems to have its own name for the phenomenon. The body-double most commonly known by the German word *doppelgänger*, is called a 'vardger' in Norwegian, a 'taslach' in Scottish and a 'fetch' in Old English. Of course many of these tales emerge from former times and are therefore less than reliable evidence. Examples from our own century are not so easy to dismiss. During World War II, a French lieutenant colonel, in charge of an Italian prisoner of war camp at Guelma in Algeria, was returning to his quarters one evening when he noticed the camp's medical officer walking around a restricted area outside the perimeter wire. When asked by his superior what he was doing, the medical officer Captain Lefebure replied smiling, 'Don't worry it's not really me, it's just my double' and promptly disappeared. When the shaken colonel checked Lefebure's quarters he found the doctor fast asleep in his bunk. Speaking of the incident the next morning, Lefebure explained that he had been taught the skill of leaving his body while serving in the Orient: whenever he felt the urge, he took his astral form for some exercise!

A trawl of the records of the Society for Psychical Research on both sides of the Atlantic will soon uncover plenty more examples of witnessed bi-location. While at college, the poet W.B. Yeats apparently visited a fellow student in his common room yet remained asleep in his own dormitory at the same time. Novelist Theodore Dreiser has described how his friend John Cowper Powys appeared in *doppelgänger* form after accepting a bet that he could project his likeness to a distant spot. According to the testimony of researchers who tested her in the pre-war period, the medium Eileen Garrett regularly travelled while in a clairvoyant trance in New York to the home of a doctor in Newfoundland; once there, appearing both visible and solid, she would return to New York with information gathered from the doctor in order to prove the reality of her powers. In the same way another medium, Mrs Mary C. Wlasek, seems, on one night in 1922, to have flown from a moving train passing through America's east coast, to a spiritualists' convention being held the same evening in Los Angeles. The clairvoyant was seen by so many people that the reality of her 3,000-mile astral hop seems to have been proved beyond reasonable doubt.

Examples continue to crop up. During the last twenty years, researchers working in the field have written graphic accounts of how their most gifted subjects have been seen to materialize in places far from their physical body. Robert Monroe, the psychic tested under laboratory conditions by Charles Tart, included in his 1972 autobiography *Journeys Out Of The Body*, several accounts in which he met astounded friends while on his soul wanderings. During his work with Dr Karlis Osis in the same decade, people have regularly seen Alex Tanous bi-locating, even when the psychic has been making no conscious attempt to do so. On one occasion, during a fly-in experiment in which Tanous left his Portland home to appear in Osis's New York office, he was seen by several witnesses who later accurately described the clothes Tanous was known to be wearing at the time. Another time, Tanous bi-located to the bedside of psychologist David Viscott who was at the time seriously ill in a Los Angeles hospital. On this occasion, the psychic's sudden materialization out of thin air was seen by doctors and nurses on ward duty.

The reason why the astral body should appear visible for some people and not others remains unclear. Yet this anomaly remains consistent with our experience of other elements of the paranormal – ghosts do seem to exist but only a few people see them and then only briefly; messages from the spirit world may be available to us all, but few individuals possess the developed psychic sensitivity to receive them. Taking this into account, researchers currently involved with the OBE phenomenon have attempted to use those with psychic sensitivity to watch for and predict the movements of their subjects during in-flight experiments. One investigator, Dr Robert Morris of the Psychical Research Foundation Research Centre in North Carolina, has even gone a step further by using animals. Bearing in mind the numerous stories of dogs snarling or barking at apparently nothing, and other displays of agitation or fear in animals during haunting outbreaks, Morris decided to see whether non-human witnesses would react in the same way to the presence of astral counterparts. In order to test whether animals showed altered behaviour in the presence of a disembodied projection, a kitten was placed in a large box and observed very carefully for a prolonged period before the experiment was due to begin. Morris's test subject, a university undergraduate named Keith Harary, who had reported having OBEs since childhood, was then invited to disengage his astral counterpart and enter the otherwise empty room, attempting to attract the kitten's attention. During those times that Harary claimed to have successfully left his body, observers saw the kitten suddenly stop running around and sit in a motionless gaze at a seemingly empty space.

Taking the experiment one step further, Dr Morris repeated the test, this time using a non-domestic animal – a venomous snake. Placed in a terrarium, the reptile was left alone in its small isolation booth and observed through a window. Its usual behaviour was to slither about its glass cage in the normal fashion, yet during the period that Harary claimed to have entered the room, it slid up the side of the cage and bit wildly at the glass. Without question the snake saw something and at no other time was this peculiar behaviour pattern repeated.

*   *   *

The importance of the out-of-body experience to the case against death is all too obvious. Biology tells us that the continuation of life is dependent upon the health of the brain and nervous system; self being a construct of the mind, and the mind a product of the brain. But if, as the evidence in this chapter suggests, we can step outside our brain and nervous system, if our consciousness is capable of functioning independently of the physical life support mechanism – the mass of cellular tissue that is the human body – then our true identity is somewhat more complex. As one researcher has put it, 'the belief that the ecosomatic state exists requires an article of faith – that there is another "me" waiting to get out.' In fact there may very well be several other 'me's' in all of us.

It is the opinion of Professor William Tiller of Stanford University, USA, that the human somatic system is supplemented by at least one and possibly several others, a structure he terms 'the human ensemble'. Tiller's own research has led him to consider the possibility that there are three levels of bodily reality each underpinning each other; hidden systems which are alike in every detail and complementary to the physical form. The professor's ideas are in accordance with the doctrine of mystics in the East and West and, if true, would go some way to explain such little understood forms of treating illness as acupuncture, a practice which presupposes the existence of a second body through which energy flows down invisible channels. The same theory might also help to account for certain medical curiosities: the way, for example, some amuptees continue to feel sensations in the limbs that they have lost, the feeling which, when severe, is labelled 'deferred pain'.

There are plenty of sound biological reasons for believing in the existence of a life field, or second bodily system. For instance, medical science has seen (but cannot fully explain) how new human cells are able to adopt the same functions and arrange themselves in the same pattern as old dying ones. Whilst in theory every individual living cell has the genetic information necessary for making another adult organism, in the higher animals the blueprint is not enough. It needs something extra for creation to take place. This 'something extra' may be the illusive second system that spiritualist healers treat through the process of the laying on of hands.

Another distinguished scientist who believed that we all possess more than one body, was the late Harold Burr of Yale University. Before his death in the mid-1970s, Burr described how 'the traditional modern doctrine, that the chemical elements determine the structure and development of the organism, fails to explain why a certain structural constancy persists despite continuous metabolism and chemical flux.' The true reason, Burr insisted, was that beneath the visible form lay a subtle electromagnetic field without which none of us could continue living. Far closer to our true selves than the heavier and more cumbersome garment of flesh we traditionally consider ourselves to be, this electromagnetic field body was likened by Burr to Prana, the life force element believed by Yogis and other eastern mystics to be the true identity of the human individual.

That there really may be such a thing as a second body is understandably a source for contention within scientific circles. Nevertheless, the march of medical science through experimental research would appear to be leading inexorably towards the very same conclusions reached by mystics and transendental philosophers long ago. Most recently, a group of Russian scientists have suggested that mental energy is itself capable of forming, albeit for a short period, a separate self or astral counterpart, which they termed the 'bio-physical plasmabody'. This, they have argued, is the source of the fabled aura which spiritualist mediums claim to be able to see, and which has been virtually proven to exist through the advent of Kirlian photography, a process itself pioneered in Russia. A source of much controversy everywhere, this amazing technique may hold the key to life's most central mysteries. Named after Seymon and Valentine Kirlian, the couple who developed it, Kirlian photography provides a startling clue to the nature of the astral double, suggesting that there is a kind of energy field which surrounds and interpenetrates the physical life form. In the Kirlian process, unexposed film is placed on a flat metal plate and the objects to be photographed laid on top. High-voltage impulses are then charged through the plate, exposing the film. When developed, the pictures invariably show not only an outline of the object but a multi-coloured aura of light. Seymon Kirlian believed this aura was a direct transfer of charges from the object of the photograph – electrical signals of the inner state of the organism.

Over the past forty years the Kirlians have photographed these strange patterns emanating from a variety of living tissues – leaves, fruits, small animals and just about every part of the human body. In the human experiments, the Russians noted not only how the vividness of the haze altered with the person's health but also with their state of mind. Subjects under the influence of drugs produced idiosyncratic auras, whilst known psychics and spirit healers reflected extraordinarily powerful auras. Most significantly of all, pictures of leaves partly cut away showed the faint yet unmistakeable imprint of the missing portion, indicating that the photographic process was picking up emissions from a second structure. According to the Kirlians, the image remained intact because the whole structure of the living object remains intact on the non-physical level.

Anyone who has undergone Kirlian photography and
seen a picture of their own hand-print emitting glowing
lights which look like iron filings cannot fail to be
impressed. However, when the Russian team announced
their early research in the post-war years many scientists
dismissed their findings out of hand, not so much because
they doubted the accuracy of the techniques involved,
but because they knew that the implications of the
results could turn the scientific world upside down.
Today controversy continues to surround the practice
of Kirlian photography but the balance of belief has
begun to swing towards the Russians. During the 1960s
in the US, Professors Thelma Ross and Ken Johnson
built their own high-voltage, high-frequency apparatus
which produced photographs similar to those taken in
the former USSR. Working with 500 subjects, Ross and
Johnson found that each person has their own psychic
finger print, a unique and recognizable pattern which,
though it may change slightly with mood, health or when
under the influence of drugs, alcohol or hypnosis, remains
characteristically theirs. More recently, at the Newark
College of Engineering, Dr Douglas Dean has produced
a comparable set of results and shown conclusively that
spirit healers produce a much stronger aura. Along with
the aforementioned William Tiller of Stanford, each of
these investigators remains convinced that the etheric
double has now been proved to exist.

From elsewhere in the world even more remarkable evidence has emerged during the past decade.
In Bucharest, Romanian physician Ion Dumitrescu has
produced a new high-voltage photographic technique
he calls 'electrographic imaging' through which medical
conditions such as ulcers, cancers, nerve malfunctions
and muscle disease can be identified. Excessively dark
patches on the patterns of the secondary system have

been shown to correspond precisely with malformations on the physical form. Once more in the USA, this time in Pennsylvania, Dr L.W. Konikiewicz has been able to achieve similar results from his own supersensitive Kirlian-style apparatus. The prospects for further research look decidedly hopeful. As one parascientist in the field of psychic imaging has put it, 'The next twenty years should see final proof that the mystics were right about man. In a hundred years' time no one on earth will believe they only have one body.'

Of course not everyone agrees with this prediction. Despite the extraordinary weight of evidence that continues to mount supporting the case for genuine out-of-body experiences, some medical figures completely refuse to accept the possibility that we are anything other than machines made out of blood, bone and muscle. Prominent among their number is Dr Susan Blackmore, a British neurologist and writer who has expressed the opinion that OBEs are really nothing more exciting than dreams, brought about during states of altered consciousness. Noting that a significant proportion of spontaneous OBEs take place at times of undue stress following accidental injury or battle wounds, or while the subject is under the influence of drugs or anaesthetic, Blackmore has contended that the ecosomatic state is triggered by an imbalance in the supply of carbon dioxide and oxygen to the brain. Pointing out that some pain killing narcotics contain opiates that could bring on hallucinogenic visions, Blackmore cites, in her book *Beyond the Body*, one personal out-of-body experience she had after smoking cannabis. Although it seemed real at the time the doctor considered it later to be no more than a waking dream. Blackmore's recollection went as follows. Having shared a joint with two college friends, the then student doctor felt herself gradually float out of her own body, exit through a window and glide over the roof-tops. Her trip seemed real enough at the time but when she checked the appearance of the building's roofs some days later, she found their formation, chimneys and ridge-tile variations were very different from those she remembered. Naturally enough, from that moment on she considered the episode to be nothing more than an illusion and held the cannabis to be entirely responsible for playing tricks on her mind.

The neurologist's experience is certainly interesting, and suggests that some OBEs may be less than they seem. However, whilst Dr Blackmore's experience must certainly have been drug induced, only a small proportion of all OBEs can be accounted for in that way. In most of the examples recorded by researchers, the subject has not been under extreme stress nor under the influence of alcohol or drugs. Many have taken place when the subject is fully conscious and not distracted in any way. Certainly the 'brain oxygen' theory would be rejected by all those who have mastered the ability to project their astral body at will. Furthermore, the out-of-body-experience is a very special one, quite unlike anything else known to man. As with those psychologists who seek to explain the phenomenon as an emotional defence against the thought of extinction, Blackmore's hypothesis entirely fails to explain the intensity of the sensation associated with being 'out'. Perhaps most importantly, neither theory accounts for the frequency of reports, either.

The sheer bulk of testimony relating to the phenomenon is overwhelming. The OBE is among the most commonly reported paranormal experiences, ranking alongside precognition and déjà-vu. Recent assessments suggest that up to ten per cent of the adult population can consciously recall being out of their body at some point or other in their lives. In their massive work *Phantasms of*

the Living, published in 1886, two members of the British
SPR, Edmund Gurney and Frederick Myers, recorded
over 700 different accounts, including many where other
witnesses received a strong impression of the presence
of the astral traveller. In 1953 J.M. Whiteman published
a report summarizing more than 500 cases of the same
condition which he described as 'detachment from the
physical body'. A dedicated parapsychologist, Whiteman
had taken the trouble to interview everyone who was
involved in these cases personally and his research has
been thoroughly checked and found to be reliable.
Over the past twenty-five years literally thousands more
accounts have been recorded by researchers on both
sides of the Atlantic. Englishman Dr Robert Crookall
devoted no less than nine volumes to the several hundred
cases that he collected. More recently, South African
investigator J.C. Poyton received 122 positive replies
to a single published questionnaire, whilst a newspaper
article published in Britain by researcher Celia Green
provoked over 300 people to write to her claiming to
have been 'out'.

But the importance of OBE to us all goes far beyond
mere experience. The evidence outlined in the preceding
pages of this chapter point towards a single logical standpoint – that a human being is more than a physical body,
and that life itself is not dependent upon the functioning
of the respiratory and nervous systems. If the real human
being, the real us, the soul, spirit, personality, or whatever we may wish to label ourselves, is truly as Koestler
said, 'the ghost in the machine', then our physical body
may very well be, as the spiritualists claim, no more than
a suit of clothes which we cast off when they are unfit for
further use. Accept this standpoint and we must implicitly
accept the considerable probability of life after death.
Some might consider it to be all the evidence necessary.

Halfway to Heaven

'Thus all things altered, nothing dies – and here and
there the unbodied spirit flies.'

Ovid

They say that no one knows what the moment of death
is like, for no one ever lives to tell the tale. This is not
true. In 1871 a Swiss geologist named Albert Heim fell
seventy feet down a sheer rock face whilst climbing Säntis
Mountain in the Alps. Astonishingly, he survived. Even
more astonishingly, the experience seems to have been a
pleasant one. According to his written account, Heim felt
no fear during his fall, only peace and serenity. His mental activity, he said, increased to 'a hundred-fold velocity'
and his surroundings were 'transfigured in a heavenly
light'. Though his descent could have lasted no more
than three seconds, the climber apparently had time to
see every major event in his life flash before his eyes, each
incident suddenly acquiring a new, deeper significance.

I acted out my life as though I were an actor on stage,
upon which I looked down as though from practically
the highest gallery in the theatre. I was both hero and
onlooker . . . then sounded solemn music as though
from an organ in powerful chords . . . I felt myself
go softly backwards into this magnificent heaven –
without anxiety, without grief. It was a great, glorious
moment!

*   *   *

By the time he hit the ground Albert Heim was a different person. A year later, having recovered from his injuries, and with his views on life and death radically changed, the geologist set about researching the recollections of other survivors of near-fatal falls. Collating the memories of thirty individuals who had similarly cheated death, Heim found that nearly all described sensations exactly like his own: an absence of anxiety or pain; an amazing expansion of time and a divine calm which swept through their souls. Even the instantaneous life review featured in more than half the cases Albert Heim investigated.

It would seem that this peculiar sense of calm detachment in the face of imminent extinction is not idiosyncratic to the mountaineering faternity, but a universal human reaction to life-threatening situations. In her autobiography, the American socialite Caresse Crosby described a feeling of 'sublime harmony' and a 'dazzling prismatic vision' of her past during her moments of near-death by drowning. In his book *The Romeo Error*, British parascientific author Lyall Watson records both his own experience following a landrover crash in the African bush, and the memories of a sky-diver from Arizona who fell 1,000 metres to break only his nose. The remembrances of both men mirror those of the Swiss climber Albert Heim in all important respects.

Why should the seeming moment of death produce peace rather than panic in the human mind? How can the multitudinous moments of a person's life miraculously appear before their eyes and be assimilated in seconds by their brain? Questions like these pose unanswerable conundrums for psychologists. But for parapsychologists they provide the key to a greater understanding of the human condition – before and after the actual moment of death.

*   *   *

In November 1949 Edmund Wilbourne, a young man suffering from pleurisy, was admitted to Crumpsall Hospital, Manchester. Already in a critical condition when he arrived, hopes of Wilbourne's recovery faded and he passed away the same night. Or so the doctors initially thought. In fact, although all bodily functions appeared to have ceased, Wilbourne's consciousness had left his body to float peacefully above his inert physical form. There, from his ecosomatic vantage point, the young man watched incredulously as nurses prepared his corpse for the mortuary. It was, he said afterwards, like looking at a motion picture rather than a scene viewed through his normal eyes. To his surprise, the pleurisy victim felt no strong emotions as the doctor below grimly pronounced the sentence of certified death. In his mind at that moment there was neither sadness at his own passing from the mortal realm, nor any desire to return to the body of flesh and blood that he had left moments before. If anything, Wilbourne felt he was in the proper and correct place. Speaking much later of his experience, he recalled watching, with a sense of detached curiosity, his corpse's face being carefully shaved with a cutthroat razor – unaware that this was standard practice in hospitals. Floating serenely just below the ward ceiling, Wilbourne lost all sense of time, and it was after drifting through space for what seemed like an eternity that he suddenly returned to his physical body which was by then laid out in the hospital mortuary. There, having fully returned to normal consciousness he called for assistance.

The mortuary attendant nearly fainted with fright as the apparently dead form suddenly sat upright and shouted for help! Edmund Wilbourne made a full recovery and remains alive today. Yet in the winter of 1949 he 'died' for over two hours and has a death certificate to prove he did not dream the whole thing.

Who said dead men tell no tales? Parapsychologists never do.

Wilbourne's experience is far from unique. In his 1988 book *The After-Death Experience*, English author Ian Wilson includes the story of a US soldier blown up by a mortar bomb while serving in Vietnam in June 1966. The infantryman, Private Jack Bayne, afterwards found himself floating in a weightless condition some yards from his own physical form and at a height of several feet above the ground. Below he could see the events of the battle continuing, where his side's position was being overrun. As he watched Vietcong soldiers removing the boots from his apparently lifeless body, Bayne found himself trying in vain to get his physical limbs to move towards his rifle. But there was no response. It was, he wrote later, as if his flesh and blood were 'nothing more than a manikin clothed inside a uniform'.

The enemy soldiers passed on leaving the American GI still floating above the scene of his own death. Some hours later, when American troops regained the position, Bayne saw 'himself' pronounced dead and put into a body bag. Transported by helicopter to a base behind US lines 'he' was left in a morgue to be embalmed. All the time the 'real' Bayne – his mind, soul or whatever he had become – remained with the body though outside it. Naturally, like the doctors who had examined him, he began to assume he really was dead. However, when the process of embalming his corpse began there was a change of medical opinion, for the first scalpel incision produced an unexpectedly great effusion of blood. Suspecting that there might still be some life in their patient, medics began pumping his heart and at that very point Bayne returned to his normal position within his earthly body. Like the Englishman Edmund Wilbourne, he made a complete recovery and astonished doctors with the story of his hours of 'death'.

At first glance the case above bears a strong similarity to those out-of-body experiences of battle-wounded war veterans described in the previous chapter. However, it differs markedly in some serious respects. For one thing, Private Jack Bayne left his body not simply for a few moments but for a period of several hours. More importantly, he had been pronounced clinically dead some time before he actually recovered. In both the case of the Vietnam GI and the Englishman who died in a Manchester hospital, all vital signs of life had ceased; the doctors who certified them dead could in each case find no trace of heartbeat nor any evidence of respiratory functioning. Examples like these – where the ecosomatic state follows a close brush with physical death – are much rarer than the standard variety of OBEs. Nevertheless, they have been reported to doctors across the world with such persistence that paranormal investigators have become convinced that these experiences are neither dreams nor illusions. Indeed, their sheer consistency would appear to suggest the probability that all of us are likely to undergo a similar experience during our last moments of earthly existence.

As medical science progresses, bringing with it more sophisticated techniques of resuscitation, the number of persons who are able to recall these experiences is on the increase. If we are to lend any credibility whatsoever to the stories they tell from their close calls with the grave then it is certain that some part of ourselves, consciousness, mind, soul or whatever, is not snuffed out when the vital functions of the body cease to operate. In terms of the case against death, the importance of that simple assessment is inestimable.

*   *   *

One of the first people to investigate the enigma of near-death experiences (NDEs) was Dr Elisabeth Kubler-Ross, a Swiss-born physician now resident in California, USA. As a professor of psychiatry in the Chicago University Hospital during the post-war period, Kubler-Ross had recognized the psychological need for those terminally-ill patients she worked with to come to terms with the idea of death. An agnostic herself, Kubler-Ross had no illusions on the subject: as far as she was concerned death was an end to everything and she never sought to sentimentalize the matter either in her own mind or in conversation with others. Even so, the Swiss doctor's opinion slowly began to change through her regular contact with patients living through their last hours of earthly existence. Far from being sad, a high proportion spent their dying moments in a joyful, even elated mood. Even patients in great pain, or those who had been previously depressed during long weeks of illness seemed to embrace the onset of death with open arms. Kubler-Ross noted that this curious mood change towards happiness often coincided with them apparently seeing, and sometimes even holding conversations with, relatives already deceased. Initially the psychiatrist assumed that these spirit appearances beside her patients' deathbeds were simply hallucinations – possibly a result of a depleted oxygen supply to the brain.

She began to doubt this explanation after personally encountering several examples where patients claimed to see the ghosts of people that they did not know were dead. One notable case concerned the death of a young Indian girl who saw her father only seconds before drawing her last breath. Kubler-Ross knew the man to be still living elsewhere in the United States, yet it transpired that he was indeed dead, having suffered a fatal coronary only one hour before his daughter's moment of death.

As the psychiatrist later wrote, the child could not have guessed her father's fate since his heart attack was unexpected. Other examples Kubler-Ross found particularly hard to account for involved children who died in hospital from injuries suffered in multiple-death crash car accidents. Knowing that the children had not been made aware of the names of those relatives who had preceded them into death, the psychiatrist was impressed by the way many youngsters seemed to instinctively know which members of their family had actually been killed and which had not. Only those who had not survived appeared at their deathbeds. Consulting colleagues in other hospitals Kubler-Ross found that the phenomenon she had witnessed was unexpectedly widespread. Elsewhere in the States, other doctors had also noticed that dying patients, including children who had been involved in road accidents and other incidents involving multiple deaths in the same family, always knew which of their relatives were already dead, for it was only they who appeared at their bedside. In no single instance that Kubler-Ross discovered, did a child or any other person mention seeing at the final moments before their own death, any friend or member of their family who turned out to still be alive.

The Swiss-born psychiatrist's observations of the curious and unaccountable behaviour of patients in the process of dying were eventually written up in the form of a comprehensive study and published. But it was a separate and even more extraordinary group of patients that really convinced the once sceptical doctor of the probability of an afterlife: those individuals who had apparently died only to recover. In such cases (of which Kubler-Ross collected dozens) patients who suffered the apparent onset of death – the cessation of the vital signs of life e.g. no heartbeat, no respiration, no blood pressure, seemingly no brain activity, and yet who were eventually resuscitated – often seemed able to recall in detail the events and even the conversations of medical staff who had been present during their period of seeming death. Invariably, these near-death survivors talked of floating several feet above their own body where they could look down upon the activity below. The sheer similarity and clarity of these individual accounts, plus the fact that they were in each case accompanied by a feeling of peace and tranquillity – a feeling already noticed in terminally ill patients – convinced the psychiatrist that the recollections were not illusory. To deepen her conviction further, those who entered into an apparent death-state only to return also talked of meeting dead relatives, in exactly the same way that those about to die insisted that they were seeing their deceased family members by their bedsides.

For Kubler-Ross, this last factor was proof that the two phenomena (of deathbed visions and NDE visions) must be connected in some fundamental way. Although those who experienced a close call with death had done so under widely varying conditions and circumstances, and although they represented a wide range of ethnic types and ages, they were quite obviously all seeing and feeling much the same thing after their hearts had stopped beating.

None of these patients had had the opportunity to compare notes with others who had undergone the experience, yet the parallels went way beyond the boundaries of coincidence. In the opinion of Dr Kubler-Ross it was only logical to assume therefore, that the NDE was something all human beings were likely to undergo when faced with the moment of death.

Around the same time as Kubler-Ross was formulating her theory of the near-death ecosomatic state, she met another respected medical figure whose own independent investigation not only seemed to duplicate her findings but went far beyond her conclusion in asserting the probability of an afterlife. Dr Raymond Moody, a philosopher turned psychiatrist from Virginia, had by the mid-1970s become intrigued by the mounting evidence for an afterlife, particularly those deathbed visions of the same type noticed by Kubler-Ross. Having studied closely all the available literature on the experience of dying, such as the pioneering 1926 work *Deathbed Visions* by the distinguished English physicist Sir William Barret and the more recent book by American Dr Karlis Osis entitled *Deathbed Observations by Doctors and Nurses*, Moody became convinced that much could be learned from talking to those whose own brush with death had been too close for comfort: people who had almost been killed in accidents or nearly died under the surgeon's knife, only to make a miraculous recovery.

To begin with, Moody's fascination with the out-of-body experience came about not through the observation of one of his own patients but following a conversation with a fellow physician, Dr George C. Ritchie who had himself 'died' from pneumonia in December 1943, while training at a US Army camp in Abilene Texas. Describing his experience decades later Ritchie recalled leaving his hospital bed and walking around looking for his uniform. Only after a few moments did he realize that the inert form he had left behind in bed was his own body! Ritchie remembered discovering to his own surprise that he had acquired fantastic powers: the ability to fly at great speeds, and to move through solid objects (including living persons), to name but two. Yet he had no tactile sensation; try as he might he was unable to touch or hold anything. Some hours later, though to him it seemed much longer, Ritchie recalled how he saw doctors pronounce him dead, finding no trace of a pulse nor breath from his lungs. It was only when the disembodied man saw a white sheet being pulled across his own face that he fully realized he had actually died and was not simply dreaming.

As he recalled to Dr Moody, he then felt a surge of emotion rise in his breast – there was no sense of alarm or panic just a profound sadness in the knowledge that his earthly existence was over.

According to Ritchie's testimony, a remarkable manifestation then occurred. The room became filled with a golden glow and he became aware of a strange and immense presence by his side. At the same time he saw flash by in a matter of only a few seconds every major event in his life. Moments later the hospital walls seemed to disappear altogether and Ritchie found himself confronted by an entirely new and wonderful panorama; a city of light standing on a hill, a place of indescribable majesty peopled by beings whose very skin seemed to give off an aura of warmth and love. He assumed that he must have ascended to Heaven, yet no sooner had he arrived at the city wall than he found himself suddenly sucked backwards to wake up inside his physical body. His return to health confounded those doctors who had presumed him to be lost; when he told them of his experiences they were even more stupefied. According to medical records at the camp hospital, George C. Ritchie had been clinically dead for twenty-nine minutes, during which time every single recordable life function had ceased.

Having heard his colleague's story, and knowing him to be a man of integrity, Raymond Moody felt it impossible not to take these strange recollections seriously. However, he thought it entirely possible that Ritchie's memories were hallucinations. It was true he knew of a student

doctor who had once related a similar story, but could not
the two examples simply be a bizarre case of coincidence?
Determined to unravel the mystery, Raymond Moody
took the trouble of interviewing patients in his own
hospital in Virginia who had also undergone close calls
with death. To his amazement he soon heard a number of
accounts which not only corroborated the feeling of being
'out' described by his colleague, but which appeared
to duplicate Ritchie's 'Heaven' remembrance in almost
every respect. Encouraged, Dr Moody set about his
research with the dedication of a pioneer, until by 1976
he had found over one hundred cases of persons who
survived a near-death experience to relate stories which
matched George Ritchie's. Many were even more bizarre
than that of his fellow doctor. Documented meticulously,
the most impressive examples were compiled in a book
entitled *Life After Life*, which when it was published in
1977, was hailed as a breakthrough in our understanding
of the afterlife state and rapidly sold over three million
copies. Few books in the history of paranormal research
have had such an extraordinary impact and it is not hard
to see why.

Through his research, Raymond Moody discovered
that almost all near-death experiencers had vivid recollections of leaving their body and since these descriptions
had much in common, he formed the opinion that the
experience of dying remained profoundly similar for all
human beings. In his introduction to *Life After Life*,
the psychiatrist constructed what he considered to be
an archetypal dying experience based upon the fifteen
elements most frequently reported. According to Moody
the 'model' NDE begins when the subject notices an
uncomfortable buzzing sound and is transported rapidly
down a long dark tunnel. Following this process, the
subject's consciousness finds itself outside the physical

body, though in the immediate physical vicinity, almost always floating several feet above their corpse. The disembodied viewer is then presented with a vision of spirits known to them – people who have gone before them into the realm of death. After this the experiencer senses an indefinable feeling of kindness and love emanating from his or her surroundings, a feeling followed by another vision, this time of a Being of Light (variously described) which seems to represent a higher spiritual entity sent as a guide. The experiencer is then directed telepathically towards a consideration of his or her achievements and failures during earthly existence. A panoramic, instantaneous, life review playback then appears before the near-dead person's eyes. Many other events may now occur, but the subject inevitably reaches a point in which he or she is asked to cross some form of symbolic barrier or point of no return. At this moment astral travellers somehow become aware that the time is not right for death and realize they must return to earthly life. Once more within the physical body, they are often disappointed at having to leave this world of sublime beauty, love and happiness.

This then is the core experience of passing into death and back again. Moody stresses in his introduction to *Life After Life* that no two NDEs are identical, nor have any that he has discovered incorporated every single one of the elements described above. Furthermore, there is no one element which would appear to be absolutely universal to all experiences, though some people (usually those who have been pronounced clinically dead for a long period of time) recall particularly vivid memories which come close to the model. As a general rule, those who went deeper into the other world were people who had been dead for longer; those who simply reported leaving their body were usually patients

whose life functions had faile
two minutes.

One aspect of the NDE v
Raymond Moody was the
time on the other side of c
profoundly moved by the
Many lost their fear of death a..
with over one hundred individual e^p
expressed distress that they had come so close ι
and more than a few were actually pleased. The absolute
conviction which Dr Moody found among near-death
experiencers also impressed him immensely. Usually,
those who returned from the valley of death were only
too willing to tell of the marvels they had witnessed.
Some would even become angry that the poverty of
their language did not enable them to describe the
things they had seen. Typically, they would say things
like, 'There are no words to express what I saw', or
'They don't make adjectives big enough.' One woman
told Moody that the next world contained more than
three dimensions, another that you could 'hear' colours
there. In almost every case the psychiatrist investigated,
experiencers remembered seeing their own lifeless form
below them, and often their descriptions of these scenes
contained details corroborated afterwards by doctors
and nurses who were attempting to resuscitate them.
It was this evidence more than any other which initially
convinced Moody that at least part of these experiences
were real. But eventually, the psychiatrist's investigation
led him a stage further: if one apparently impossible part
of these recollections were true, then why not all of them?
It seemed logical enough, and besides, there were some
interesting parallels.

Though not a spiritualist himself, and whilst sceptical
of mediums' descriptions of the so-called Summer Land,

could not help but notice how many experiencers'
ections bore marked similarities to the astral planes
piritualistic philosophy. According to almost all of
oody's subjects, sensory perception in the soul state
was heightened far beyond their ordinary powers –
another noted feature of spiritualist tradition. Whilst
none of those interviewed could recall a sensation of taste
or odour, most were able to see far more clearly than
usual. One man recalled that his vision was tremendously
more powerful (like a telescope), whilst another reported
an all-round visual capacity that could look 'everywhere
and anywhere' at once. Yet another spoke of having eyes
'like a zoom lens' with which he could see close-up the
minutest of details. The unimpeded and swift movements
of the consciousness from place to place at the speed of
thought was perhaps the most frequently reported of
all the experiences, mirroring precisely the beliefs of
occultists with regard to the afterlife state. Almost all
of those who reported meeting dead relatives recalled
the ability to transmit and receive messages telepathically – an aspect of the spirit world which ties in with
descriptions received through mediumistic communications throughout the last hundred years and more. In
no single case which Moody uncovered did damage to
the physical body adversely affect the spirit counterpart;
however, the disembodied (ecosomatic) persons were
unable to touch or contact any material counterparts
they continued to see on the physical plane. Often it
was this very sense of isolation, an awareness of being
alone and unable to reach their loved ones, which seemed
to coincide with the first appearance of other spirits –
usually those of dead relatives – who arrived specifically
to tell the experiencer that their hour of death had not
yet arrived. In more than a few cases, astral travellers
returned to the material plane believing they had met

their own guardian spirits, those souls who, according to spiritualistic beliefs, are given the specific task of guiding an incarnated human soul through its passage of mortal life.

In almost every case in which it was a feature, the part of the experience which most profoundly affected the subject was the dramatic appearance of the Being of Light. According to Moody's book, this unearthly form was always shrouded in a brilliant aura though its physical features varied. Its identity remains obscure although in each case experiencers recall it as emanating an indescribable level of holiness. At no stage was any experiencer frightened of this awesome presence but always felt at ease in its company; some even felt drawn towards it by an irresistible magnetic attraction. It was Moody's opinion that the various disparities between descriptions of the Being were largely a function of the individual traveller's religious background or lack of it. Christian experiencers interpreted it as Christ (one or two actually claimed it to be Jesus) whilst a Muslim believed it to be Mohammed and a Jew simply an angel. Many called it the 'spirit of love', though the manifestation was far from impersonal.

In almost every experience in which the Being of Light appeared, a life review followed, though experiencers insisted that it held nothing in common with their normal memories. Those in Moody's sample compared it to a three-dimensional picture reel which evokes the emotions associated with every stage of the person's life. Moody himself noticed how the information displayed in the life review seemed beyond the capacity of any normal human mind consciously to assimilate and yet according to his subjects, it was always rapid, chronological and accurate. Such was the speed of the playback that it was over in a few moments, despite containing the most

206

Surviving Death

extraordinary detail – a thousand separate incidents, a million words spoken, heard and overheard, joined intelligibly in their minds. Understandably, it was a phenomenon which most astral travellers found amongst the hardest to describe.

As for the barrier stage, the point of no return beyond which travellers felt instinctively the true afterlife world began, there were further variations. To some it was a bridge, to others a gate, to many a stretch of water. But no one doubted its meaning.

For most experiencers the end of their soul ride seemed characteristically hazy. Very few actually recalled the return to their physical bodies; almost all simply remembered waking up sometime later. However, among those who did remember the moment of re-entry most believed their disembodied spirit returned to their physical form through the head, being sucked in through what seemed to be a funnel-like motion. It was almost, one said, 'like a genie returning to its bottle', the narrow neck in this case being the brain and spinal column. Those who remained conscious during this phase of their astral flight recalled their re-entry to be swift.

By the time Raymond Moody began writing up his research into the book which would eventually earn him a million dollars, he had already become convinced that the stories he heard over and over again were the clearest evidence for human survival of death yet to emerge. His reasoning was simple. The repetition of key features was so great that coincidence had to be ruled out; the emotional intensity with which these astral flights were recalled weighed heavily against the likelihood that they were hoaxes. For his part, the investigator rarely doubted the integrity of those he spoke to. As he wrote in *Life After Life*, 'The people I have interviewed are functional, well-balanced personalities.' No matter whether they were Muslim or Christian, atheist or agnostic, each of those who had undergone the near-death experience knew extinctively that the place they visited during those critical moments was as real, and perhaps even more real, than the world of matter that they had briefly left behind. Many, believing their personal afterlife experience to have been unique, had for years, kept quiet about their memories for fear of ridicule. When Moody assured them that they were not alone in what they had seen, they were greatly relieved and grew even stronger in their conviction that death is merely a transitional stage.

The publication of *Life After Life* caused a sensation around the world and opened the floodgates for a number of other books based on parallel investigations. One of the most comprehensive studies was undertaken by Dr Michael Sabom, a cardiologist at the University of Florida. Ironically, Sabom was originally a sceptic of Raymond Moody's work, holding strong reservations about the extravagant claims the psychiatrist appeared to be making in *Life After Life*. Having attended a lecture given by Moody in Chattanooga in the November of 1977, Sabom bluntly told the author that he found his evidence impossible to take seriously, since he had never himself come across a patient who would recall such an experience. Moody pointed out that not all those who experienced the afterlife state volunteered the information. Had he bothered to ask these people? Though basically still a disbeliever, Michael Sabom decided to conduct a limited survey himself. To his astonishment the third patient he spoke to reported a near-death experience of the classic Moody type. With his prejudice shaken to the roots, Sabom began his own in-depth study into cases of patients whose life functions ceased briefly during open heart surgery, or following cardiac arrests. His findings were published in 1979 under the title *Recollections Of Death*: *A Medical Investigation*. Covering over one hundred cases, it provided the clearest possible evidence that the type of experience uncovered by Moody is a truly universal phenomenon.

Dr Sabom was one of several medical experts to follow in the footsteps of *Life After Life*. In 1978, Dr Maurice Rawlings of Tenessee's Chattanooga Diagnostic Center, hit the US bookstalls with his own analysis of NDEs entitled *Beyond Death's Door*, whilst in 1980 Dr Kenneth Ring, a professor of psychology from Connecticut, published his own findings entitled *Life at Death*: *a Scientific Study of the Near Death Experience*. Throughout each of these works the features of individual case studies tend to repeat each other like an intricate spider's web of cross references. Statistical analysis of the material also substantiated Moody's belief that there was such a thing as a near-death core experience. Kenneth Ring, for instance, found that NDEs were reported by almost half of those who came close to dying, a ratio confirmed both by Moody and the other writers above. Each of these investigators came to the conclusion that it did not seem to matter which way a person approached death, be it through illness, accident or suicide. Nor did a person's previous religious faith make the experience more or less likely to occur since religious and non-religious people had NDEs in roughly equal numbers.

For those who, like myself, have taken the time to read through them all, the most outstanding feature of these works is their sheer consistency of content. It is equally hard not to be impressed by the intensity with which these experiences are described. The near-death experience, unlike the more common out-of-body experience described in the previous chapter, often has a profound significance upon the lives of those who live to bear witness to it. Many speak of an indescribable elation, a never-to-be-forgotten sensation of peace and happiness: 'Completely unlike anything else I have ever experienced . . . perfectly beautiful, beautiful feeling,' said one of Ring's case studies; 'Perfect, perfect, bliss', reported another to Sabom. Even those who attempted suicide or had been suffering trauma or severe distress immediately prior to their entry into the ecosomatic state, reported the same overwhelming sensation of peace, once they had left their bodies. Almost all those studied by doctors Moody, Ring, Sabom and Rawlings insisted their close encounter with the shadow of death had changed their view of their own place in the scheme of things. Many said that it made them feel better people, more caring towards others, more philosophical towards everyday troubles. Some turned towards religion or became interested in occult philosophy and several claimed to have developed a heightened sense of moral principles. Few, if any, remained wholly unaffected.

While serious research into the near-death experience has begun only within the last fifteen years, the experience itself has been reported for centuries. Both the pre-Christian Greek biographer Plutarch and the early Christian Bishop Augustine of Hippo wrote accounts of warriors who died, only to recover telling stories of meeting dead comrades-in-arms. In his history of the English Church and people, the eighth-century English monk, the Venerable Bede, relates the tale of Arthur Cunningham, a Northumbrian man who died one night only to return to life the following morning, sitting upright with such suddenness that those mourning him fled in fright. According to Bede's eighth-century chronicle, Cunningham told of a flight through darkness, followed by a vision of lovely surroundings, a strange place in which he met a man shining with light who told him that he must return to 'live amongst men once more'.

Many hundreds of years later, the eighteenth-century mystic and scientist Emmanuel Swedenborg described man's state immediately following death in terms which concur exactly with the archetypal near-death experience Moody outlined in his introduction to *Life After Life*. When the bodily circulation ceases, wrote Swedenborg, 'man becomes separated from his corporeal part. During the transition from this world to the next, the newly dead meet spirits and angels who communicate through thought rather than speech.' In the spirit world, wrote the German mystic, 'time and space are subject to the soul's mind and the newly dead will find their powers of sight and movement are incredibly enhanced.' Instructed by his previously departed friends and relatives as to the state of eternal life, the newly deceased person is then shown a visual representation of his own past, 'from earliest infancy to old age'. Only when this process is over may a man go before the light of God.

Swedenborg claimed to have gained his knowledge of the afterlife state not from a personal near-death experience but through regular mediumistic contact with the world of spirit. Even so there are many examples prior to the twentieth century where persons have recovered from an apparent state of death to recount extraordinary stories which bear close resemblance to those later uncovered by comtemporary researchers. In his 1987 book *The After Death Experience* English author Ian Wilson includes the case, from the America of the 1860s, of a Mormon farmer who died for several hours after having his hand seriously mangled in an accident. Also the more well known example of Dr A.S. Witzer of Kansas, who died of typhoid fever in the summer of 1889, only to be awakened two days later when he heard church bells ringing to mark his passing. Both men recounted stories of the 'life after life' variety. The similarities between the description of the afterlife state written by Emmanuel Swedenborg 200 years ago and those recounted by near-death survivors in our own age cannot be pure coincidence. And there is an even earlier account – this time from an ancient manuscript of Eastern antiquity – which outlines the process of dying in the much the same terms. The *Bardo Thodol* (Tibetan book of the dead) is a work compiled by Eastern sages thousands of years ago and handed down through generations by word of mouth. First written down some time during the ninth century and translated into English in 1927, the *Bardo Thodol*'s purpose is not merely philosophical. A manual to be studied and used, it gives the reader the precise knowledge he or she needs to pass through the portal of death with the minimum of unease. The book was traditionally read aloud as part of a funeral ceremony or beside a deathbed to prepare the departing soul for the transition they were about to make to the next world. In particular it warns the dying not to become confused and drawn backwards towards earth by the emotional ties they might continue to feel for those left behind.

The descriptions of the moments following death contained in the Tibetan text bear unmistakable parallels with the first hand experiences of those who have narrowly survived death in our own time. According to the *Bardo Thodol*, the soul-man enters a swoon upon death and wakes to find himself floating in a void. Here he finds himself surrounded by disturbing and even frightening visions which may very well include his own corpse. Perhaps unsure of whether or not he is still alive, the soul-man may not know what to do next, but soon he will become aware of undreamt-of powers. In his new body, the soul-man finds himself able to travel at fantastic speeds, being wherever he wants to be in the blinking of an eye. Indeed, there are no physical constraints placed upon him. If a man is deaf, blind or crippled in his earthly life, he will have found in death that his facilities have returned and all his senses have become heightened to a degree previously unknown. According to the *Bardo Thodol*, the soul-man is then presented with a mirror of his life's deeds, good and bad, and will be asked to judge for himself whether he has earned the right to continue upwards towards the higher Bardos (a Tibetan term for astral plane) or whether he must return to reincarnate in the mortal sphere once more, where there will be a further opportunity to continue his soul development.

The American researchers conducting studies into the near-death experience during the past two decades have been quick to draw parallels between their own patients' remembrances and the experience of death outlined in the ancient Buddhist text. As Raymond Moody points out, it would be illogical to assume that all contemporary witnesses to the near-death experience could have previously read the *Bardo Thodol*; indeed, most Westerners today have never heard of the Tibetan book. It is hard to imagine how twentieth-century Americans can have had their own perceptions of the dying experience influenced by the obscure beliefs of ninth-century Asian mystics.

Just as key features of the near-death experience seem to cut diametrically across religious, cultural and ethnic boundaries, so the very earliest works devoted to the nature of the afterlife world have much in common. The idea of the soul flying free following the onset of physical death would appear to be a universal human idea, perhaps predating even the origins of the *Bardo Thodol*. Anthropologists have noticed how tribes from as far apart as West Africa, Australasia and the Pacific islands, all share a belief that, upon death, the human spirit rises and views its own body from a vantage point high above. Ancient Egyptian hieroglyphic engravings discovered upon the walls of the Pharaoh's tombs show a king's 'ba', or soul, fluttering bird-like above his mummified remains. Since the elevation of the soul to a vantage point is the single most consistently experienced of the fifteen 'core' elements identified by Dr Raymond Moody and his fellow researchers, the Egyptian myths may have more in common with reality than superstition.

Other elements of the classic or model near-death experience also feature in many ancient legends. The life review is a particularly common feature, being mentioned not only in Hebrew and early Egyptian papyrus remnants, but also in accounts of Viking legends dating from before the Norman Conquest, and woodcuts which have survived from early medieval Christian Europe. As for the experience of meeting dead relatives, anthropologist Irving Howell, writing in a 1940 study of the Canadian Salteanix tribe, cites several examples where tribal members suffering from near-fatal fevers reported afterwards seeing their ancestors in the spirit realm. Professor Mary Eastman, who more recently has made a similar study of customs among the Sioux Indians of Dakota, has uncovered similar evidence. Elsewhere in the world, anthropologists have found that the belief that friends and relatives are met upon death is held in ethnic cultures as far apart as New Zealand, Pakistan and Polynesia.

That a comprehensively similar mythical view of the afterlife's early stages can have emerged independently from so wide a variation of cultural backgrounds is a mystery for which experts of the theory of the development of human society have no ready answer. But the latter-day research conducted by specialist medical teams in university hospitals across the United States offers an intriguing probability – that the legends are not legends at all, but fact. Naturally, many remain less than convinced and the evidence for the survival of the human consciousness seemingly provided by the near-death experience has been vigorously challenged by members of the medical establishment and other sceptics of an afterlife. Critics of the research undertaken by specialists only rarely question the probity of those who have survived a close call with death; rarely do they dispute the qualifications of those researchers who have interviewed them. Instead, their objections focus upon the purported reality of the experience itself. Possible alternative explanations offered for these near-death memories are numerous and varied, but they have key elements in common. Broadly speaking, sceptics assert the following non-survivalist scenarios: (i) Patients who seemingly die only to recover, were not really dead in the first place. (ii) Their brains and nervous system continue to function unobserved by those attempting to revive them. (iii) Their so-called memories are merely hallucinations brought about by their abnormal condition.

Specifically, disbelievers have pointed to a number of ways whereby the brain can be fooled into believing it is experiencing reality which is in fact an illusion. One idea put forward suggests the dying person is suffering from a form of delirium brought about by diminishing oxygen supply to their brain cells – a condition termed hypoxia which has been known to induce hallucinations in the minds of mountaineers climbing at high altitudes. Another theory, suggested mainly by psychiatrists, relates the after-death experience to a rare medical condition known as autoscopy. The autoscopic phenomenon occurs when a person under extreme psychological stress sees a mirror image of him or herself – a vision which, as some doctors have pointed out, bears comparison with accounts of people looking down upon their own bodies from a distance several feet above. A further suggestion advanced by sceptics is that the administration of narcotic drugs to the seriously injured might in itself create the hallucinogenic condition under which the near-death experience regularly occurs.

For my money, the doubters are wasting their time. Even the strongest disbelievers in the literal reality of the near-death experience are honest enough to admit that none of these explanations, whether taken individually or collectively, can account for the sheer consistency and similarity of recollections. Morcover, not only do these natural explanations fail to provide a general theory for the mystery, they do not even stand up with regard to the examination of many individual cases. The hypoxiac state, for instance, differs markedly from the ecosomatic state in a number of ways. Generally speaking, those suffering oxygen deficiency demonstrate irritability, sluggishness of thought and (afterwards) poor memory recollection; in contrast, those who enter the ecosomatic state following the cessation of bodily functions recall, usually with intensity and clarity of detail, heightened emotions bordering on euphoria and enhanced powers of vision and concentration. As Dr Michael Sabom has pointed out, countering the hypoxiac explanation, there have been no reports of hypoxiacs recalling sensations of floating or leaving their body.

In the same way, the second explanation – the autoscopic phenomenon (mainly associated with the mental condition of schizophrenia) would seem to differ in important respects from that of the near-death experience. According to the testimony of those who suffer autoscopy, their illusory 'self' can be seen with apparent life and movement, whereas the physical body seen by those in the ecosomatic state appears exactly as it is in

reality, inert and motionless. Viewed dispassionately the
autoscopy theory falls down on a number of counts, not
least because only very few people who return from death
are themselves schizophrenics. Indeed, any explanation
which looks towards the possibility that near-death
experiencers are suffering from a type of personality
disorder must be entirely lacking in credibility.

The third 'natural' explanation mentioned above –
that the ecosomatic state is an illusion brought about
by the application of narcotics – seems to many sceptics
to be the strongest possibility. But here once again
researchers into the near-death experience have their
own counter-objections. Whilst it would be true to
say that pain-killing narcotics (many of which have an
opium base) are regularly administered to dying patients,
it would be quite wrong to assume this applies to all cases
of near-death experience. In every study carried out by
researchers to date, there are many instances where the
subject received no drugs or other medication (including
anaesthetic) prior to leaving their body. Moreover, as
Dr Raymond Moody pointed out in his breakthrough
work, the majority of drugs administered to patients in
hospitals have no effect on the central nervous system.
Once again there would appear to be no sound basis
for an objective refutation of the ecosomatic state based
upon the purported hallucinogenic drugs hypothesis.

Even though alternative physical explanations for the
near-death experience evidently lack credibility, many
psychologists persist in believing they are little more than
dreams based on archetypal images and subconscious
wish-fulfilments. This blanket denial of the evidence
seems to me to have little to recommend it. It may
be true that the sensation of floating or flying during
normal sleep-state dreaming is common, but even so,
most dreams are disjointed affairs containing clearly

unreal elements, whereas the early part of the near-death experience corresponds to real physical locations. The vividness of the experience, and the clarity of the recall both differ greatly from that of a normal dream, the details of which are often jumbled in the person's mind and quickly forgotten upon waking. Those who return from a close brush with death never forget the experience.

Perhaps the strongest evidence of all is the fact that, upon reviving, patients have occasionally gained access to information to which they were not privy, describing events around them which took place after their bodily functions had ceased. One typical example concerns Sir Oliver Oyston, a distinguished British soldier who recalled an astral flight he experienced while critically ill with typhoid in a Boer War field hospital. Considered a hopeless case by doctors treating him, Oyston felt himself rise from his physical body one night and float unhindered through the walls of wards and beyond. In one small room some distance away from his own bed, he witnessed the unpleasant sight of a young surgeon undergoing death agonies from the same illness. The next morning Oyston recovered to tell astonished medical staff of his nocturnal soul flight. Doctors were able to confirm that details of the young surgeon's last moments were exactly as Oyston described.

Medical science has no explanation for the way in which those who are clinically dead – showing no signs of respiratory function, heartbeat or electrical nerve functions – can report knowledge of events taking place around them in the operating theatre or scene of an accident. There is an abundance of such examples, however, in all the books written by US investigators over the past fifteen years. Some are truly breath-taking in specific detail. For example, in 1974, a female patient of Dr Kenneth Ring, who 'died' on the operating table, afterwards told the researcher how she saw dust on top of the operating theatre lights while floating just below the ceiling. The woman also described accurately a sequence of numbers which appeared on a machine wired up to her physical body, a detail later corroborated by the anaesthetist present at the time. Dr Maurice Rawlings, meanwhile, recalls in his book *Beyond Death's Door* how he helped to revive a student nurse who had attempted suicide by hanging herself from a coat hook. By the time Rawlings found the girl she had stopped breathing and her face had a bluish pallor, but after the surgeon had administered the kiss of life she began to show signs of recovery. Still, the nurse remained in a coma for several days and it was not until some weeks afterwards in conversation that Rawlings realized she had undergone an ecosomatic experience. She was not only able to describe precisely his attempts to resuscitate her, but also the clothes he had been wearing on the day of her suicide attempt.

Even sceptics of the near-death experience admit there is much in these stories which cannot be explained. In his book entitled *The After Death Experience*, the English writer Ian Wilson, a noted debunker of matters paranormal, includes several interesting cases including one reported by Professor Kimberly Clark of the University of Washington. Clark's example involved a woman who was suffering a cardiac arrest while in the hospital; she afterwards recalled floating upwards through several floors, finally ending up in a storeroom she had never physically entered, and that she was unlikely to know existed. There, while on her astral journey, she noticed an old tennis shoe laying discarded on top of a locker, out of the sight of normal vision. Intrigued by her story, Dr Clark set out to check these details and found them to be in all ways correct, even down to the tennis shoe's manufacturer. In the words of the American doctor, 'Only someone who was twelve feet tall, or was floating just above the ceiling, could have noticed it there. In any case the woman had never been in the room.'

For Dr Clark this single remarkable story was concrete evidence that out-of-body flights occurred. In fact such accounts abound in the researches of near-death experience investigators. In his *Recollections of Death*, Dr Michael Sabom published no less than six in-depth descriptions from patients who recalled in meticulous detail accounts of their own operations, purportedly viewed while floating above their body. Comparisons with surgeons' notes confirmed the accuracy of the memories. One investigator, Dr Elisabeth Kubler-Ross, has even uncovered examples of visual descriptions recalled by the physically blind – descriptions containing accurate and verifiable facts such as the colour and designs of surgical garments worn by doctors and other medical staff who attended their resuscitation. Needless to say, there is no conceivable way a blind person could be aware of such details through any natural process, yet the return of sight is entirely in accordance with spiritualistic belief regarding the nature of the astral counterpart. Once more, given the inability of sceptics to construct a physical or psychological explanation for these enigmas, one is inevitably drawn towards the probability that the parapsychological explanation is nearer the truth.

The universality of the near-death experience is demonstrated most strikingly when one considers that even young children appear to undergo the same process. In the early 1980s a Seattle paediatrician, Dr Melia Morse, made a special study of young patients in the city's children's orthopaedic hospital. In conversation

with youngsters who had suffered temporary clinical
death (mainly through cardiac arrest or drowning), the
doctor discovered that many recalled experiences which
had much in common with those collected in the earlier
research of doctors Moody, Sabom and others. One
eight-year-old diabetic girl who recovered from a near-
fatal coma remembered floating above the operating
table. A six-year-old boy whose heart had stopped
beating when complications set in during routine ton-
sillitis surgery, recalled going down a long dark tunnel
towards light. A sixteen-year-old who died for almost
ten minutes after a circulatory collapse, afterwards spoke
of going 'halfway to Heaven'. Crosschecking a total
of thirty near-death cases with a sample of similar
number who had simply been unconscious for extended
periods of time following concussion and treated in the
hospital's intensive care unit, Morse found that none
of the second group displayed similar recollections. He
deduced therefore that the core near-death feelings (of
travelling down a tunnel towards light, meeting dead
relatives, seeing heavenly visions) were specific to cases
in which patients underwent a period of physical death
or came very close to it. At the same time, he dismissed
entirely the notion that these children had undergone an
experience based upon what they expected death to be
like. Clearly, none would have read the Tibetan *Bardo
Thodol* or been familiar with aspects of Eastern mystical
philosophy, and the fact that many came from atheistic
family backgrounds further lessened the likelihood that
their minds were grouping together fantasies based upon
stories learned in Sunday school.

A similar study by Margot Grey, a member of the
British Society for Psychical Research, has recently
produced complementary evidence to that uncovered
by Dr Morse. One example which particularly interested

Grey concerned a Pakistani girl who, whilst apparently dying from an extreme toxic condition, seemed to meet her great-grandfather – a man whom she had never seen in life, nor even in a photograph.

Having recovered from the ailment which brought her to the brink of physical death, the girl was able to describe her great-grandfather's appearance in detail. When told the story, neither of her parents believed it until a group of relatives flew to Britain for a wedding the following year. Looking through a photograph album, the girl was able to point out the face of the man she had seen during her near-death experience. It was indeed her great-grandfather who had died many years before she was born.

The controversy surrounding the near-death experience, which began in earnest with the publication in 1975 of Dr Raymond Moody's *Life After Life*, shows no sign of abating. On one side there are the sceptics who, often ignoring the most convincing cases, continue to assert the enigma to be a dream or malfunction of the brain; on the other side we have those who claim NDEs prove that the human consciousness survives physical death. The fact that most of those who have undertaken NDE research fall firmly into the latter category, has tended to cast a shadow over the partiality of their conclusions. Yet this is surely unfair. Whilst some researchers such as Raymond Moody may occasionally have been overzealous in making claims for the value of their work, the fact remains that a truly staggering body of documentary evidence now exists to support the notion that the human mind and the human body are not inseparable. To write off such evidence wholesale, as some rationalists attempt to do, is an act of intellectual dishonesty.

Are those who undergo such experiences really dead

at the time that they are supposed to have left their body? Hard though it may be for some to accept, distinguished medical figures on both sides of the Atlantic consider this to be a facile question. According to every established method of distinguishing between the states of life and death, many patients really have died only to be resuscitated in modern hospitals. As medical science progresses, it is inevitable that the number of such cases will increase. Speaking of her own findings in an interview published in *People Magazine* in November 1975, the Swiss psychiatrist Dr Elizabeth Kubler-Ross wrote, 'I have investigated cases from Australia to California, including patients from the ages of two to ninety-six. I have found . . . very clear cases from all over the world. One had been dead for twelve and a half hours. All these people experienced the same thing.' It could have been any one of a dozen researchers talking. Kenneth Ring, now head of the newly founded International Association for Near-Death Studies at the University of Connecticut, concedes that his work will always fail to satisfy all critics. But his own opinions on the subject remain undiminished, 'I do believe – not just on the basis of my own or others' data regarding near-death experiences – that we continue to have a conscious existence after our physical death and that the core experience does represent its beginning, evidence of things to come.' Although Kenneth Ring dislikes the word soul because of its religious connotations, he admits 'with considerable intellectual reluctance', that the Being of Light so often seen during NDEs would appear to represent a higher self or aspect of God. Michael Sabom, once a disbeliever, has carefully considered and eventually rejected alternative explanations for NDEs such as dreams, hallucinations, induced delusions or mental impressions caused by drastic changes in the brain prior to death. Whilst noting that some drugs such as LSD produce visions which can include features similar to some aspects of the NDE (such as trips down a tunnel), Sabom is certain that the application of hospital anaesthetic would not produce similar chemical changes in the dying brain. Nor, for him, would such a physiological viewpoint explain how so many of his patients accurately reported the details of resuscitation efforts that occurred while they were unconscious.

Since these men and women began their research a decade and a half ago the true value of the near-death experience has remained a subject of much controversy and interest. As of 1987, at least forty scholars and researchers in the United States alone were active in NDE research. The International Association for Near-Death Studies publishes *Anabiosis*, a scholarly journal on the subject, and one can find psychiatry text books describing NDE research in university libraries across the country. It is no exaggeration to say that virtually every single expert currently working in the field would appear to have reached virtually the same conclusion: namely that all existing data relating to the moment of death is more consistent with transition than extinction.

Perhaps in the years to come medical investigations into the enigma of NDE will be accepted as proof of the survival of the human spirit. I tend to feel, however, that no matter how overwhelming the evidence eventually becomes, many will still prefer to ignore it. For those who have already been on the other side – the experiencers themselves – there is no need for further proof. They have seen beyond the veil for themselves and know that the Valley of Death is not a frightening place. For many who have been close to death, their brief return trip to the next world has marked a turning point in their earthly lives. No longer half-believing in the afterlife as an abstract possibility, they see it as both real and inevitable. 'Seeing is believing' is as true for the believer as it is for the sceptic. Perhaps we should envy them. As the Buddha wrote: 'Better than the life of a hundred years of the man who perceiveth not the deathless state, is the short life of a single day of the man who senses the deathless state.'

The Phoenix Fire Mystery

The soul of man is like to water;
From Heaven it cometh
To Heaven it riseth
And then returneth to earth,
Forever alternating.

J.W. Von Goethe
Song of the Spirits over the Waters

I have lived before many times. Or at least so I am reliably told. Perhaps I'd better explain. In the early 1980s, while attending a circle for developing psychic awareness, I found myself surrounded by people who not only claimed the ability to speak to the dead, but also to recall a multitude of past lives going back thousands of years. This did not mean that they were unique as a group. It was simply that, as psychics, they could tune in to their own pasts, whereas most people forget their previous lives at the moment of birth. If today, the idea of rebirth seems highly plausible, then it certainly did not appear so at the time. Although impressed by their evident sincerity, there seemed to be little in their remembrances to indicate a first hand knowledge of historical eras. At the same time, I became convinced that many were creating remarkable pasts to justify a belief that they had been given special spiritual missions in their present incarnation.

Some even seemed to feel that they were the reborn souls of saints and minor biblical characters. I was actually

assured by one lady, in deadly earnest, that I was myself
the reincarnation of a high priest who had worked in
the Temple of Greatest Mystery where Jesus had been
initiated as the Christ 2,000 years before!.

The psychic self-aggrandizement so prevalent among
this group prejudiced my mind against the possibility of
reincarnation for several years. Not so today, however.
For whilst the claimed recollections of these 'old souls'
should continue to be taken with a large pinch of salt,
there has emerged over the last two decades evidence of
a different kind, and in such quantity that it now seems
ridiculous to deny it.

In the summer of 1979, a San Fransisco child psychotherapist named Dr Helen Wambach was presented with
a case so mysterious that at first she did not know where
to begin to unravel it. The subject was Jeremy Anderson,
a four-year-old boy from Waukomis, Oklahoma. The
child's problem was that he had spent most of his young
life believing he was somebody else. A hyperactive child
who suffered constant nightmares, Jeremy had, since the
age of two, made up stories in which he invariably died
violently, almost always in the same manner – crashing
a car head-on into a heavily laden wagon. Although
family doctors had been unable to understand the force
disturbing Jeremy's mind, or the peculiar intensity of his
fantasies, Jeremy's parents noticed an uncanny similarity
between their son's daily play-deaths and the real-life
traffic accident which killed his uncle, James Houser,
some twelve years before. Indeed, Nancy Anderson,
Jeremy's grandmother, had come to believe the boy was
the spirit of her dead son returned to earth. Her conviction
was reinforced by the fact that her living grandson always
insisted his true name was Jimmy and frequently refused
to answer to his own Christian name.

A modern day example of reincarnation from Middle

America? To begin with Helen Wambach was sceptical. As a practising psychotherapist well acquainted with the complexities of the young mind, she was inclined to search for a more down-to-earth cause for the boy's regular traumas. Gradually, however, the sheer consistency of the child's imaginings began to undermine her faith in a conventional explanation. Moreover, as hypnotherapy progressed, Wambach realized that the Anderson enigma bore marked similarities to a famous case of purported reincarnation from India – the Shanti Devi story. Born in Delhi in 1926, the young Shanti Devi had claimed, almost from the moment she had learned to speak, that she was the returned soul of a merchant's wife from Muttra, a town some one hundred miles from her home in the capital city. Although most people refused to believe her, not least her own family, Shanti Devi's story was eventually strengthened when her supposed former husband, a merchant named Kedar Nath, confirmed many details the girl had given of his deceased wife's life. Subsequently, when taken to her former home in Muttra, the child was able to recognize relatives and even pinpoint the place where 'she' and Kedar Nath had hidden a box of money many years before.

The apparent similarities between the Indian girl's story and that of her own patient troubled Dr Wambach greatly. Knowing full well that rebirth is central to the faith and culture of the Indian sub-continent she had never considered the mystery from earlier in the century to be trustworthy evidence for reincarnation. She was also well aware that few people in the United States would lend credence to a similar story involving a boy from a Mid-Western state; indeed she remained far from convinced herself. Even so, the mystery had to be unravelled somehow. . . .

Putting her professional reputation on the line, Wambach

suggested that the Anderson family join her in a trip to the scene of James Houser's last moments – the spot where he died along with a friend in a collision with a wagon in 1967. For all concerned it was a risk that proved worth-while. Despite having never been there before, young Jeremy Anderson became highly emotional when they approached the scene of the fatal accident. Through his sobs he described to astonished listeners how he had once lived in the body of another person and died after being thrown clear from the still-moving vehicle twelve years before. All the details the child remembered were in accordance with the known facts of the crash which claimed his uncle's life. All, that is, except one – Jeremy Anderson insisted that he had been driving his friend's car whereas the police accident report concluded that Houser, who did not hold a driving licence, was occupying the passenger seat at the moment of impact. To Dr Helen Wambach this seemed a flaw which significantly lessened the likelihood of true past-life memory; ironically, it was to provide the key detail which eventually convinced her that some form of reincarnation had occurred.

Investigating the circumstances of the 1967 accident further, Dr Wambach contacted not only the state police department but the undertaker who had prepared James Houser's body for burial over a decade before. The man clearly recalled noticing chest injuries to the corpse which were, he felt, consistent with those suffered by a driver, rather than a passenger. It was a detail of which none of the Anderson family had ever been aware, thus cancelling out the possibility that the child's memory of the incident could have been built up from descriptions overheard from adult family members. From that moment on, the mind of one West Coast psychotherapist was open to possibilities undreamt of by Sigmund Freud. Today Dr Wambach runs a practice in which patients are encouraged, under hypnotism, to recall past lives; few fail to do so and she has many hundreds of cases on record to prove it. Can it really be possible that some people have actually lived before, and if so is it true of the whole of mankind? As we shall see in the next two chapters, the evidence for reincarnation is perhaps more compelling and more significant than anything we have so far considered in the case against death.

Helen Wambach was correct to follow a line of enquiry that sought to establish concrete proof for reincarnation – the US medical authorities would lose no time in condemning a fellow professional who chose to reject established psychiatric procedure in favour of a half-baked esoteric hypothesis. However, whilst the majority of the medico-scientific establishment continue to laugh at the notion of past-life memories, recent statistical evidence suggests that Wambach's theory may well have found a more positive response among the general public. In 1982, a Gallup poll uncovered the startling fact that nearly one American in four believed in the strong probability of rebirth. The United States was by no means exceptional among Western nations. A similar survey published in the British *Sunday Telegraph* three years earlier, reported reincarnation belief running at twenty-eight per cent in the United Kingdom, whilst a *Times* questionnaire the following year showed much the same story – twenty-nine per cent affirming belief from a response of over 1,300 adult readers.

In the East, where the major religions hold rebirth as a central tenet of their creed, these would be surprisingly low figures; in the Western developed countries, where reincarnation has played little or no part in the development of Christianity and Judaism, the figure seems unaccountably high. Belief that we have all led many lives is certainly on the increase, a fact which must in itself be of considerable interest not only to an investigator like myself but also to theologians and social psychologists. Yet the idea of reincarnation is by no means new to Western thought. Indeed, those who affirmed belief to the opinion pollsters can count themselves as being among celebrated company. When we look at the history of the past two centuries, the list of famous names who shared a belief in the philosophy of rebirth is quite remarkable. The roll call includes rulers Napoleon Bonaparte and Fredrick the Great of Russia; philosophers Immanuel Kant and Friedrich Nietzche; statesmen Benjamin Franklin and David Lloyd George; scientists Thomas Edison and Pierre Curie. Both the industrialist Henry Ford and the soldier George Patton recalled past lives; humanist Albert Schweitzer and pioneer psychologist C.G. Jung saw valuable truths in the idea of transmigration a hundred years after thinkers Thomas Carlyle and Henry Thoreau had reached the same conclusion.

Those of an artisic bent – authors, painters and composers – figure more commonly than any other group: Goethe, Balzac, Tolstoy, Victor Hugo, Emerson, Edgar Allan Poe, Herman Melville, H.G. Wells, W.B. Yeats, D.H. Lawrence, Henry Miller, Walt Whitman and J.B. Priestly . . . all of these writers could recall earlier existences or believed passionately that their present incarnation was not their first. Likewise, Wagner and Mahler, Gauguin and Salvador Dali each knew they would be reborn in different bodies. Actors are also richly represented, notable believers from the modern era including Sylvester Stallone, Peter Sellers, Glenn Ford and, of course, Shirley Maclaine, the Hollywood actress who makes something of a cottage industry from her own pastlife recollections.

Some readers will no doubt be surprised that so many Western figures of proven mental calibre should have chosen to embrace this 'absurd Oriental superstition'. However, this is to misunderstand the truly universal nature of the doctrine of pre-existence and the reasons for its impact upon the development of human society, East and West. Moreover, to describe it as a 'superstition' would be to ignore the vast amount of hard evidence that has emerged during the present century – documented case histories which lead towards the conclusion that we have all experienced previous lives and are destined to return again and again after our present existence is over.

We need not look far to discover a pattern of rebirth in the visible world. The natural cycle of death and regeneration appears all around us. The ebb and flow of the tides from which water rises in vapour and falls once again as rain; the perpetual alternations of day and night, waking and sleeping; the eternal following of winter by spring. So fundamental is the theme of this underlying cyclic system in all levels of the manifested universe, that many great thinkers East and West have concluded that a similar system of palingenesis – continuous death and rebirth – must apply also to the unseen realms of spirit. Such a belief is by no means confounded by revealed scientific truth. Indeed, the centuries-old Taoist philosophies of ancient China appear to be born out by recent discoveries in the invisible microcosm of the sub-atomic world, where particles are instantaneously obliterated and created in continual transmutation from matter to energy and back again. Using radio telescopes to look out into the incomprehensible vastness of the universe, astronomers have discovered the death and rebirth of entire galaxies and solar systems, while within our own bodies, even as we go about our daily business, millions of cells are dying every hour to be replaced by others newly created from ingested material.

It is the realization that death is merely nature's way of bringing about new life that underpins the philosophies of the great reincarnationist religions of the East. Hindu belief in transmigration holds that all life – human, animal, plant and mineral – is tied to a wheel of personal fortune, a wheel upon which souls travel in an upward spiral of learning gained through trial and error. Their personal destiny (karma) leads them through hundreds of incarnations and thousands of years from beast to man, from tyrant to saint, until their souls eventually reach a state of perfection. Only then, when they have achieved this purified level do they cease to be reborn into the world of matter. Under the karmic law of cause and effect, a soul's progress (samsara) may lead it to rise or fall, and incarnations, which can be of either sex, are always the most appropriate for the degree of development attained. Each individual's destiny is their own responsibility and severe transgressions can result in a future incarnation in the body of a beast. Thus karma can be likened to a game of cosmic snakes and ladders, though each player's fate is not subject to chance. No soul may count itself unlucky to be inhabiting a particular body, even that of a cripple, for each incarnation has been chosen according to that soul's level of spiritual understanding. We get our just deserts, no more, no less.

Buddhist teachings are profoundly similar to Hindu beliefs, although Buddhists hold the view that each separate incarnation is simply a facet of the previous one, rather than a complete, journeying soul. Following death, Buddhists believe that the personality, by then separated from its physical chains, passes across a threshold into a realm beyond our conscious knowledge called the

Bardo-state, a multi-dimensional plane of pure being which is far closer to reality than anything we might know on earth. Here (in a way I have outlined earlier with regard to the teachings of the Bardo Thodol) the discarnate human entity may meet other souls it knew on earth, and be subjected to sensory illusions at once more pleasurable or more frightening than any formerly imagined possible. Whether this realm is pleasant or unpleasant will depend on the person's previous life; in the Bardo-state a man may make his own heaven or hell. In one Buddhist text it is written, 'As men think, so are they, both here and hereafter . . . as the sowing has been, so will the harvest be.' Thus the discarnate soul travels this wonderland of the dead for a variable duration until it finally realizes that it must return to earth to continue its progress upon the karmic cycle. Before it chooses its next life it must review and judge its thoughts and actions in the previous one, and as the time for the reunion with the earthy plane draws near, its consciousness is cloaked in forgetfulness, the new-born child recalling little or nothing of the Bardo world it has so recently left behind.

Although Hinduism and Buddhism contain subtle differences in religious interpretation, their similarities are more striking. Both religions share the dual conceptions of transmigration and the gradual karmic purification of the spirit through successive lifetimes. Both hold that only through achieving perfection can a soul step off the wheel of life into a permanent heavenly state, or as Buddhists term it, 'nirvana'. It is not surprising therefore, that both great faiths should share roots in the pre-Christian world of south-east Asia. Gautama Buddha, the avatar who could recall 500 lives before his enlightenment, lived between 563 and 483 BC. The Upanishads, the Bible equivalent of the Hindu creed, were probably written during the previous century. Both religions would seem to have had their beginnings in the Indian subcontinent.

Most Westerners assume, erroneously, that the emergence of the two major Eastern faiths marked the advent of the doctrine of reincarnation in human thought. Nothing could be further than the truth, nor was the East its starting point. The *Eleusinian Mysteries*, a Greek tract written fifteen centuries before Hindus adopted the karmic principle, mentions the 'sorrowful wheel' of death and rebirth. The idea crops up once more in the *Orphic Mysteries* from the seventh century BC, and again in the writings of Plotinus and Plato, particularly in the latter's *Theory of Reminiscence*. Across the Mediterranean there is much evidence that reincarnation was an old belief at the time of the Pharoahs (the phoenix itself is an ancient Egyptian symbol), whilst the early religions of the Northern Europeans – the Gauls, Celts and Druids – all bear strong affinity to the idea of the cycle of death and rebirth throughout all things.

All available evidence now suggests that belief in reincarnation was a truly worldwide concept throughout early civilizations – 'among the primordial affirmations of mankind', in the words of the great psychologist C.G. Jung. The idea was no less strong among tribal cultures. Ethnologists studying the belief systems of the Tlingit and Haida Indians of Alaska have noticed marked similarities to the Hindu doctrine of karma. Similar studies elsewhere in the world have shown comparable beliefs to underlie religions in native cultures as far apart as West Africa, Venezuela, Australia and Lebanon. As one researcher has written, 'The idea of rebirth would seem to be anthropologically innate.' Given the near-universal acceptance of rebirth, one can only wonder why it plays so small a part in Christian theology. In fact, this may not always have been the case, though for the past 1500 years it certainly has been. Historical evidence only recently discovered by Catholic scholars has demonstrated that in the year AD 553 an important meeting of church leaders, the Fifth Ecumenical Council, under the direction of Roman Emperor Justinian, anathematized (cursed) the doctrine of the pre-existence of souls. Any Christian who thereafter professed a faith in reincarnation would face excommunication or death, and rebirth was effectively excluded from orthodox Christianity from that moment onward.

Could the early Christians have embraced reincarnation? Some verses of the New Testament suggest that they did. In Matt. 16: 13–14, Jesus asks his disciples who the ordinary people believed he was. They replied: 'Some say thou art John the Baptist; some Elias; and others Jeremias; or one of the prophets.' Since all those listed were long-since dead, apart from John who had been executed the previous year, it would not be too difficult to draw the conclusion that first-century Jewish belief encompassed the possibility of the soul's return. Later the Messiah confided to his followers that John had been the returned soul of Elijah who lived centuries before. Intriguingly, the closing lines of the Old Testament include Malachi's prophecy which seemed to confirm the Lord's words: 'Behold, I will send you Elijah the prophet before the coming of the great and dreadful day of the Lord.' Saul of Tarsus, in his letter to the Galatians 4: 19, touches upon the reincarnation theme when he talks of mankind, 'travelling in birth again until Christ be formed . . .'. The key word is surely *again*. The idea of a soul slowly evolving towards a state of perfection, or Christhood, bears marked similarity to the Hindu idea of the karmic wheel leading towards a plane of pure consciousness where further rebirth becomes unnecessary. The basic principle of karmic law, cause and effect, may

play little or no part in received Christian theology, yet it
is echoed throughout the Testaments. Jesus himself said
that, 'Those who live by the sword shall die by the sword,'
whilst Paul warned that, 'As ye sow, so shall ye reap',
words which surely bear more than a passing resemblance
to the Buddhist text quoted·earlier.

Whatever these Biblical references may or may not
prove, there is firm historical evidence that some early
Christian groups such as the Gnostics, as well as some
Jewish sects, most notably the Essenes, certainly *did*
believe in the palingenesis of the human soul and suffered
persecution for it. Centuries later the Cathars likewise
held to a doctrine of metempsychosis – continual rebirth
until a level of purity is reached which allows the soul
to be delivered into Heaven – before they and their
ideas were systematically exterminated by the Inquisition.
The Cathars, like the Gnostics before them, accepted
that Jesus was an example of a soul who had achieved
perfection through many previous lives, and not a divine
entity separate and distinct from the rest of the human
race. It is a doctrine which has much in common with the
attitudes of Eastern devotees to their own avatars. These
early groups might have had a much greater influence on
the development of the Christian tradition had it not been
for their ruthless suppression by the established religious
authorities of the day. As it was, this lost chord of Christian faith played almost no part in the development of
European religious thought until the nineteenth century
saw the emergence of Theosophy and the birth of the
Spiritualist movement.

Of course the fact that rebirth has been a near-
universally held belief for thousands of years in virtually
every part of the planet at some time or another, does
not in itself constitute proof of its reality. After all,
the majority of people during most of the same period

also thought the world was flat! In order to establish whether these faiths have a grounding in firm evidence we must look closely at those people who today claim remembrances of past lives. Here, inevitably, the most interesting will be instances in which people can recall factual details to which they could not conceivably have gained access in their present incarnation. Some, like the bestselling memoirs of actress Shirley Maclaine, are useless. Whilst they might be entertaining to her fans, her descriptions of the past contain few details which can be verified and virtually nothing that might not otherwise have been studied by any reasonably intelligent adult with access to a public reference library. Fortunately for the serious investigator, some past life remembrances are a different matter entirely. . . .

Children, especially those very young, are unlikely to have the opportunity to acquire great knowledge beyond their immediate childhood experience and it is no surprise that investigators consider the most interesting past-life recollections to be those which come, literally, from out of the mouths of babes and sucklings. There is no shortage of examples, the cases of Jeremy Anderson and Shanti Devi being just two among literally hundreds recorded over the past century. Viewed objectively the evidence they provide is mind-blowing. In many cases children have not only accurately described people, places and customs about which they could have no knowledge; some have even manifested bizarre and alarming signs of their former selves, usually birthmarks corresponding to wounds suffered at their earlier moments of death. Others show peculiar psychological traits incompatible with their age: hungerings for adult pleasures such as alcohol, tobacco or sexual intercourse. A few find it hard to acclimatize to their new sexual identities and follow instead the dress and habits of the opposite gender. In such cases it is extremely rare for their personality disorders to be cured through conventional child psychiatry.

One of the most dramatic examples to emerge from the modern era is the case of Reena Gupta, from New Dehli, India, who was less than two years old when, in 1966, she first told her grandmother she had a gharada (husband), a wicked man who had killed her and now languished in prison for his crime. Reena was not believed, but as she grew up, she never lost the conviction that she had lived and died before. Consequently, she would often infuriate her mother when, on shopping expeditions to the market, she would search for familiar faces from the past, hoping that such a recognition might meet with a favourable reaction. Then one day by chance, a teacher friend of Reena's mother called Vijendra heard a tragic story about a Sikh family which involved the murder of a young wife by her husband; the dead woman was named Gurdeep Singh. Realizing that the background of the Sikh's history closely mirrored events recalled by Reena Gupta, Vijendra tracked the family down to their home which was situated in another suburb of the Indian capital. There, finding the dead woman's gharada was in prison for the killing, she spoke to the parents of the murdered Gurdeep Singh. Though reluctant at first, they eventually agreed to meet Reena who recognized them immediately and without introduction as her own mother and father. In their astonished presence, the little girl recalled many events of her former childhood, including the origin of the unusual nickname by which Gurdeep's younger sister had been known. Subsequently, when she was taken to meet other members of her former family, the girl was able to recognize them also, and several years later, when an adolescent in the 1970s, she even agreed to pose for a photograph with 'her' suspicious and somewhat bemused murderer husband.

Another Indian case, this time from the previous decade, would appear to be even more conclusive. In 1953, as soon as two-year-old Ravi Shankar had learned to talk coherently, he began to mention his former life in a neighbouring district. If Ravi's parents found his utterances disturbing they were far more shocked when he told them that he had been brutally murdered while still a boy, identifying his assailants by name and occupation. Two years later when Ravi was four, a man who had heard about his odd memories visited Ravi's family and told them that his own six-year-old son had been killed some nine months before Ravi's birth. The man was anxious to find out the identity of his own son's killers and wondered whether there was truly a connection between the two boys. He ended up being quite convinced that there was.

To begin with Ravi recognized the man and correctly guessed that his occupation was a barber. Secondly, when he described several of his previous-life toys – a wooden elephant, a ball on an elastic string, and a toy pistol – it became clear that the barber's son had also owned such items. Moreover, Ravi was also able to describe a ring owned by his former father, always kept in a locked desk. His account of the murder incident seemed to the bereaved man to be even more strikingly accurate. Like the man's son, Ravi said that he had had his throat cut, and the names and occupations of the men he identified as his slayers matched those of two men who had been arrested by police for the murder but later released due to lack of evidence. In a further corresponding detail, Ravi suggested that he had been eating guavas immediately prior to the fatal attack and this too proved to be the case with the barber's son. Connections between the two

boys were not confined to Ravi's memory. Not only was
the child too afraid to venture near the area where the first
boy had been killed, but his physical body seemed also to
bear witness to the crime. When Ravi was three months
old an eerie scar had appeared on his neck. Some two
inches long and a quarter inch wide, the mark appeared
to have the stippled quality of a scar, and one doctor who
examined the boy described it as looking much like, 'the
old scar of a healed knife wound'.

Though many examples of past-life recall arise out of
Eastern countries they are by no means the majority. In
1981, Romy Crees, a toddler from Des Moines, Iowa,
began telling her parents that she was a married man
named Joe Williams who had died several years before
in a motorcycle accident, leaving a wife Sheila, and three
children. Little Romy pleaded to be allowed to go and
see her family, who she said, lived in Charles City, a
community some hundred and forty miles away from
Des Moines. As devout Catholics and therefore firm
disbelievers in reincarnation, Romy's parents were more
inclined to think their child was possessed by the Devil
than the returned spirit of another person. However,
when an exorcism failed to remove the impression from
the girl's mind, the Crees called in a child psychiatrist
named Dr Hemendra Bannerjee.

In the same way that Dr Helen Wambach had become
convinced by the intensity of young Jeremy Anderson's
recollections of his moment of death, Bannerjee quickly
came to realize that his own initial scepticism was
unfounded. An expedition to Charles City was arranged
during which the toddler was able to identify correctly
many locations, even finding her alleged previous home.
There, the death of Joe Williams in a motorcycle accident
was confirmed by his widow Sheila, along with several
other key details of their relationship that could hardly

have been guessed by a two-year-old child living a hundred miles away. The parents of Romy Crees were left with little choice but to accept reluctantly that rebirth was the most likely explanation. Meanwhile, Dr Hemendra Bannerjee has, like Dr Helen Wambach before him, reviewed his own psychiatric practice to include the possibility of factors stemming from past lives.

Most researchers of the reincarnation enigma seek to verify cases by corroborating details obtained through interviews with established historical records. The first person to adopt this qualitative approach was Dr Ian Stevenson, director of the division of parapsychology at the University of Virginia. Stevenson's book *Twenty Cases Suggestive of Reincarnation*, has become a classic of the genre and his lifetime of research (which continues today) provides us with the most authorative body of evidence supportive of reincarnation available in any language.

Dr Stevenson originally became interested in the possibility of rebirth after hearing a curious story from an Alaskan Indian village. The tale concerned the apparent return to earth of one William George Senior, a fisherman who, shortly before his own death, told his son that he would be reborn from the womb of his son's wife; people would, he said, know that his prediction had come true since birthmarks upon the baby's skin would correspond with blemishes upon the old man's body. In August 1949 William George Senior drowned in a fishing expedition; sure enough his daughter-in-law became pregnant and gave birth to a son bearing birthmarks uncannily similar to those of his grandfather. As a mark of respect he was named William George Junior. Thereafter, the growing William demonstrated a precocious knowledge of his namesake's old fishing haunts, as well as extraordinary skill in making catches. Visiting the Indian village for himself and staying with the family, Stevenson concluded that the boy's knowledge of his dead grandfather's ways and habits 'transcended what he could have learned by normal means'. Apart from the similarity of the birthmarks (which photographs proved to be virtually identical), the investigator found nineteen separate points of major correlation regarding information known only to the grandfather and grandson. With his curiosity aroused, Stevenson began his life's work – the hunting down and analysis of memories of previous lives. It is a quest which has taken him across every continent of the world and brought him into conflict with both scientific and religious establishments.

In a typical Stevenson case, a child (usually between the ages of two and four) starts to tell its parents, and anyone else who will care to listen, that he or she can remember being someone else. The child's statements concerning its previous life are nearly always accompanied by behaviour which is alien to the child's background but which harmonizes with elements of the past existence. According to Stevenson, these recollections may increase in intensity between the ages of two and four but are only rarely remembered after the age of five, for reasons which remain unclear. This pattern is repeated irrespective of the child's religious or cultural background. As a general rule Stevenson found that rebirth was taking place in every corner of the globe and following a pattern which was largely repeated whatever the child's religious or ethnic background. There were, however, one or two minor variations. For example, the likely interval between lives tended to be shorter in those cultures that held reincarnation as an article of faith. Gender swaps seem to occur with greater frequency among cultures that believe them possible, such as the Burmese and the Kutchins of north-west Canada, less so among peoples who rejected this possibility, like the Syrian Druse and the Tlingit Indians of Alaska.

Whatever background or country a child came from, a disproportionately high number of reborn children recalled violent deaths and in these cases the children's memories were more often likely to centre on the events immediately preceding their former self's last moments. Stevenson himself has speculated that the sudden intensity of violent death experiences might enhance individual memory recall in a way that the less intense experience of gradually fading health through natural causes might not. If this is true it would certainly explain why the number of violent deaths recalled so evidently exceeds the known mortality rates. It would also help to explain why so many children who remember former lives suffer from phobias connected with the cause of their earlier death. Stevenson's case files are full of examples where children who previously drowned or were knocked down in road accidents exhibited pronounced fears of water and automobiles in their present lives. Birthmarks corresponding to deadly wounds suffered in a previous life seem strikingly common too. The case of the Alaskan Indian family was the first among more than 250 examples Stevenson has so far discovered where birthmarks on children are somehow linked with an aspect of their former lives or deaths; most often the marks bear similarity to injuries – knife wounds or bullet holes suffered during the critical moment of the previous incarnation's death. In more than twenty of these cases, evidence such as medical records and autopsy reports have substantiated the reincarnation hypothesis.

Despite all this startling evidence, the American parapsychologist recognizes that rebirth is hard to prove conclusively: the reason he titled his first major

work, *Twenty Cases Suggestive of Reincarnation*, empha-
sizes that cases can only suggest the phenomenon. In
it he put forward examples from cultures as far apart
as Brazil, Sri Lanka, North America and the Middle
East. None have satisfactorily been explained without
reference to some form of palingenesis, nor could they
reasonably be; yet the researcher is aware that it would
be equally true to say that none of his cases are without
flaws, nor does he personally expect to find one that
is. According to Stevenson, the most an investigator
in the field of reincarnation research can hope for
is to investigate the available facts thoroughly, keep
painstaking records, and eventually produce a body of
evidence that, taken as a whole, could not easily be
ignored.

Dr Ian Stevenson is not the only investigator currently
working in this field. Comparable studies undertaken by
researchers in Europe have uncovered a similar pattern.
During the 1980s the British husband and wife team,
Peter and Mary Harrison, unearthed dozens of cases of
children being apparently reincarnated in the United
Kingdom. Generally these memories were found to be
most intense during the period when the child was
aged between eighteen months and four years, a detail
which concurred with Stevenson's findings. In 1983 the
British couple published research from twenty-six of
their most interesting cases in a book entitled *Life
Before Birth*.

In the majority of the cases described, the former lives
of these children were brought to the notice of their
parents by the spontaneous flashes of insight triggered
off by everyday activities or play experiences. Seldom
were the children believed until their repeated versions
became so consistent and detailed that they could no
longer be ignored. Certainly, it must be said that many

of the case histories unearthed by the Harrisons are as striking as anything revealed in the books of their American counterpart. One Irish girl, Angela Mahoney from Cork, recalled at the tender age of twenty-two months, working as a nurse during the last century in Barclay House, a large building in the English town of Poole, Dorset. Although the building was now used as a bank, enquiries confirmed that it had been used as an infirmary prior to 1900. Three-year-old Carl Edon from Middlesbrough, had vivid recollections of being killed in a crash in a former life as a Luftwaffe pilot during World War II. Evidence supporting the reality of Carl's past existence was not only to be found in the accurate drawings he was able to reproduce of the various badges and insignia of his flight command, but in detailed descriptions of the inside workings, levers, controls and dials of his Heinkel aircraft's cockpit. To his parents' amazement he even knew the dimensions, performance and bomb payload of the World War II flying machine. When checked against published descriptions of the equipment and uniforms, they proved to be perfectly correct to the last detail.

Other convincing past life recollections described in *Life Before Birth* included that of a girl who remembered being her own great grandmother, a boy who recalled being killed in a battle while a soldier in World War I and a girl who lost her life as a young child in the famous Scottish Tay Bridge disaster of 1879. By far the most impressive example of a corroborated story, however, was the memories of Nicola Wheater of Keithley, Yorkshire, who recalled her former past as a young boy, John Henry Benson, who lived and died in the West Yorkshire village of Haworth during the late nineteenth century.

It was just after Nicola's second birthday that the girl's

parents began to sense that something was strange about their child. 'Why am I a little girl this time?' she would say, 'Why aren't I a boy like I was before?' At first Nicola's parents were nonplussed by these questions but as her stories of a previous life in Haworth grew more coherent and detailed, her mother Kathleen gradually began to take them seriously. Where had the name Benson arisen from she wondered? The surname was entirely unfamiliar to her. And why did the girl's story never change unlike most childhood fantasies?

According to young Nicola's tale, she had lived a hundred years before, the brother of two younger sisters and a child of a man who worked on the railway. Her old house she said was in a road called Chappel Lane near some railway lines. She, or rather John Henry, had regularly played there and it was during one of these games that he had been knocked down by a train and killed. Because Nicola's recollections of those last tragic moments were so intense, Kathleen Wheater decided to take her daughter to Haworth, a place neither of them had ever visited. Initially, she had hoped to put an end to the girl's story by showing her how different the place was in reality from her own imagination. It didn't work. In fact Nicola knew her way around the village very well, confidently directing her mother down unmarked roads to the very building she had occupied a century before, one of four old greystone terraced houses. Its address was 12 Chappel Lane. Stunned, Kathleen Wheater went to the local parish church to see whether a register of births and deaths still existed for the area. Her heart stopped when, turning over the faded yellow pages she found recorded, on 20 June 1875, the birth of a baby boy, John Henry, to a family named Benson who resided at 12 Chappel Lane. The father was employed as a railway plate layer.

Evidence for John Henry's accidental death at an early age proved more difficult to come by since no hospital records for the area were still in existence. However, a copy of the *General Census of 1881* unearthed by reference librarians in the Bradford Metropolitan Council Offices, strongly suggested that the boy did not survive for very long. The census showed no record of a Benson male child still living six years after John Henry's birth at 12 Chappel Lane although the document included the names of two daughters, Hephyibah, and Sallis, born in 1877 and 1888 respectively. This would appear to confirm Nicola's belief that John Henry had two young sisters at the time of his death. So, although Nicola Wheater's story of the boy being killed by a train remains unconfirmed, all the established facts seem to fit in with its probability and as a case of genuine past-life recall it remains hugely impressive. It was no surprise therefore that the story became the focus of a BBC television programme entitled *Many Happy Returns*, broadcast in 1990. Among the millions who watched it many must have had to reassess their opinions about the possibility of rebirth. Certainly, Nicola Wheater's mother is in no doubt about the clue to the mystery. 'I always knew it must be true,' she was quoted as saying. 'I realized pretty soon that if she was making it up the story would probably alter but it never did. She must have come back to life. How else could she have known so many real facts, especially so long ago and in a place she had never been to?' How indeed?

Many people who have read *Twenty Cases Suggestive of Reincarnation* and Dr Ian Stevenson's later books on the same subject have become convinced that rebirth is really in operation. Nevertheless, there are some who remain less than impressed with the evidence. One sceptic is Ian

Wilson, the English writer whose books *Mind Out of Time*, and *The Afterdeath Experience* have attempted to debunk systematically much of the evidence for survival, from ghosts to out-of-body experiences. Being a Catholic, Wilson is particularly hostile towards reincarnation, claiming for instance that Stevenson's methods are less than scientific and his case histories selected carefully to support his own theories. Pointing out that many of the American's aides are themselves Buddhists or Hindus who are already committed to a belief in transmigration, the British writer asserts that their impartiality must be questioned. Likewise, the Englishman argues that the vast majority of Stevenson's examples come from cultures which embrace the doctrine of reincarnation, that is to say India and the Far East. This background, according to Wilson, makes most of the evidence suspect and he notes a number of specific examples where Indian children from the lower Hindu castes have claimed to come from a higher caste previously. The tendency towards upward mobility, writes Wilson, raises the possibility of wishful thinking on the part of the child, or even the conscious collusion of ambitious parents hoping to extract a more favourable position for their offspring.

Just how valid are these criticisms of the American's research? The fact that many of Stevenson's cases arrive out of south-east Asia is unsurprising since roughly half of humanity lives in that area of the world. It would, however, be quite wrong to suggest that an overwhelming majority of the researcher's examples come from there. When, in 1974, a full review of Stevenson's cases to date was made by independent writer Dr J.G. Pratt, he found that only thirty per cent of cases came out of reincarnationist cultures. Stevenson's files comprised (up to that time) a total of 1,339 individuals who claimed to recall past lives, of which by far the largest source nation was the USA – 342 excluding examples from Red Indian and Eskimo tribes. Only 135 had arisen from India, despite that country's prodigious population, whilst 111 were reported from Great Britain, a country with a population of only fifty million. A more up-to-date analysis of Stevenson's work since 1974 has not been made, but the fact that so many cases prior to 1974 came from non-reincarnationist cultures much surely refute the suggestion that cultural background is the major deciding factor.

As for Wilson's criticism of the impartiality of Stevenson's helpers, it is a fact that many of his fellow researchers believe in the doctrine of rebirth and karma; whether or not this automatically debars them from establishing genuine proof is another matter. Certainly it would be hard to find anyone willing to spend their lives scouring the world for such examples unless they held some sort of interest in the subject. In any case, we all have opinions and preconceptions. Is Ian Wilson himself, as a Catholic convert, strongly prejudiced against the possibility of reincarnation from a theological standpoint? Personally, I see no reason why this should make him unfit to comment upon the subject. The acid test here, as with any branch of scientific research, is whether or not investigations have been carried out in a thorough, professional and responsible manner.

From this standpoint, criticism of Stevenson's techniques of assessing and evaluating evidence is difficult to sustain. Commenting upon his own methodology in approaching a case of possible reincarnation Stevenson writes: 'I have to use the methods of the historian, as well as the psychiatrist. I have to gather testimony from as many witnesses as possible. It is not uncommon for me to interview twenty-five people in regard to one case . . .'. Anyone who has read the 354 pages of documented evidence contained in *Twenty Cases Suggestive of Reincarnation* or the subsequent three-volume work entitled *Cases of the Reincarnation Type*, cannot fail to be impressed by the care Stevenson takes to ensure that his subjects are revealing facts about past lives which they could not otherwise have gleaned from conversations or newspaper cuttings. Reviewing some of Stevenson's findings in *Look* magazine in 1970, Dr Gertrude Schmeilder, a professor of psychology at City College in New York, described the American researcher as, 'A most careful and conscientious person of great intellectual ability and high professional standards. He has a most painstaking approach to the collection and analysis of data.' Another distinguished academic, Dr Albert Stukard, chair of the Department of Psychiatry at Pennsylvania University, was quoted in the same article as saying that Stevenson always took the 'appropriate investigative controls'. It is a dedication to establishing the truth that has characterized the American's methods right up until the present, including his most recent publication. At no point during the past thirty years has anyone seriously questioned the researcher's probity, nor has it ever been proved that one of his many child case studies has invented past lives to make money or gain fame.

More often than not children who talk about their former lives on earth are discouraged by their parents from talking about the subject to others. Among Stevenson's studies there are even examples where such children have been rejected by their peers and severely beaten by adults. Though in most cases the child lives in reasonable travelling distance of its past life predecessor, it rarely wishes to leave its new home environment and go in search of its old family.

Although it challenges many of the basic assumptions

that underlie the religious and philosophical concepts of Western society, Stevenson's research has stood both the test of time and the hostile intellectual onslaught of his professional critics. Whether sceptics like it or not, the fact remains that a considerable number of very young children from virtually every country in the world have recalled past lives and exhibited a knowledge of adult ways which seems impossible to account for naturally. One of Stevenson's subjects – a five-year-old Lebanese boy named Imad Elawor – made fifty-seven verifiable statements about his previous life as a tuberculosis victim called Ibrahim Bonhanzy. Fifty-one turned out to be, in the researcher's words, 'dead right'. This is by no means an isolated example. In those cases that Ian Stevenson has studied most closely, roughly ninety per cent of all verifiable memories proved to be accurate. Unless we accept that the American psychologist has consistently and consciously falsified his records, evidence of such complex cross-referenced correlations cannot be dismissed as the product of childhood fantasies or coincidence. Logically, on any objective analysis, we must accept that the phenomenon Ian Stevenson discovered really is throwing up some quite extraordinary possibilities regarding the nature of human existence.

But what possibilities? Are these apparent memories of previous lives evidence of true reincarnation or is there a more likely alternative explanation? Intriguingly, some parapsychologists have put forward the suggestion that the phenomenon of apparent past-life recall need not involve rebirth at all. One theory that has gained ground over the past fifteen years suggests that memories of previous lives are gained through a subtle form of psychic osmosis – a type of unconscious extrasensory perception (ESP) through which the receiver unwittingly gains information by dipping into a vast pool of knowledge buried in a substratum of the collective human mind. This idea presupposes that the concept of the collective unconscious pioneered by the psychologist C.J. Jung is correct. The theory is unprovable from a practical standpoint, but even on a purely hypothetical level it fails to answer the various enigmas thrown up by Dr Stevenson's research. For example, it cannot account for those instances where children have been born with birthmarks relating to their previous existence.

One Eskimo boy investigated by Stevenson claimed to be the reborn spirit of an uncle who had died while he was still in the womb. Several marks on the old man's body, including a surgical scar in his back, were evident on the child's skin. When Stevenson examined the mark on the child's back closely, he found evidence of a surgical-type excision bordered by tiny round marks lined up like stitch wounds. What made this example doubly exciting to the researcher was the endless set of recollections of the dead man's past life which checked out as being entirely true. In such an example, which is far from unique among Stevenson's many case studies, the ESP hypothesis cannot be held responsible, unless we add to it the possibility that the scar markings were merely coincidental. This is surely unlikely.

A further alternative explanation which has found favour among a few parascientists is the generic theory. This idea presumes that past-life memories might be inherited – transmitted from parent to child in a manner not dissimilar to the way in which DNA patterns, containing the basic physical information of the parents' bodies, are carried through to the newly-born infant. Dr Ian Stevenson rejects the generic theory on the grounds that it fails to explain how children can become aware of knowledge (dates, places, names etc.) of which their parents were unaware. What is more, in all of the

American's research only a minority of reincarnated children claim to be the returned soul of a parent or grandparent.

If tales of past-life recall seem impossible to explain in terms that do not involve some form of rebirth, then proving reincarnation to be a fact is at least as difficult. Since the researcher must inevitably rely on first and second-hand testimony the possibility will always remain that the facts uncovered will be distorted. In this branch of investigation there can be no laboratory tests, no double-blind controlled trials. Recognizing the difficulty of his position, Dr Stevenson concentrates upon examples of those who, in their supposed last existence, died at an early age, thus increasing the likelihood of finding the dead person's friends and relatives, living witnesses who might then be able to confirm details of the reincarnated person's account of their former life. In cases where the past life recalled is from much further back in time this is not possible and research into such examples throws up a new set of dangers. Some of these cases, initially impressive, later prove to be rather less than they once seemed. . . .

Nineteen years ago just such an example aroused considerable interest in Britain. In 1974 a book was published in London entitled *Second Time Around*, and subsequently came out in New York under the title of *Twice Born – The Total Recall of a Seventeenth-Century Life*. The book, written by an Englishman named Edward Ryall who was then resident in the Home Counties, purported to be the waking reminiscences about the author's previous life as one John Fletcher, a yeoman farmer born in 1645 in the Polden Hills of Somerset. According to Ryall's account he (Fletcher) had taken part in the Monmouth Rebellion before marrying and siring two sons, and finally being killed in a battle against the army of James II in the year 1685. In its sheer wealth of detail, Ryall's account went far beyond most other reports of past lives. Its depiction of seventeenth-century English rural life was extraordinarily complete, containing many obscure details, such as the customs of West Country people, all of which were confirmed as accurate by historians of the period. A five page glossary was included in the publication to list all the obsolete expressions and redundant words that characterized Fletcher's prose, and investigations proved that many dates, family and place names included in *Second Time Around* were historically correct. A check of the seventeenth-century calendar showed that key events in the supposed lifetime of John Fletcher would have indeed taken place on the same days of the week as Ryall described in his book.

For many people the enigma of John Fletcher appeared to be a near-perfect case study of genuine reincarnation. *Second Time Around* sold in large numbers and a BBC television documentary screened soon after its publication, left millions of viewers in little doubt that an extraordinary mystery had been uncovered. However, the following year one or two experts, most notably the aforementioned journalist and author Ian Wilson, began to have doubts. Examining the parish records of Ryall's former lifetime years, Wilson could find no evidence of Fletcher's birth, nor records of the birth, marriage or baptism of his son, which Ryall claimed had taken place in a particular church. Many other details were certainly correct, including the name of the vicar serving the community during the mid-seventeenth century, but these facts could have been easily researched. Finally, other journalists became suspicious after Ryall proved unhelpful to a local historian who wished to trace John Fletcher's farm. When pressed, the author was unable to locate the place, even though he had reckoned in his book to know its exact whereabouts. By the time Ryall died in 1976 his published past-life memoirs had become a bestseller on both sides of the Atlantic, but many were already convinced that his creation was nothing more than an elaborate historical fantasy.

The furore which followed the debunking of *Second Time Around* provides a lesson for parapsychologists everywhere. The rule is that when working in this field, one must treble-check every claim, no matter how convincing the witness involved. Clearly in Ryall's case this did not happen. Even Dr Ian Stevenson admitted at one point to be 'deeply impressed' by the Englishman's story, describing Ryall himself as a man whom he found to be 'honest and sincere'. He was wrong. Yet, just as one fraudulent medium does not rule out the possibility of spirit communication, so one rebirth hoaxer can in no way invalidate the work that Ian Stevenson and other researchers have put in over the past two decades. By and large, past-life recallers are otherwise unremarkable – they are neither disturbed, neurotic nor attention seeking. On any other subject they would doubtless be considered as wholly reliable witnesses. Only because their stories seem so incredible do we doubt them.

To remind ourselves how astounding these stories are it is perhaps worth examining three of the most famous examples to have arisen during this century, examples in which parents have lost children at an early age only to find them returning in the body of their next offspring.

On 15 March 1910, Alexandrina Samoa, a five-year-old daughter of Catholic parents, died in Palermo, Italy. Several months later her mother Adela, the wife of a medical doctor, had a dream in which Alexandrina appeared, cradling a baby in her arms, saying that she was 'coming back'. Adela's husband dismissed the dream as the product of grief and, since their religion forbade them to believe in reincarnation, he insisted his wife speak to no one else about it. Nevertheless Adela was convinced the dream would come true, even though an ovarian operation the previous year had made it seemingly impossible for her to bear more children. Her belief was not misguided: she became pregnant and gave birth to twin girls in the November of the same year. One, which bore birthmarks in the same place as her dead sister, was named Alexandrina as a tribute to her memory. As the second Alexandrina grew up she began to seem more and more like her predecessor, playing the same games and sharing aversion to the same foods; like Alexandrina (1) she was left-handed even though her twin sister was not.

It was not until the girl was aged ten that the Samoas came genuinely to believe her to be a reincarnation. One day in the spring of 1921 Adela told her daughters that they would be visiting the town of Monreale the following week. Immediately, Alexandrina pronounced that she had already been there and described the town in considerable detail. It was, she said, the place where you saw 'red priests' unlike any in Palermo. When her mother asked how she knew all these things, Alexandrina replied that Adela had taken her there when she was young, accompanied by a woman she described as, 'The neighbour with scars on her forehead'. Adela knew that Alexandrina (2) had never visited Monreale. In fact the only time she had herself been to the place was many years before, when she went accompanied by her first child and a friend who was suffering at the time from cysts on her forehead. Casting her mind back, Adela recalled how, in the main square of the town, they had seen a line of Greek priests wearing bright red vestments of a type unknown in Italy. Afterwards nothing would ever convince the mother that the soul of the first girl had not truly been returned to her.

From a medico-psychological viewpoint the Samoa case is easier than some for non-believers in reincarnation to account for. Sceptics would say that the mother's dream was wishful thinking; that the apparently miraculous birth of twins was a result of an incorrect medical diagnosis; that the so-called past-life memory of the second Alexandrina might have been based upon knowledge overheard during the first ten years of her life. The birthmarks could be no more than a genetic trait, the girl's apparently similar personality might have developed under the direction of a mother hoping to find a common link between the two girls. On balance of probability, the convoluted 'natural' explanation for the Italian mystery might appear singularly unconvincing, but it shows once again the difficulty researchers have in establishing cast-iron evidence for reincarnation.

An example from the United Kingdom bears a strong similarity to the Samoa experience. In May 1957 sisters Joanna and Jaqueline Pollock, aged eleven and six respectively, were killed when a car mounted the pavement in their home town of Hexham, Northumberland. Soon after the tragedy, the girls' father John Pollock became convinced (for reasons which he has never been fully able to explain) that their two souls would return in the bodies of other children. When, in 1958, his wife Florence announced that she was again pregnant, his belief grew into the certainty that she would give birth to twin girls. This feeling was so strong that he even argued with a gynaecologist who told Florence Pollock that she was carrying a single child.

The father was right to trust his own instinct. On

4 October 1958 Mrs Pollock gave birth to twin girls. John Pollock's belief was further reinforced when it was noticed that one of the twins, christened Jennifer, had a white line on her forehead in the place where her dead sister Jaqueline had cut herself badly after falling off a bicycle. The same girl also had a birthmark on her hip which corresponded to a similar blemish on the skin of the deceased daughter. The other twin, Gillian, had no birthmarks whatsoever, yet this in its own way was also slightly odd, since the twins were monozygotic – formed from the same egg.

When the girls were just four months old, the Pollock family moved to Whitley Bay, some miles away from Hexham and they did not return to their old district until three years later when John Pollock took his family out on a day trip. Both husband and wife were amazed by the way in which their young children showed recognition of the parks and play areas frequented by their earlier daughters. They were even able to recognize the road in which they used to live. Subsequent events convinced the Pollocks that the souls of their dead children had actually returned. Around the age of four, the twins began to suffer nightmares of a disturbing intensity. After waking they would recall the sudden deaths which ended their previous lives, describing the scene of the accident in graphic detail. These dreams were to continue for several months until, having reached the age of five, both girls ceased to be tormented by the past trauma. Now, long-since grown up, they can remember nothing of their former lives, yet John Pollock and his wife Florence remain convinced that their dead daughters did return, just as John predicted they would.

The last case to be considered in this chapter is amongst the most unusual for the child involved remembers clearly, not only the details of her short life on earth, but her premature death and the events surrounding her burial. In 1963 a baby girl was born to a young couple in Leeds, England. Christened Mandy, the infant was found to have congenital heart problems and lived only a few months. It was a traumatic time for Mandy's mother Gillian. Partly due to her inability to cope with the bereavement, the couple split up and later divorced, their one surviving child, a five-year-old girl named Carol, going to live with her father. A few years later, Mandy's mother remarried a man called George Seabrook, and together they had three children: Wendy, Sean and John. In order to save Gillian from reactivating her past grief, the subject of her dead child from a previous marriage was never discussed. But when, in May 1972, Gillian gave birth to a fourth child by her second husband, the baby bore such uncanny resemblance to her lost girl that she decided to call it Mandy as well.

In the fullness of time similarities between the two children were to prove somewhat greater than appearances. In 1974, during a family outing, the Seabrooks happened to be passing the cemetery at Hunslet on the outskirts of Leeds, where the first Mandy had been buried. Though never before taken to that part of the city, Mandy Seabrook became animated as the car approached the cemetery railings and jumped up and down on her mother's lap shouting. 'Look mummy!' she cried, 'that's where you put me in the ground, remember?' Horrified, her parents could say nothing in reply. Not only was it impossible for the child to know anything of her half-sister, it was beyond belief that she should have recognized the spot where the girl's body had been laid to rest. But much more was to follow. Not only did Mandy (2) subsequently show knowledge of the first girl's life, she could even remember specific details of her funeral (the fact, for example, that her mother Gillian

had almost fallen in the grave after slipping and losing
her balance from the wet soil). Incredibly, the child also
went on to describe to her parents a tiny silver bracelet
engraved with roses and crosses which Mandy (1) wore
on her wrist when she was buried. It was a present from
Gillian's first husband's brother, and engraved especially
for her with the words, 'To darling Mandy from Uncle
Patrick'. Mandy (2) recalled the inscription exactly even
though she had never met nor even heard of the man in
her present incarnation as a Seabrook.

'Mandy sent shivers down my spine,' recalled Gillian
Seabrook. Her second husband, meanwhile, said that
the child's memories had left him, 'struck by an electric
current'. Though a physical resemblance between the two
babies had been recognized from the very beginning by
Gillian, both parents insist to this day that they never
looked for a connection between the two girls or held
out any hopes regarding reincarnation. Curiously, one
further detail of Mandy's recall seems to back up the
Seabrook's innocence. As well as the silver bracelet,
Mandy (2) said that a yellow fluffy ball had been buried
with her infant self. Gillian Seabrook knew this was not
true yet casting her mind back she recalled that Carol,
her other daughter from the first marriage, aged five
at the time of baby Mandy's death, had once made a
pompom of yellow wool at school and given it to her
baby sister as a present. Since Mandy's coffin had been
laid out on the night before the funeral with the coffin
lid open, it seemed just possible that Carol could have
placed it inside the casket without her mother realizing
it. But did she? When Gillian Seabrook next saw her
eldest daughter she questioned her on the subject. It
was true – Carol admitted that she had hidden the
ball of wool underneath the dead baby's body as a
parting gift.

Today, Mandy Seabrook would appear to be undisturbed by her recall of death and has grown up into a well-balanced young woman. Naturally she has no fear of death; neither have her family. Once a religious agnostic, George Seabrook has no doubt that we all survive: 'I used to think that when you were dead, you were dead. I don't think that now.' Gillian Seabrook adds, 'If you had told me once upon a time that all this was possible I would have said no. Now I just can't not believe in it.'

Do tales of apparent reincarnation hold a wider significance for the rest of us? Does reincarnation take place on a universal level, or are such examples as those mentioned above simply further evidence of what we already know – that, on rare occasions, fate and coincidence sometimes go hand-in-hand with the more obscure faculties of the human mind to spin an unfathomable web of contradictions? Dr Ian Stevenson, whose research remains the world's most comprehensive study of the phenomenon, urges caution before we accept that any single example is really a case of rebirth, no matter how extraordinary it may seem. However, asked to judge his research as a whole, he is less reticent. Even in one of his earliest essays on the subject entitled *Evidence for Survival from Claimed Memories of Former Incarnations*, which appeared in 1959, Stevenson could write, 'I will say therefore, that I think reincarnation must be a plausible hypothesis . . . a large number of cases in which the recall of true memories is a plausible hypothesis should make that hypothesis worthy of attention. I think the number of cases on record confers that respectability. . . .'

And so indeed it continues to do. Since that paper was written thirty years ago, reincarnation has come to be taken seriously by academics and the general public alike. Many new examples are contained in Stevenson's most recent work *Children Who Remember Previous Lives*, published in 1987. By and large, the American's new book covers the same ground as that of his earlier works and, therefore, continues to leave many of the central questions regarding reincarnation unanswered. Yet as we shall see in our next chapter, there is a field of research that has gone much further towards proving that the enigma is not isolated to a few thousand special cases but, more probably, relates to all our yesterdays. Far from being the annihilation of consciousness that many of us fear, the process of human death may very well turn out to be, as Wordsworth said, nothing more than 'a sleep and a forgetting'.

Chapters of Experience

'The endless legacy of the past to the present is the
secret source of human genius.'

Honoré De Balzac

Of the 4,000 types of mammal in existence on this planet,
the human species is undoubtedly the one born most
vulnerable, entirely unable to defend or care for itself,
and wholly dependent on its parents for its wellbeing.
Whilst many other species appear to have from birth
the genetically imprinted instincts which allow them to
progress swiftly towards a pattern of adult behaviour
necessary for survival, the human infant mind seems to be
much more of a blank canvass. Though it will eventually
reach great heights, its development is painfully slow and
seldom varies in timescale. But not all children fit neatly
into this pattern.

If, as much evidence would seem to suggest, the rebirth
of the human soul is a fact, it must surely go a long way to
explain those curious examples of infant prodigies that
occasionally appear down the centuries – youngsters
whose ability and intelligence seems not only to be
preternaturally in advance of their peers, but is beyond
the reach of all but a handful of adult minds. Well known
examples of this curious syndrome include Wolfgang
Amadeus Mozart, who could produce piano concertos
at the tender age of four, and English radical philosopher

John Stuart Mill, who spoke fluent Greek when aged only two. There are plenty of less famous instances. José Capablanca was an illiterate Cuban child whose mastery of the game of chess enabled him to beat world champions before his fifth birthday; Miguel Mantilla, a Mexican two-year-old, had a mathematical mind which could calculate seven-digit root numbers faster than a computer. Jean Louis Cardiac, the French wonder child, could repeat his alphabet at three months and translate Latin into French or English at three years, whilst Christian Frederich Heinecken, the so-called Infant of Lubeck, talked in complete sentences only hours after his birth in 1721. A mere two years later, he was able to recite the entire Bible off by heart in either Latin, French, English or his native German tongue. Ironically, neither of these last two geniuses survived their first six years.

Innate skills in infants often seem even harder to explain than feats of the intellect. When, on 12 March 1953, an eight-year-old Italian girl named Gianella brilliantly conducted the London Philharmonic Orchestra in works by Wagner, Hadyn and Beethoven, it proved to be her 123rd professional performance, yet the child was considered by non-music tutors to be not particularly bright. Aged six, Blind Tom Wiggins, the sightless son of a 'negro slave from Georgia', discovered he could play the piano in any style, despite never having had lessons. Although he became a world-famous entertainer, Wiggins never learned to write, remaining a near-idiot with a low IQ and pitiful vocabulary until his death in 1908.

It is beyond the capacity of educational psychologists to imagine how such extraordinary abilities could develop in minds so young, and unsurprisingly, reincarnationists claim infant prodigies to be simply displaying gifts they acquired in a former existence. However, since so few of us are born genuises, we might well wonder what the rest of us have learned during the past lives we are all supposed to have had. The question is an essential one, for behind it must lie the key to such perennial riddles as the true meaning of life and the nature and purpose of creation itself. Some profess to already know the truth. Those who adhere to the doctrine of the karmic path think of the mortal plane as a training school to which incarnated souls return again and again, learning new lessons and overcoming fresh difficulties. Through a succession of trials, triumphs and reversals the soul moves upwards towards perfection. It is a spiritual ascent rather than an intellectual one, and through its voyage of discovery the soul-mind must cast aside such emotions as greed, selfishness, materialism and the vain pursuit of personal glory. We are all on the same path and only when the awareness of the human race has grown through this continuous process of rebirth can the greater plan for the future of mankind be fulfilled.

As a general principle, the doctrine of karma is embraced not only by the ancient religions of south-east Aisa, but also by theosophists, spiritualists and, strangely, many humanists in the West. What is far more interesting from the parapsychological viewpoint, however, is the fact that much of the modern-day research into claimed remembrances of former lives upholds aspects of the karmic theory. Dr Ian Stevenson, whose extensive studies were discussed in the previous chapter, has found many instances where the personality of a child seems to have been formed by experiences gained during a previous life. Stevenson is not alone in believing that the human personality develops prior to conception. Dr Helen Wambach, the clinical psychotherapist whose investigation into the case of young Jeremy Anderson of Waukomis began several years of study into similar

cases, has noticed how those people able to recollect
past lives generally retain some fairly close identification
with their earlier personality. In Wambach's opinion,
based on her study of over 750 subjects, the larger, new
personality absorbs the former one, but discards such
'superficial' details as race, sex or religious persuasion.
Wambach claims to have found that, in accordance with
reincarnationist religious thought, each new incarnation
has been chosen by the soul to develop knowledge, to
experience emotions and – in the doctor's own words –
'straighten out past mistakes'. Heredity is rarely a factor
in reincarnation it seems, for, according to Wambach's
sample, eighty per cent of subjects felt certain they
had chosen their previous incarnations as well as their
present one.

It is not really surprising that the idea of the karmic
path is gaining more supporters in the West. From a
purely rational viewpoint it must be seen to make sense.
Who but a saint could be expected to learn all of life's lessons in the space of a single span averaging seventy years?
Who from a personal experience of one incarnation could
see life's every vicissitude? No individual can be at once
rich and poor, master and slave, healthy and diseased,
murderer and victim. In order to learn and grow we all
need the opportunity for education. The rotational cycle,
unlike Christianity's one life doctrine, offers all souls an
equal chance to participate in the spiritual evolution of
mankind. In addition, from the point of view of fair
play, the karmic path has rather more going for it than
the Western concept of salvation. Christians believe that
we either ascend to heaven or descend to hell on the basis
of our record over a single earthly existence. Given the
world we inhabit, this is profoundly unjust as clearly we
do not all get the same life-chances; any future which
is based on a single lifespan's trials would seem to fly

in the face of natural justice. As one cynic has pointed out, it seems as though the Christian God is asking all his students to sit the same exam at the end of their course when half of them never got the chance to attend any lectures! The moral superiority of the karmic creed is even more evident when we consider those people who have little or no opportunity whatsoever to prove their soul to be worthy of heavenly reward: individuals such as the severely mentally handicapped or children who die in infancy. Significantly, most Christian theologians duck this issue altogether, realizing their own faith cannot offer a satisfactory explanation for these anomalies.

In contrast, there are no logical contradictions to karma. All incarnations are chosen before birth and their circumstances, both bodily and external, are the result of past deeds. We each make our own bed and we must lie on it. If we do not receive adequate redress for our strivings in this life then surely we will in our next incarnation. Nor are these rewards and punishments arbitrary: each receives their just deserts exactly measured upon the cosmic scales of justice. There are no sharp divisions between heaven and hell; all is relative. Yet karma is not a fatalistic doctrine. It predestines nothing; it neither creates nor designs. In the karmic mind-world it is man alone whose thoughts, plans and actions cause reactions and the adjustments of destiny. When bad thoughts or actions occur they are like discordant musical notes in an otherwise perfect classical arrangement; a pebble making ripples on the surface of a previously still lake. Seen through the light of karma, we may now begin to understand why some are born with very great privileges whilst others are condemned to live out their span in the conditions of deprivation and misery into which they were born. The fault is truly in ourselves and we need not blame heaven, God or providence for the injustices of the manifested world.

Of course the philosophical perfection of karma will not in itself convince the majority of people who continue to labour under the illusion that life ends in death and the bodily corruption of the grave. The nihilists, who believe life is nothing more or less than an accident of chemical and biological principles, will doubtless point out that very few of us actually remember anything about our past lives and therefore gained nothing from the experience. It is an argument which entirely misses the point of karma. As adults much of the formative period of our present lives – our early childhood – is now completely lost in the furthest recesses of our memory, but psychologists insist these early years do much to evolve our mature personalities. In fact nothing we have ever experienced is truly forgotten, as regression through deep hypnosis has proved beyond doubt. It is this same technique of regression that during the past twenty years has produced the most striking evidence that we have all lived before. Under hypnosis thousands have recalled past existences with a clarity and emotional intensity incredible to those who witness it. Some display a wealth of historical knowledge impossible for them to have acquired in their own lives; others (like the children whose spontaneous recollections have been studied by such researchers as Dr Ian Stevenson) remember factual details which prove upon investigation to be correct. Few who undergo past-life regression remain unmoved by the experience. Most believe their remembrances are genuine and feel profound relief in the knowledge that the death they feared so much will in reality mean so little.

*   *   *

In March 1983 an Australian television documentary gripped viewers across the subcontinent and impressed many who had hitherto been sceptical about the possibility of soul migration. *The Reincarnation Experiments* involved four housewives from Sydney, who were seemingly transported back through the centuries under the influence of hypnotherapist Peter Rouser. One, Cynthia Henderson, recalled her life as a French aristocrat using colloquialisms not heard in France for centuries. She revealed her former home to be a chateau, situated near the small village of Fleur. Although the woman had never visited Europe, she easily led a film crew to the location where, sure enough, a ruin of the building still stood. Another housewife tested, Helen Pickering, recalled her previous existence as James Burns, born in the Scottish town of Dunbar in the year 1801. As proof of her past life, Helen Pickering drew plans of Aberdeen's Marshall College where Burns had studied – plans which, although very different to the building which presently occupied the site, bore uncanny resemblance to a set of plans later discovered within the archives of the Scottish college. As the television documentary pointed out, it would have been impossible for Mrs Pickering to have seen the records.

Although the term hypnotic regression has only entered the wider public consciousness during the past couple of decades, its history goes back almost a century. Its first practitioner was Albert de Rochas, a Frenchman who used mesmerism to heal patients of psychosomatic disorders by transporting them back across eternity. One of Rochas' most successful subjects was Marie Mayo, who remembered several former existences. Under hypnosis she became, by turns, a fisherman's wife who had committed suicide at the age of twenty, a clerk who lived at the time of Louis XVI, and the wife of a gentleman in the French court of Emperor Napoleon III. Names were given which upon examination proved to be people who had really existed, yet few other medical practitioners took Rochas' evidence seriously, preferring instead to believe the mesmerist had prompted his subjects to concoct a series of fantasies.

Another pioneer of the regression technique was John Bjorkham, a Swede who conducted several hundred case studies, many of which he cross checked with verifiable facts to discount the possibility of coincidence. Bjorkhem's experiments during the early part of this century led another researcher, Englishman Dr Alexander Cowan, to undertake a similar line of investigation. In 1950 Cowan published details of more than a thousand rebirth cases in his book *The Power Within*. Originally sceptical about reincarnation, he had begun his research by attempting to disprove Bjorkhem's belief that genuine recall of past lives through hypnotism was possible. Eventually, however, forced by the weight of contrary evidence, Cowan came to the conclusion that many psychic disorders such as fears, complexes and phobias have their root cause in the inherited memories of traumatic incidents from previous existences. The Englishman's case-files produced a few ripples in the medico academic establishment, yet it was not until 1952 and the celebrated case of Bridey Murphy, that past-life regression began to arouse the interest of the general public.

Bridey was the name of a girl from nineteenth-century Ireland, the former identity of housewife Virginia Tighe from Colorado, USA. Her discovery was made under the direction of amateur hypnotist Morey Bernstein who thereafter wrote a bestselling book on the mystery. At first the Bridey Murphy case seemed like a gift from heaven to those who believed in reincarnation.

Although Mrs Tighe had not been to Ireland herself, under Bernstein's hypnotism she was able to recall a huge amount of detail relating to local events and customs, plus a host of obsolete Irish words, all delivered in a convincing Gaelic brogue. Whilst details of her birth, marriage and death could not be verified (since no records existed in Ireland before 1864), many people found the hypnotic performance too convincing to doubt. So enthralled were the American public by the enigma that the story even became the subject of a Hollywood movie. Doubts arose, however, when it was discovered that Virginia Tighe did actually have some Irish family connections, a fact which she had previously withheld from the press. Speculation about a hoax intensified when it became clear that, as a young woman, she had lived in Chicago next to an aunt whose own maiden name had been Murphy. Sceptics lost no time in claiming that Tighe must have either colluded with Bernstein to perpetrate a fraud, or drawn unknowingly upon subconscious recollections of stories told by her elderly Irish relative. For their part, both Tighe and Bernstein denied any collusion, either conscious or otherwise, and remained steadfast in their belief that Bridey was real. But whatever the truth of the matter, and in this case it will surely never be known, a question mark had been placed over the reliability of the regression technique which proved hard to erase.

The inauspicious start provided by the mystery of Bridey Murphy has tended to cloud the judgement of many otherwise objective researchers in the field of parapsychology. This is sad because whatever doubts remain over the Bridey Murphy enigma, plenty of regression cases since have proved highly resistant to similar suspicions. Particularly convincing was English teacher Margaret Baker's apparent recall of the life of Tyzo

Boswell, a gypsy horse trader born in 1775 and killed by lightning in 1831. It was in 1978, under the direction of hypnotherapist Maurice Blake that Baker, of Tetford, Lincolnshire, first realized she had lived before. Speaking in the rough, gutteral language of her former self, not only was her detailed knowledge of the traveller's way of life uncanny, but came replete with Romany expressions which neither Baker nor Maurice Blake had ever heard. Although she consciously remembered nothing of her past life, the teacher was, while under hypnosis, able to lead investigators to the graveyard of St Mary's Church where Tyzo Boswell had been buried more than 150 years before. The exact date of his death by lightning, said by Baker to be 5 August 1831, was later confirmed by parish records.

Clearly a case like this is a sceptic's nightmare. The regression of the English school teacher is convincing not only for the verifiable facts given, but also for the physical transformation that came over her. Anyone who has ever heard a tape of Tyzo Boswell's deep, gutteral and obviously male voice coming from the mouth of Margaret Baker cannot fail to be astounded. This aspect of the regression phenomenon was brought home to me personally when I watched English hypnotist Joe Keeton working with a group of volunteers in Birmingham more than ten years ago. The dramatic changes in voice patterns which took place were matched only by distortions in facial muscles which had to be seen to be believed. Tapes played from regressions of past cases were equally amazing. In one half-hour I heard voices which described lives over three centuries. The sheer intensity with which the more meaningful events in these lives were remembered was truly incredible to behold. I will never forget hearing the last desperate words of a child who died in a Victorian house fire: 'Mummy, mummy, help me!' Occasionally, during other regressions I witnessed, a facial transformation would accompany the past personality's presence. Those who recalled old age became haggard and drawn, whilst creases in the faces of older subjects would seem smoothed out when recalling a previous youth. The physical changes could be even more dramatic, and some researchers have recorded instances where regressed individuals manifest the appearance of medical conditions consistent with past-life memories, such as muscular spasms in the faces of stroke victims. One British subject I saw actually developed a livid rope burn around her neck when recalling her hanging, whilst another who died from a beating, manifested extensive bruising all over her body.

At no stage could I have been persuaded to believe that what I was witnessing was either a fantasy or some bizarre practical joke. Yet neither at that time was I ready to embrace the obvious alternative conclusion that those people, and therefore probably all of us, had really lived before. I have long-since changed my mind. By the time I met Joe Keeton in 1979 he had become convinced that many of the phobias which affect the human mind are derived from pre-birth memories. Since then a similar position has been reached by several other regressionists including a number from the USA who now base their entire medical practice on the validity of past-life therapy. Healing the scars of centuries is an expensive business and Californian therapists charge hundreds of dollars per session of hypnotism. Whilst the mainstream medical authorities remain deeply uncertain of regression therapy, its advocates have claimed extraordinary cures through the process of mining the soul. Indeed, not only do they believe they can cure psychosomatic problems such as phobias, allergies and addictions, but some insist that a past-life link exists for every physical disease and boast recorded cures for chronic ailments including cancer, arthritis and multiple sclerosis.

One Californian therapist, Dr Edith Fiore, has gone so far as to say that, 'There isn't a single physical problem that can't be solved by good past-life treatment.' And she has several thousand case studies to prove her point. For some problems, says Fiore, there is an all too obvious cause. She believes obesity, for instance, is more often than not the result of the oppressed memories of a person who starved in a previous incarnation, whilst migraine sufferers may be the reincarnated souls of persons who suffered scalping or other serious head wounds. One teenage insomniac whom Dr Fiore treated, recalled under hypnotism his former life as an American GI which ended when he was bayoneted to death while sleeping on a beach during the Pacific War. Dr Fiore is certain that genuine reincarnation is the true source of past-life recollections rather than viewing them as aspects of a collective or ancestral memory. A longtime disciple of Freud, she rejects entirely the notion that these former identities are mental constructs or fragments of a sub-personality. Her reasons for accepting reincarnation as the most likely cause of pre-birth memory are the often instantaneous cures which coincide with the liberation of a suppressed past-life memory. According to the Californian doctor, 'If someone's phobia is eliminated instantly and permanently by the remembrance of an event from the past, it seems to me to make logical sense that the event must have happened.'

Another American hypnotherapist, Dr Morris Netherton of Los Angeles, agrees. Netherton first became aware of his own past life when, under the hypnotism of a colleague, he recalled a miserable former existence in a nineteenth-century Mexican lunatic asylum. Under regression he felt the pain of being kicked in the stomach by a guard, an injury which caused internal bleeding in exactly the same spot where he, the twentieth-century medical practitioner, was suffering from an ulcer. Simply as a result of that recognition the ulcer never flared up again, and from then on the Los Angeles doctor began to use regression regularly in his own practice. As Netherton believes that his patients must relive the most traumatic moments from their previous lives, especially their births and deaths, a visit to his surgery on a typical day will find men and women screaming, weeping or moaning, in foreign languages or in voices inappropriate to their sex. In Netherton's experience, the sexual and racial identity of his patients matters little, nor is their attitude towards reincarnation relevant. Under hypnosis, past-life recall inevitably begins whatever the person's religious viewpoint. With regard to his own opinion on the subject, Morris Netherton is as incautious as his Californian counterpart Dr Fiore: 'Many people go away believing reincarnation is symbolic, metaphorical; but what's the logical answer? That it actually happened!'

The conviction that literal reincarnation lies at the root of the regression enigma was a view strongly supported by an English psychiatrist, the late Dr Arthur Guirdham. Commenting on the evidence obtained both by American regressionists and the investigations of Dr Ian Stevenson, Guirdham was moved to write in an article published by a British medical magazine, 'To disbelieve the facts which lay behind reincarnation evidence, one would need to be a mental defective.' Oddly enough, Guirdham's own interest in reincarnation sprang not from hypnosis but from a careful cross-referencing of medical symptoms with patients' recurring dreams and psychic revelations. Noticing that an illness or depression in a living patient seemed to correspond with tragic happenings in what were (Guirdham had originally assumed) imagined previous lives, the psychiatrist began to investigate more deeply under hypnotism. When the factual details contained within these imagined lives correlated closely with actual events and personalities from the past, Guirdham realized that he had uncovered a far deeper mystery.

Dr Guirdham's conclusions that some diseases continue to manifest through the cycle of incarnations has been supported by evidence from several countries. The severe bouts of bronchitis which afflicted a top Canadian fashion model named Bonham Bright, proved beyond the diagnosis of doctors in her home city of Toronto, but under the direction of hypnotherapist Beverly Janus they were traced back to her death as a young Eastern European Jew in a German concentration camp. Once she knew the sickness which killed her earlier self had no power over her new body, Bright realized that she had nothing to fear in her present incarnation. She never suffered from bronchitis again. Likewise, the seizures which gripped an American woman named Shirley Kleppe Moran throughout her first twenty-seven years of life, baffled medical practitioners until, under regressive hypnosis, she traced the root of the problem to her suicide as a sixteenth-century French courtesan. The fits never returned. One of the most remarkable regression cures to date concerns a thirty-nine-year-old female patient of Dr Edith Fiore who had undergone twelve unsuccessful operations for bone-marrow cancer before turning to regression therapy as a last resort. Taken back through time to an incarnation as high priestess in a cult which practised human sacrifice, the woman saw herself ritually drinking the blood of her victims and realized that her present condition (cancer of the bone-marrow stops the healthy production of new blood cells) was actually a karmic punishment. However, this experience was sufficient to lift the burden of guilt

and her next set of medical tests revealed her body free
of cancer. A full account of this and other miracle cures
is to be found in Dr Fiore's book entitled *You Have Been
Here Before*. It is not recommended for those who wish
to continue disbelieving.

Whilst a growing number of cures seem to have been
effected through soul-mining regression, some ninety-
eight per cent of the medical establishment remains
determinedly reluctant to embrace the possibilities this
new branch of therapy opens up. If few doctors admit that
past-life regression has a therapeutic potential, fewer still
among the medico-scientific establishment would support
the idea that hypnotic memories are genuine evidence
of former lives. Since the controversy began with the
Bridey Murphy case in the early 1950s, psychologists
have been busily putting forward alternative theories for
the phenomenon.

Writing in the newsletter of the Association for
Transpersonal Psychology in 1978, Dr Arthur Hastings, a
respected psychiatrist, proposed ego-gratification to be at
the root of many regression cases. 'These experiences,' he
argued, 'are often vivid and plausible but I think we must
say that there is no reliable proof that they are memories
of a past life.' Dr Hastings personally believed that, once
placed in a suggestible state of relaxation, regressed
persons simply let their imagination run wild, creating
ever-more glamorous former selves. The question posed
by Hastings is one that parapsychologists working in
the reincarnation field already accept. Even Dr Ian
Stevenson, himself a believer, finds much evidence
gained through the regression technique vaguely troub-
ling and warns that under hypnosis, 'The subconscious
part of the mind is released from ordinary inhibitions and
may then present in dramatic form a new personality.'
The reservations expressed by the American researcher

have encouraged firm non-survivalists to further suggest
that past-life memories are really manufactured under the
direction of the hypnotists themselves. Pointing out that
stage hypnotists can lead people to behave in a bizarre
manner, often performing a plausible, if stylized, impression of almost any person or thing, sceptics argue that
under much deeper hypnotism more profound changes
could conceivably take place in the human mind, perhaps
opening up channels of creative thought and memory
recall beyond the conscious capacity of the person
involved. In the late 1970s a Russian physician named
Dr Vladimir Raikov set out these objections in a paper
entitled *Artificial Reincarnation Through Hypnosis*. The
article described a series of experiments Raikov had
undertaken in which hypnotized students were made to
believe they were the returned souls of famous people.
A music student who was told that she was a virtuoso
violinist, began to play in a style reminiscent of her 'dead
self', whilst an art student, given to believe he was the
soul of a famous Russian painter, managed to paint
with a skill and style well beyond his personal ability.
Dr Raikov's point was made clear enough.

But damning though this evidence might appear at first
glance, the alternative explanations offered by sceptics
of reincarnation cannot be described as wholly convincing. It is difficult to imagine, for example, how
the ego-gratification syndrome that Dr Arthur Hastings
identified could account for more than a tiny percentage
of regression cases, since very few past lives recalled under
hypnosis are those of famous or noteworthy people,
and the vast majority reflect mundane and insignificant
existences. The idea that hypnotists deliberately direct
their subjects towards a fantasy construction is similarly
misleading. Regression researchers like Dr Edith Fiore
and Joe Keeton take considerable care not to lead their

subjects, allowing them instead to find their own past lives. The likelihood that subjects are merely attempting to please their hypnotists is a possibility firmly rejected by the researchers themselves. Answering the question in her book *You Have Been Here Before*, Dr Fiore wrote that if her patients had been fooling her for so long they should all be nominated for Academy Awards. Having listened to and watched thousands of examples of regression, the American doctor became convinced there was 'no deliberate, nor conscious attempt to defraud. The tears, shaking, the gasping for breath and actual physical manifestations are all too real.' Witnesses who have seen a regression at first hand will find it difficult to argue with Dr Fiore's comments. I have myself heard a woman recalling her terror at being burned as a witch; the pain of those last moments was all too real in her mind – it was as if it were happening again. How could such vivid recollections be summoned up at a moment's notice with all the attendant anguish and distress involved, if they in no way reflect actual remembrances? How might ordinary people effect so totally the mannerisms and voice patterns of those whose class, culture, race and even gender may be completely different from their own?

In order to appreciate fully the unlikelihood that regression is in some ways consciously or unconsciously faked, one needs to remember the way in which hypnotism works. At the lower levels of a trance – those used by stage hypnotists – subjects become relaxed, are able readily to accept suggestions, and may be persuaded to undergo temporary personality changes. Usually the subject does not remember much about these events afterwards, undergoing a sort of spontaneous amnesia, and on this level only superficial psychiatric analysis may take place. Deep trance hypnotism, the type practised by past-life regression therapists, is a rather different matter

for, once in the deep trance state, the subject has little
chance of doing other than what they are told. Mainstream psychiatrists accept without question that, whilst
under a deep trance, patients' minds can be so completely
taken back to a very early age, that their handwriting will
conform to samples taken from their old school books.
There is even evidence that hypnotized subjects recalling
childhood go back to the appropriate physiological level.
Examination of eye movements indicate that when people
are regressed to an early age, their ocular coordination
either degenerates or improves to the level that prescrip-
tive evidence indicates they enjoyed at the time. It is a
fact that would astonish most opticians and has proved to
be clinically impossible to create artificially. Yet, such is
the power of hypnotism that even the changing patterns
of neurophysiological responses during the first months
following birth have been precisely mirrored during
experiments into early-life regression.

All this supports the contention of conventional medical practice that regression into one's early years is a
proven phenomenon. If such hypnotic states produce
accurate memories from babyhood then surely it is only
logical to assume that the same method can be trusted to
produce past-life memories. Indeed, to argue otherwise
is to stand commonsense on its head. However, there is
fortunately another way of establishing whether regressed
subjects are reporting genuine recollections and not just
daydreaming. Electroencephalographic studies carried
out by scientists in Sacramento, USA, have shown that
past-life memories occur when the brain level measures
8.3 cycles per second. When the subconscious state is
altered – when the conscious mind is invited to interfere
– the pattern alters immediately. Another machine, called
a biosometer, was used by the same investigators to meas-
ure galvanic skin response, the minute secretions from

the skin pores which show whether a person is telling the truth. Effectively lie detectors, both techniques proved beyond any reasonable doubt that the regressed subjects, without exception, fully believed in their own memories. Or, to put it another way, they proved that the memories were real.

In assessing evidence for past-life regression, the most impressive examples are always those where related details can be crosschecked against known facts. Sadly, this is easier said than done, for many subjects recall lives from long ago. More importantly, as adults they have undoubtedly gained access to material from which some part of their subconscious mind might draw. This second factor has led many convincing cases to come under suspicion and it is a problem recognized by those regression hypnotists who have dedicated their lives to uncovering evidence for genuine reincarnation. Occasionally, a case which initially seems of considerable interest, eventually has to be discarded on these grounds.

In 1979, when I first met Joe Keeton, the English hypnotist, he had by then conducted over 11,000 separate regressions. Always searching for perfect proof, he was pinning his hopes on Pauline McKay, a young woman from Manchester who under hypnosis recalled details of her life as Kitty Jay, a West Country servant girl who had committed suicide in the eighteenth century. McKay's recollections were particularly vivid and when Keeton made enquiries at Exeter Central Library, the chief librarian confirmed many of the details given by 'Kitty Jay,' including several old place names no longer used. What was more, the suicide story was correct down to the last detail – the girl hanged herself at Canna Farm on the edge of Dartmoor. However, this in itself proved to be an unexpected barrier to the proven likelihood of actual reincarnation, for the site of 'Jay's Grave' had become something of a legend locally, reputedly being haunted. Moreover, the full story of the servant girl's death is included in several books on British ghosts.

Even though Keeton believed Pauline McKay's assertions that she had never read such books, it destroyed the case he had been attempting to build. The girl need not have been deceiving herself either, since it has long been observed how the human brain is capable of storing in its darkest recesses virtually every single sense-impression that has ever entered it. This hidden memory or cryptomensia, has been regularly put forward by sceptics eager to explain the most intriguing examples of past-life regression. Do they have a case or is reincarnation still the most probable explanation?

Extremities of cryptomensiac activity are almost as unbelievable as rebirth itself and it is small wonder that many have been wrongly taken to be evidence of such. In 1906, the British Society for Psychical Research investigated a medium known in their records as Miss C. Under a trance, the medium took upon herself the persona of a distinguished medieval lady called Blanche Poynings, a spirit who claimed to have once been the maid servant of the Countess of Salisbury. Her knowledge of the culture of the earlier era was truly extraordinary and few among those who encountered 'Blanche Poynings' doubted that her spirit had returned. However, the truth was a little different. After several extraordinary sessions SPR members asked the entranced Miss C if there was any way they might check the facts she had given. She replied; 'Ask E. Holt.' E. Holt proved to be none other than Emily Holt, a Victorian historical novelist whose fiction *Countess Maud* contained every detail of Blanche Poyning's life story. Though Miss C insisted that she had herself never read one of Emily Holt's novels, the only rational assumption the SPR could make was that she had done so and forgotten it consciously. Meanwhile, her subconscious mind in some way stored the pages as though on photographic plates.

An even more extraordinary case of cryptomensia, this time resulting from supposed past-life regression, concerned a thirteen-year-old Norwegian schoolgirl who conjured up the personalities of no less than eight previous incarnations, under the hypnosis of Finnish psychiatrist Dr Reima Kampman. Ranging from a Babylonian woman who lived over 2,500 thousand years ago to a Russian girl who died of tuberculosis in post-revolutionary Leningrad, the teenager's recollections seemed entirely authentic. Most impressive were the memories of Dorothy, a twelfth-century English peasant girl who liked to recite a poem she called the *Summer Song*. Not understood by her hypnotist, the words were eventually identified by university lecturers who specialized in the Middle-English period, as being those of a seven hundred-year-old lyric called the *Cuckoo Song*. Understandably, the Finnish psychiatrist considered this at first to be a prima-facie case of reincarnation. However, the mystery was differently solved when, some years afterwards, again under hypnosis, the Norwegian girl recalled borrowing a song book from her local library which contained a version of the *Cuckoo Song*. Although she had never properly read the book, let alone learnt it by heart, a brief glance at the page seems to have been enough for the child to hold the obscure verses in her mind for all time. At once the existence of Dorothy, the twelfth-century peasant girl, seemed remote.

Taking the cases of cryptomensia outlined above as the starting point for a generally sceptical overview of all hypnotic regressions, English author Ian Wilson attempted in his book *The After Death Experience* to analyze what he saw as the crucial flaws in one of the most sensational series of past-life regressions to surface during the past twenty years: the Bloxham Tapes. Arnall Bloxham, an English doctor who lived near Cardiff, began regressing friends and volunteers in the early 1970s. One of his first subjects, a young Welsh swimming instructor named Graham Huxtable, became Ben, an eighteenth-century master gunner on the British warship *Aggie*. Describing an engagement with the French fleet Ben's voice grew loud and raucous, his speech containing the sort of obscure nautical terminology that Graham Huxtable could hardly have known. When Huxtable listened to a tape of his trance utterances he professed astonishment, confirming that he had never been to sea nor had any interest in naval history. So realistic were the sailor's accounts of life aboard an eighteenth-century British Man O'War, that upon hearing them, ex-Lord of the Admiralty Earl Mountbatten commissioned a Royal Naval historian named Owen Warren to verify the accuracy of the accents, dialect and expressions used. In due course Warren confirmed their accuracy and both aristocrat and academic became convinced the regression was authentic. To Bloxham's irritation, however, a trawl of naval records uncovered no reference to the vessel's name nor its commander, who Ben identified as a Captain Pearce. And so, whilst Graham Huxtable's trance-induced recall demonstrated considerable knowledge of peripheral details, speech archaisms and naval customs appropriate to the period he appeared to be reliving, the central facts of the purported former life remained elusive, thus leaving the story unproven.

Soon afterwards, however, Bloxham found an even more striking example which seemed at last to offer proof of reincarnation beyond reasonable doubt. Jane Evans was the pseudonym of a woman who was able to recall seven past lives: a Roman living in the Britain of the first century AD, a Jewess murdered in a pogrom in York, a Parisian prostitute, a maid servant from the Loire Valley, a serving girl in the reign of Queen Anne, a lady-in-waiting at the Spanish Court, and, most recently, an American nun who lived and died in a convent in Des Moines, Iowa. Each of Jane Evans's pasts provided a wealth of evidence suggestive of reincarnation, especially those which showed expert historical knowledge of Roman Britain, or the geographical accuracy of the Loire Valley, a region which the twentieth-century English woman had certainly never visited. In terms of cross-reference by far the most impressive evidence was her recall of the life of Rebecca, the Jewess who claimed to have died in an anti-semitic riot in the York of 1190. Historical records showed that there had indeed been such an uprising of violent anti-Jewish feeling and an expert on the period, Professor Barrie Dobson of the University of York, was moved to astonishment by Rebecca's accurate reconstruction of the massacre. The one major weakness in her story concerned her claim that, before their eventual slaughter, she and her family had hidden in the crypt of a church. The problem was that the church she described, St Mary's Castlegate, had no crypt.

For a time it seemed that the former lives of Jane Evans could not be proved. Then, incredibly, six months after her regression, workmen renovating the floor of St Mary's discovered remains of a hitherto undiscovered room with vaults and arches. As Arnall Bloxham later wrote, it was the clearest possible evidence of reincarnation for, if no living person had known of the crypt's existence then the fact remained unguessable to the present-day mind of Jane Evans. The implications of the case were staggering. Predictably, not everyone concurred. Casting his usual sceptical eye across the enigma, author Ian Wilson

justifiably pointed out that Jane Evans's knowledge of
Roman Britain could have been gleaned from history
books; likewise, her geographical awareness of the Loire
Valley might have been picked up from any one of a
number of travel magazines. Despite her protestations
that she knew little or nothing about either of these
subjects, the cryptomensiac faculty (already proven to
exist to a phenomenal degree in some individuals) might
bear responsibility. However, when faced with the enigma
of Rebecca, Wilson's objections were less easy to uphold.
Minor discrepancies between the spelling and pronunciation of actual twelfth-century words and those used by
the regressed woman seem of little importance, set against
the number of genuine historical facts she could recall.
Also, the fact that there were (as Wilson contends) over
forty other churches in York at the time would appear
to be of questionable relevance, since Rebecca clearly
describes St Mary's Castlegate – a fact accepted by a
genuine expert of the period, Professor Dobson. With
the discovery of the previously hidden room underneath
the church, cryptomensia can, in this instance at least, be
ruled out entirely. Absolute proof of reincarnation it may
not be, but surely one must go very far before finding an
alternative explanation that makes more sense.

Remarkably, since the case of Jane Evans was first published in Arnall Bloxham's *More Lives Than One*, in 1978,
an even more striking example of regression has emerged
from a London-based group of Joe Keeton's volunteers.
The subject was a journalist named Ray Bryant who, in
1983, began writing a series of features on regression
for the local *Evening Post*. Under Keeton's hypnosis,
Bryant recalled several former identities including that
of a soldier named Reuben Stafford who fought in the
Crimean War before returning to England to spend
his last days as a Thames boatman. As recalled by

Bryant, Stafford's life ended when he was drowned in an accident in 1879. After witnessing the manifestation of the Victorian soldier, two of Keeton's research team, Andrew and Marguerite Selby, attempted to find documentary evidence of the man's existence.

In the Guildhall Library, London, the couple were fortunate enough to find a roll call of Crimean War casualties. Among those listed was one Sergeant Reuben Stafford, then serving with the 47th Lancashire Regiment of Foot, who was wounded in the hand at the Battle of the Quarries, a little-remembered skirmish that had taken place during the siege of Sevastapol. It also gave details of Sergeant Stafford's subsequent career, in which he won medals for bravery. At the next opportunity for regression these very same details came unprompted from the mouth of Ray Bryant. The date, location and name of the battle were recalled by Stafford as well as his regiment. All were exactly correct. This was by no means the end of the Selbys' research. Spending some days at the General Register of Births, Deaths and Marriages they eventually located Reuben Stafford's death certificate which showed that, having drowned (accidently or not), the ex-soldier had been buried in a pauper's grave at East Ham. Under regression, the date of Stafford's death and burial were also given by Ray Bryant.

Is there any way these facts could be known without the operation of some form of reincarnation? In the regression of the journalist the possibility of cryptomensia hardly arises, since the details of the long-since dead soldier's war record would have remained safely away from public gaze. Unless one assumes that Keeton and his volunteers have abused their chosen occupation by perpetrating an elaborate fraud, the return to life of the Crimean War veteran in the body of the twentieth-century journalist would seem to be an odds-on bet.

* * *

Outstanding individual examples like the one outlined above are probably the closest we will ever get to proving that pre-birth regression really does involve returning to an actual past life. However, it is by no means the only evidence we have. Recent studies have shown how statistical analysis of regression therapy recollections upholds the probability that reincarnation lies at the bottom of the mystery. When American psychologist Dr Helen Wambach opened her practice in Walnut Creek, California, she made detailed case notes of all her patients. Looking at a study of 1,088 regressions Wambach found that, regardless of the sex of their present incarnation, her patients in past lives seemed to divide evenly across the gender barrier: 49.4 per cent female; 50.6 per cent male. This proportion not only upholds the beliefs of reincarnationists concerning the sexless nature of the human soul, but is in exact accordance with actual population gender distribution. The same proportions were reflected in smaller samples, even where there was only a single sex being regressed.

A socioeconomic breakdown of Wambach's regressions also corresponded closely with established historical evidence. Less than ten per cent of those who underwent regression recalled lives of the upper-class, whilst the vast majority relived a miserable existence of poor food and inadequate shelter. As might be expected, an analysis of remembered lives closer to the present age showed that the proportion of middle-class lives grew larger, thus reflecting the actual growth in prosperity during modern times. Wambach's statistics also closely mirrored US racial distribution even though her patients were overwhelmingly white. Easily the most important statistical evidence produced by Dr Wambach's work in California is her refutation of one of the key arguments so often used by opponents of reincarnation – the population conundrum. The present number of souls incarnated on earth is clearly higher than ever before and growing all the time, a fact which leads sceptics to ask where these 'new' people are actually coming from. The argument cannot be lightly dismissed. The world population doubled between Christ's death and the sixteenth century, doubled again by the nineteenth century and is now nearly five times as great as it was then.

Once again, Helen Wambach's statistics may hold a clue to the mystery. Having noticed a shorter and shorter period of time between incarnations as the centuries passed, the American analyst decided to construct a test to prove whether or not the frequency of regressed lives followed the actual birth rate. Her sample, over one thousand volunteers, were asked to choose three lives at random from the past 4,000 years. When fed through a computer, the statistical breakdown of the responses reproduced the precise curve of estimated overall population growth on earth during the same period. Unless Dr Wambach has allowed enthusiasm for her own reincarnationist beliefs to persuade her to falsify deliberately these figures, rebirth in some form seems the only tenable explanation for the various statistical links. The results of a sample comprising of a thousand volunteers recalling several thousand lives can hardly be explained in terms of coincidence when they corrolate so closely to the known distribution of sex, race, socioeconomic classes and the population growth curve.

Inevitably, there will still be those who choose to ignore this evidence and concentrate instead upon what critics have labelled the 'fundamental flaws' in the case for past-life reality. How, they ask, can a sixteenth-century French peasant understand modern English as spoken by an American psychologist and reply in the same language and retain distinct traces of a twentieth-century accent? On the face of it, this logical contradiction might seem unanswerable. Yet it misses the point. All hypnotists accept that, under regression, a part of the subject's normal consciousness (of their present incarnation) is functioning. Naturally, this present personality would choose to communicate in a medium through which it can be understood, and in many cases regression hypnotists, such as American Dr Edith Fiore, preface their regression by telling their subjects to conduct communications in English. So the contradiction is explained easily enough. Interestingly, however, there have been occasional examples where knowledge of a foreign language appears through the mouths of regressed individuals, and where such inexplicable cases occur spontaneously we see once more the clearest imaginable case for belief in reincarnation.

The incidence of unknown and sometimes dead languages echoing from the mouths of modern speakers (termed, as we have already seen, as xenoglossia) has been recorded from our own century and before. In November 1930 a four-year-old girl living in Warsaw was found to be able to speak fluent Gaelic, even though her parents knew only Polish. In the same year, a New York physician named Dr Marshall McDuffie discovered that his twin toddlers were able to converse in an unknown vernacular. He thought it was a made-up tongue until a professor of ancient languages, who visited the household as a guest, heard the McDuffie children speaking and pronounced it to be Aramaic, a language current at the time of Christ. In 1958 Dr Ian Stevenson conducted a lengthy investigation into the xenoglossiac abilities of a thirty-seven-year-old Philadelphia housewife who was able to converse in fluent Swedish under the hypnotic direction of her physician husband. The woman never studied the Scandinavian language nor associated with Swedes, and in specially designed modern language aptitude tests her low scores proved that she had no unrecognized ability for picking up languages. Yet whilst in a trance, she could identify artefacts from a Swedish museum, using their correct (old) Swedish names, and experts in the Scandinavian language confirmed her usage to be archaic and laced with expressions appropriate to someone living in that country several hundred years previously.

More recently, regression hypnotists have found patients with similar xenoglossiac abilities. One American eleven-year-old studied by Dr Morris Netherton was able to talk at length in an ancient Chinese dialect, whilst in Toronto, a Canadian child psychologist recalled his days as a Viking warrior in Norsk, the precursor to modern Icelandic. The same subject also remembered living as a young man in Mesopotamia in AD 625, and proceeded to write in the language of the day. Samples were verified by experts in ancient Middle-Eastern culture in Washington, who confirmed the language to be Sassamid Pahlavi, a form of writing not used since AD 651, and which bears no relation to modern Persian. Not surprisingly, these learned men were unable to offer even a tentative explanation for the way in which the Middle-Eastern vocabulary, with its own peculiar set of grammatical rules, had entered the mind of the Canadian psychologist.

As the last decade of the twentieth-century dawns, interest in reincarnation has reached an all-time high. Given the number of publications to appear on the subject during recent years, it is perhaps not surprising that more people believe in rebirth than ever before. Certainly the evidence of four decades of extensive research into the phenomenon speaks for itself. It is an established fact that thousands of children around the world can recall previous existences and there are tens of thousands more adults who have recalled post-life memories under hypnotic regression. Although most of us brought up in the Western tradition find reincarnation hard to accept a dispassionate study of the evidence contained in the last two chapters must surely give pause for thought. The fact that the vast majority of cases outlined above come from Western sources and not from reincarnationist countries, only strengthens the reasons for believing the evidence. On any objective analysis, these stories are probably true.

From a philosophical standpoint, the cycle of rebirth and karma offer much to those who despair of the seeming chaos of moral inequality, injustice and evil in the world. Under karmic law, the rank, character, circumstances and opportunities awarded in each successive existence depends upon the qualities, deeds and attainments of that soul during its preceding lives. We get precisely what we deserve in the end. Once the collective mind admits that this ancient theory is true, then all philosophical difficulties of moral justice vanish. Can we prove that karma exists? Some believe we can. Although regression studies into the workings of karma have so far only been carried out on a rough-and-ready basis, it does appear that a high percentage of those successfully regressed back through several former lives feel an awareness of the operation of a cause-effect principle linking their incarnations. This fact, coupled with the statistical evidence gathered by Dr Helen Wambach examined above, can only lead to the assumption that reincarnation happens to us all and that we are each one of us subject to the same karmic law. The non-believers may claim otherwise, but to deny the evidence from forty years of research would seem irrational to say the least. It is significant that no studies carried out during the same period succeeded in weakening the case for reincarnation and many former sceptics have turned into believers as a result of their own investigations. By the same token there have been no philosophical or theological traditions to emerge during the past 5,000 years that seem more satisfying or uplifting than that of the karmic cycle. Accept it and the total experience of humanity begins to form a perfect panorama of poetic justice. It is at once a vaster, grander scheme than most of us hitherto imagined, one worthy of the mind of God.

That a startling upsurge of interest in reincarnation is underway can no longer be doubted. Opinion poll figures between 1969 and 1979 in the United Kingdom showed a rise from eighteen to twenty-eight per cent expressing personal belief, and a similar increase over the same period has been recorded in the USA. Belief among those under the age of twenty was somewhat higher, so it is reasonably safe to assume that the same poll conducted today would show a continuation of the upward curve. As the 1990s begin, it is quite probable that one person in every three on both sides of the Atlantic may now accept the idea of rebirth. Yet surveys from the late 1950s showed that fewer than three in every hundred polled accepted reincarnation. Is this huge rise simply a response to the many books and documentaries that have appeared on the subject in the recent decades? Or is there a deeper, more mysterious reason for the fundamental shift in opinion? Some look towards the latter possibility. Those who believe in the millennium think that the world is about to enter a new age, in which mankind will come to realize once again many of the old truths of existence (such as reincarnation), throw off its materialistic ways, and inherit its true spiritual identity. It will be a new era when wars will be replaced by peace, starvation by plenty.

Up until very recently I have been less than hopeful about these predictions of a better tomorrow. However, one cannot help but be struck by the dramatic events on the world's stage which have coincided in a quite startling way with the celestial prophecies of the 'New Age timetable'. Curiously, the key to my change of opinion is the planet Pluto, an unattractive lump of rock, ice and methane frost revolving billions of miles away on the farthest edge of the solar system. Discovered by astronomers as recently as 1930, Pluto was long before known to astrologers, to whom it symbolized the cycle of death and rebirth. According to astrological lore, the planet exerts a particularly potent force on human affairs when it is at large (in conjunction) in the sign of Scorpio. These periods, one of which we are currently living through, occur every 248 years; the present period began on 27 August 1984 and will last until 10 November 1995.

In his book *The Case for Reincarnation*, published in 1984 to coincide with the start of the present Pluto-Scorpio axis, Canadian author Joe Fisher points out that truly momentous events have taken place during past conjunctions of sign and planet. In the final chapter of his book he explains how astrologers believe the present age – the one at the millennium – could be richer in changes than all the others, including wars and political upheavals. Fisher goes on to predict that the changes will be at their height in the period beginning in the autumn of 1989 when Pluto is at perihelion, its closest to the Sun. It is difficult to imagine how this prophecy could have been proved more correct. The second half of 1989 saw the most far-reaching political transformation in Europe since the end of World War II. Not only have the Communist dictatorships lost power, but the rapidity of the revolutions was both unprecedented and unexpected. No one writing in 1984 could have conceivably predicted that a single year, half a decade in the future, would see a redrawing of so much of the world map. Indeed, no one writing in January 1989 might have guessed that the next twelve months would see a Solidarity Government elected in Poland, the end of the Berlin Wall, and the crumbling of the whole Warsaw Pact edifice. Nevertheless, as Fisher's Astrological Survey predicted, the pace of change reached its height after September 1989 and as I write these words in the autumn of 1992 it shows little sign of slowing. If anything, history seems to have gone into overdrive. The past two years have seen revolution and counter-revolution in Romania, a bloody civil war in Yugoslavia and the complete reunification of Germany. The triumph of democracy and the failure of a military coup in the Soviet Union, not only ended the Cold War, it also led to the demise of the world's largest country as a single entity.

Never in the history of the world has there have been such a concentrated period of political upheaval. Are the astrologers right in saying that the human race as a whole is undergoing a form of collective rebirth? Are we all living through a form of global regeneration from which we will emerge into the much vaunted Aquarian Age? Time alone will tell but can it be coincidence that following the conflagration in the Gulf world leaders East and West are talking openly of a new world order? Whatever our collective futures, more and more of us are beginning to realize that our present life is not our first and that we will each individually return at some preordained moment in the future. If the recognition of this fact teaches us to have greater respect for each other and greater faith in ourselves, then an awareness of our true destiny may play a part in building a better world.

On Reflection

Death be not proud, though some have called thee
Mighty and dreadful, for thou art not so:
For those whom thou think'st thou dost overthrow
Die not, poor Death; nor yet canst thou kill me.

John Donne
Death

In his now famous interview given to the *Scientific American* in 1920, inventor Thomas Alva Edison set out the logical argument for believing that contact with the dead was possible in the following terms: 'If our personality survives, then it is strictly logical and scientific to assume that it retains memory, intellect and other faculties and knowledge . . . therefore, if personality exists after what we call death, it is reasonable to conclude that those who leave this earth and survive would like to communicate the fact with those they left here.' Although Edison never achieved his ambition to create a mechanism subtle enough to capture the vibrations of the spirit realms, he was surely right in his basic assumption that the dead wish to show that they remain alive. Over the past century they have chosen a variety of ways of doing so, mostly on a mental level but on other occasions through a direct imprint on the physical world. These latter examples are often among the most startling.

*   *   *

On a warm, sunny morning in August 1971 Señora Maria Gómez Pereira, a resident of Belmez de la Morelada, a village near Córdoba in southern Spain, awoke to find that a peculiar portrait of a human face had appeared overnight on the tiles of her kitchen floor. Although the sight of the face did not particularly frighten her, Señora Pereira became alarmed when sightseers arrived in large numbers to view the manifestation. So she decided to get rid of it. After scrubbing with detergent failed to remove the image she told her son Miguel to break up the floor with a pick axe and lay a new surface. The renovation was duly carried out but the Pereiras' lives had only just returned to normal when new and even more clearly defined faces began to appear spontaneously in the fresh cement. Among these was that of a middle-aged man whose identity was recognized by elderly residents of Belmez as being that of a villager who had died many years before. They were certain that his body had been laid to rest in a long since disused cemetery upon which Señora Pereira's home now stood.

Inevitably the Belmez phenomenon drew the interest of the parascientific community. One expert, Germán de Argumosa, analyzed the concrete and confirmed the absence of any known pigment or dyeing agent; only a paranormal explanation seemed possible he concluded. In November 1971 the visages were carefully cut from the floor and mounted behind glass. Following their removal, the floor was excavated and several metres down some human bones were found, reinforcing the probability that the house had been built on a site of a graveyard. Moreover, old photographs appeared to lend credence to the views of local people that it was the faces of those buried in the graveyard who were now imprinted on the Pereira's kitchen floor. From that moment on, no one in Belmez doubted the existence of the hereafter.

Celebrated though it has become, the Spanish house of faces is merely one example among dozens to emerge from various countries around the world. In 1923 damp stains appeared on the wall of Christ Church in Oxford, stains which bore the clear and unmistakable profile of the late dean of the college, Henry Liddell. None who saw the phenomenon could explain it in terms other than the preternatural. Had Liddell, a believer in the afterlife, returned to prove his continued existence to his old students and fellows? There seemed no other logical explanation. The Christ Church manifestation may confound those sceptical of an afterlife, yet it makes considerable sense to occultists who believe that the world of spirit interpenetrates the physical world of matter. The ability of spirit-mind to affect matter is evidenced by the way that the dead sometimes appear spontaneously on photographic exposures, and the long established capability of poltergeists to move physical objects. As we have seen, the electronic voice phenomenon currently being researched in Europe and America provides further evidence.

Without doubt direct contacts are becoming more frequent. Most recently the power of spirits to interfere in the mortal plane through the manipulation of technological apparatus suggests that we may be in for a real breakthrough in channelling in the very near future. In December 1984, Ken Webster, an economics teacher at a secondary school in Chester, installed a BBC microcomputer in his sixteenth-century cottage home on the Welsh border. The machine worked normally until one night it began to display curious messages on the screen, messages which made perfect sense yet which appeared without the influence of a human operator. No one actually saw the machine in the process of creating, but the transmissions, some as long as 400 words, continued to appear for months. Using the vocabulary and idioms of sixteenth-century English, they were signed Tomas Hardern, apparently the ghost of a man who had lived on the site of Webster's cottage some four hundred years previously.

How the discarnate mind of such a person could comprehend the detailed functioning of a BBC micro is open to question. But the transmissions (over 300 in all) were real enough. They have since been analyzed by linguist Peter Trinder who found a total vocabulary of 2,877 words of which 120 had never been recorded before. All but sixty-five of those recognized were in use during the sixteenth century and both the spellings and semantics of the language proved to be consistent with sixteenth-century usage. Trinder dismissed the possibility that Webster could have subconsciously affected the machine during his hours of sleep; in his opinion only someone who had lived at the time could have written the lines.

This is not the only example we have of ghosts flashing up messages on computers. In 1987 an Amstrad PC1512, installed in an architect's office in Stockport, England, would regularly collect mediumistic messages during the hours of darkness. Even when it was left unplugged it would be found the next morning with the screen glowing and the ghostly lines entered. When technical experts stripped it down and inspected every component, they found absolutely nothing out of the ordinary. Elsewhere in the world, the introduction of information technology has not been ignored by the spirits. In addition to the numerous phone calls from the dead outlined in chapter four, there have been several instances of ghosts apparently leaving messages on answering machines, shattering the argument that these phantom phone calls might just be the imagination of receivers. In Luxembourg, two researchers into electronic voice phenomenon, Jules and Maggie Harsh-Frischbach, regularly return home to discover coherent transmissions from deceased colleagues on their answerphone tape recorder. As our own information technology continues to become more sophisticated, so more spirits may choose to take advantage of it. As British author Lyall Watson has wryly commented, the days of the phantom fax may be just around the corner.

For those discarnate souls determined to prove their continued existence, the possibilities opened up by these technological breakthroughs must be a great relief. Certainly, channelling through the mind of a mortal psychic seems to be an exhausting and frustrating process. In the spirit words of Professor F.H. Myers, a founding member of the British Society for Psychical Research and later part of the Cross-Correspondence team of spirit contacts, mediumship difficulties were like 'standing behind a sheet of frosted glass which blurs and deadens sound – dictating feebly to a reluctant and somewhat obtuse secretary.' The inherent obstacles involved in communicating between worlds may go some way to explain the frequent unreliability of messages from beyond the grave. Just as it is only to be expected that some mediums will be more capable than others, so some spirits inevitably vary in their own sensitivity. Yet the considerable disparity between the best and worst spiritualistic communications should not blind us as to the probability that mediumistic phenomena are real. Whilst many messages might be the product of unconscious ESP between medium and sitter, or the result of mythopoeia (the human mind's proven capacity to create detailed stories and characters), they cannot account for such examples as the Cross-Correspondences or the many instances of precognitive messages which have been proven true only after a period of time has passed. Nor do they explain transmissions received from so-called drop-in communicators who interrupt seances to give information unknown and irrelevant to any of those present, but which later proves to be spectacularly correct. In fact, however hard the sceptics might try to argue otherwise, the supernatural remains the most likely cause of spiritualistic channelling. James Hyslop, co-founder of the American SPR, summed up the case for mediumship best of all. In 1905, after receiving an extraordinarily impressive series of messages through the mouthpiece of clairvoyant Leonora Piper, Hyslop carefully weighed up the reasons for disbelief, including telepathy, fraud, or the more convoluted alternatives of split personalities and mythopoeia. In the end he wrote, 'I prefer to believe I have been talking to my dead relatives in person. In truth it is much simpler.' A similar argument could be applied to virtually all the evidence for the case against death included in this book.

Ghosts have been seen by millions in every country and culture. The presence of invisible but seemingly intelligent and autonomous forces have been discovered in houses around the world, their activities recorded on film and audio equipment and witnessed by scientists, priests, politicians and policemen amongst many others. Spiritualist mediums have not only received messages which contain knowledge known only by their supposed contacts, but some have exhibited miraculous feats such as healings, levitation and incombustibility. Hundreds of thousands of people have reported out-of-body experiences, and the ability of the human mind to operate beyond the confines of the five bodily senses has now been proven in numerous laboratory tests. The similarity between the memories of those who have revived after the cessation of vital life-signs is difficult to explain within the rationalist world view, but conforms precisely with the experience of dying described in ancient Tibetan texts. As for the reincarnation evidence, hundreds of children have recalled previous lives in detail, many exhibiting birthmarks corresponding to injuries suffered at the moment of their previous deaths. Tens of thousands of adults have claimed similar recollections under the influence of hypnotic regression. As we have seen, all these separate strands of evidence point towards the simple fact that we cannot die.

If we choose to reject this evidence we must find alternative explanations for each and every enigma. It is the 'natural' explanations which fail to satisfy. To explain away the appearance of ghosts without recourse to the supernatural, one would need to postulate that millions of people down the centuries had hallucinated; were deceived by tricks of the light; misidentified natural phenomena; were insane, half blind, or drunk at the time the alleged sightings took place. If we reject poltergeists, we must surely assume that those who report them are liars or hysterics, including, presumably, those members of scientific teams who have investigated them on numerous occasions. If we label all spiritualists as charlatans, we must dismiss their apparently genuine transmissions as lucky guesses, or find some other non-mechanistic theory to account for them, such as ESP. We must also ignore more than a hundred years of psychic research on both sides of the Atlantic. Any non-paranormal explanation for the out-of-body experience phenomenon would need to assume the existence of a hitherto undiscovered mental faculty; the similarity between the tales of those who were resuscitated must be marked down as mere coincidence. The testimony of those who recall past lives must also be put down to extended synchronism, unless it is assumed that researchers into past-life recall are cynically manipulating their findings to fit their chosen hypothesis. Clearly, no explanation based on the split personality syndrome could account for physical signs on children's bodies which correspond to past-life experiences, so these once again must be put down to coincidence.

Is this rationalist standpoint really the most likely explanation for these various mysteries, all of which seem to point towards the reality of a life beyond death? The philosophical device of Occam's razor tells us that in order to solve a mystery it is always best to opt for the simplest explanation. As James Hyslop wrote, it seems rather more straightforward to accept the possibility of an afterlife than it is to create a series of evermore complicated hypothetical possibilities which taken together help to reject it. After all, what purely mechanistic theory can account for the way that spirits act upon physical matter through such diverse paranormal phenomena as phantom pyromaniacs or instantaneous cures? Indeed, try as I might, I have been unable to find a sceptic prepared to hold to this logical standpoint in the face of the evidence I and other researchers have uncovered. By contrast, the dualistic vision of the world, both seen and unseen, appears on reflection to make the most perfect sense. The different strands of evidence can be collated and cross-referenced to form a consistent model of the paraphysical world through which there runs a philosophy which is not only intellectually satisfying but spiritually uplifting. In a curious way it is also profoundly scientific.

Just as Eastern religions teach that the world is an illusion, so spiritualist mediums in the West are told by their guides that the world around us lacks objective reality. Today at least one branch of mainstream science – the new physics – is lining up on the side of the mystics. Just as Einstein's Relativity Theory swept away the old concepts of space and time, so the development of quantum mechanics has gone even further, showing how our basic understanding of reality is false. Today's experts working in the field of sub-nuclear physics have proved conclusively that the apparent stability and solidity of our planet is in itself a mirage. The pen that I am holding to write these lines seems solid enough to me yet it is really a shifting play of tiny particles rotating in violent orbit. Even my hand, my brain, my whole body, is mostly empty space populated by trillions of electrons swarming in frantic motion. In a sense, our bodies are already patterns of energy, no more, no less. On the sub-atomic level, we are indistinguishable from the inanimate objects which surround us. Only our minds separate us from other things and it is our minds alone which makes the vital difference. Perception is all.

To physicists, the evidence of our eyes and ears is a lie. As the astonomer Sir James Jeans wrote, 'Things are not what they seem; it is the general recognition that we are not yet in contact with the ultimate reality.' A mystic in his later years, Jeans felt that mankind's consciousness was in grave need of development. As things stood the human race was imprisoned in a dark cave, its back to the light, watching flickering shadows on the wall and perceiving them to be all that there was. Another great scientific mind of the modern era, Sir Arthur Eddington, put it even more succinctly, 'Something unknown is doing what we don't know what.' But cracks are beginning to appear in the fortress wall of ignorance. The most important discovery of the new physics is the considerable probability that mind and matter are interrelated in the most fundamental way. Our individual and collective experience of reality is shaped not only in a passive way but also in an active sense. In other words, there is a paraphysical interaction not only between our own minds and our own bodies, but between the minds and the bodies of those who inhabit the world around us, perhaps even the very fabric of everything around us. Many modern physicists will even argue, albeit so far quietly, that mind, matter and energy cannot exist independently of each other. In the words of Sir Arthur Eddington, 'The stuff of the world is mind stuff.'

The implications of all this for the case against death are crystal clear. If mind and matter are truly insepa-rable, then psychic phenomena begins immediately to fall within a logical framework. Even more importantly, it opens up the distinct probability of life existing on other realms of vibration. Another world existing out there beyond our senses. Mind stuff too, only more so. The German physicist Max Planck was one who eventually reached this conclusion. Another was the Nobel Prize winner Wolfgang Pauli. Since then, the discovery of such particles as the photon (a pulse of light which has no mass and no charge) suggests that two different worlds might exist together – one mass and the other anti-mass. The march towards new horizons continues.

During the past two decades the brilliant American nuclear physicist Arthur Young has constructed an ingenious theory which links together sub-atomic phys-ics, consciousness and the phenomenon of light. Young has pointed out that light, like colour, has no mass yet is real nevertheless. On a sub-atomic level, light is even able to create protons and electrons with mass and charge even though it is without charge or energy in itself. Could this be an insight into the structure of the ideo-plastic other-world spoken of by returned souls and those who undergo near-death experiences? A world where thought can alter reality without the heavier constraints of the world of matter? A world where dreams and nightmares quite literally come true?

This is one for the great scientific minds of the next century to prove. One thing, however, is clear among all this metaphysical speculation: namely that if human individuals do survive physical dissolution, then it is their minds which continue to exist. But what exactly is a mind? Or indeed a self? Clearly, if mediumistic transmissions are to be believed, the newly dead take with them their memory facility, beliefs and the conceptual view of reality they held in earthly life. On one level this seems natural and self evident, but it leaves us with a problem. For throughout our earthly existence we change many times. My mid-thirties personality is different from my personality half a lifetime ago. In another thirty years my attitudes and opinions may differ radically again. So which is the real me? Some spiritualists maintain that our souls are like diamonds with many facets. In reality we have many selves, formed through many incarnations, all of which we meet one by one after death. Together, it is then possible to understand fully past mistakes and weaknesses, strengths and triumphs. Nevertheless, only in the higher realms of vibration are the different aspects of the primary self or 'true' soul wholly reunited. Seen in this sense, death is only a gateway to further change – just one part of the soul's progression.

This process through different spheres or levels of consciousness leads on to second or third deaths as unwanted parts of the soul-personality are sloughed off. Stripped of illusions about itself, the soul undergoes a mental metamorphosis like an unfolding butterfly emerging from a crysalis. Former identities are entirely lost since they were helpful only to gain experience on the upward path.

The awakened soul willingly gives up that part of itself which it once believed to be so vital for it now views reality with a widened consciousness and becomes aware of the distinct thread of purpose underlying apparently separate events in a former existence. The succession of past lives is now recognized as in no way arbitrary but as simply reflecting a hidden pattern and purpose. Thus an individual life is seen with true perception as a mere fragment, a piece of a jigsaw, a strand of a web, shaped by former incarnations. Throughout this cleansing process, the spirit is assisted by higher souls first viewed as separate entities but later recognized as higher manifestations of its own soul-mind. For at the purest level, all selves are part of the larger mind or greater self, a single thought in the mind of God. Each reincarnated self might be likened to a cell in a single complex organism. A point of consciousness dwelling in the greater consciousness or 'over-soul' of the creative principle. As Alexander Pope wrote in his *Essay on Man*,

'All are but parts of one stupendous whole, whose body Nature is and God the soul.'

This then is the soul at its most awakened, realizing that a higher individuality lies above us unchanged and unaffected by both birth and death. Here alone is true immortality. The human personality, which is in itself nothing more than a changing series of thoughts, sensations and emotions, a moving cycle of states of consciousness in constant flux, will not survive this process nor would it be desirable for it to do so. The personality certainly does survive death for a while, as evidenced by spirit communication from deceased relatives. In time though, it will choose once more to incarnate on earth to follow its karmic path of destiny.

Rather than a plane of perpetual bliss, the afterlife world is a plane of rest and learning. Each reincarnated 'I' is not truly separated, for all separation is an illusion; we are like tiny crystal droplets held in a great ocean, each as single points of consciousness dwelling in the greater mind's infinite experience. As the Bible said, 'We live and move and have our being in Him.' In the cycle of birth and rebirth, the individual stream flows as part of a great river. No life truly begins afresh nor is any life ever really finished. We all continue somewhere and somewhen. Sexual union does not create life but merely creates the conditions for a new human incarnation to become manifest.

And so the progression of life is ever upward. A soul will not have to live forever beyond death with all that is evil and sinful in its being, but with that which is wisest and best. Eventually, through karma, the worst in our nature shall die as that part of us ought to die. Only the good will live as that part of it ought to live. Thus, truly there is no death. We have nothing to fear from the icy hand of the grim reaper. The scorpion's sting is removed and we need worry no more about the prospect of personal annihilation. The cycle of birth, death and decay are necessary to the process, though meaningless in themselves. Our future happiness is assured as we already exist as part of the infinite self or God, or whatever label you wish to place upon the universal mind. Try as we might, we can never become separated. Jesus, who understood this most perfectly said, 'I and the Father are one.' The same is true for all of us though we have yet to realize it. Now is the time to do just that.

Knowledge of the advances made in the field of parascience during the past two decades is slowly entering the public domain. As the reality of our survival beyond the moment of physical death seeps into the collective consciousness of the human race, it will inevitably begin to alter our attitudes towards ourselves and each other. If it helps to provoke a shift away from the blind materialism and the 'me first' culture which has grown up during the present century, then it cannot come a moment too soon. The threat of a nuclear Armaggedon may have receded with the end of the Cold War, but the prospects for a peaceful, secure and just world seem as remote as ever. The collapse of the Communist dictatorships in Eastern Europe, a welcome development as it might be, has also exposed old rivalries and ethnic hatreds. Meanwhile, the gap between the poor and the rich grows wider and millions of children starve to death each year – victims of an economic system in which they have no hope of competing. As the next millennium approaches, we are faced with the possibility of a threat to the environment so grave that the entire planet seems suddenly to be in danger.

In some ways it is difficult to imagine a less rosy picture. If as a race we do not take responsibility for our actions now it may soon be too late. I have no doubt whatsoever that you, I, all of us, will survive death. Whether we will survive the extinction of the human race, however, is anyone's guess.

Glossary

Akashic Records A universal record of all human activity believed by mystics to be held in the ether.

Apportations The appearance of solid objects out of thin air.

Astral Body A non-physical counterpart to the physical form.

Astral Planes Higher levels of consciousness which, according to spiritualists, are inhabited by discarnate souls.

Astral Projection A technique of leaving the body at will.

Aura Life energy field surrounding all living things.

Automatic Writing Messages written by a medium under the direct control of a spirit guide.

Bardo Tibetan name for astral world.

Bi-Location Being in two places at one time.

Bio-Plasma Body Russian parascientific term for astral counterpart.

Channelling Modern American term for mediumship.

Crisis Apparition An apparition seen at the moment of physical death or great trauma.

Cryptomensia Hidden memory.

Doppelgänger An apparition of one's self.

Dualistic View Theory of reality that embraces two co-existing levels of reality: mind and matter.

Earth-bound Spirit A soul tied to the material world

through insufficient knowledge or spiritual development.

Ecosomatic state The sensation of being outside one's physical body.

Ectoplasm Substance exuded from some mediums during a trance.

Electroencephalographic Reading Medical instrument measuring brain wave activity.

Essenes Early Jewish sect remarkable for ascetic practices.

Etheric Substance Believed by mystics to fill all space and provide a medium for mental transmissions.

Gnostics Heretical Christian sect who interpreted scriptures through a mystic philosophy, embracing reincarnation.

Karma Eastern reincarnationist term for the sum of one's good or bad actions through successive incarnations.

Kirlian Photography Process purportedly capturing aura on film.

Living Ghost An apparition of a living person.

Mechanistic View Materialist theory of reality which rejects all evidence that cannot be contained within current biological or physical laws, including the human survival of physical death.

Mental Mediumship Where a medium receives and interprets mental impressions only.

Metempsychosis Word for reincarnation, derived from Celtic language.

Mythopoeia The subconscious creation of stories.

Nirvana In Bhuddist theology, an extinction of personal self and an entry into oneness with the creative principal, or Godhead.

Occam's Razor A philosophical device to test the truth. If presented with two apparently contradictory possibilities, choose the most likely first.

Palingenesis Rebirth, derived from Greek language.

Parapsychology An investigation into the paranormal which places the unseen potential of the human mind at the centre.

Parascience A scientific laboratory-based approach to the investigation of the paranormal.

Physical Mediumship Where a medium exhibits various supernormal powers for others to see.

Place-Centred Spirit An apparition tied to a specific location.

Post-mortem Ghost An apparition seen within twenty-four hours of physical death.

Psychokinesis The ability to move or change physical matter by thought.

Regression Hypnotic method through which a person is taken back to relive the past.

Samsara Indian term for one's path of learning through incarnations.

Stone Tape Theories A hypothesis that thought patterns sometimes remain locked within physical matter and are thereafter spontaneously replayed as apparitions or sound.

Veridical Hallucination A ghost which imparts knowledge unknown to the percipient.

Xenoglossia The ability to speak in unlearnt languages.